Always the Mountains

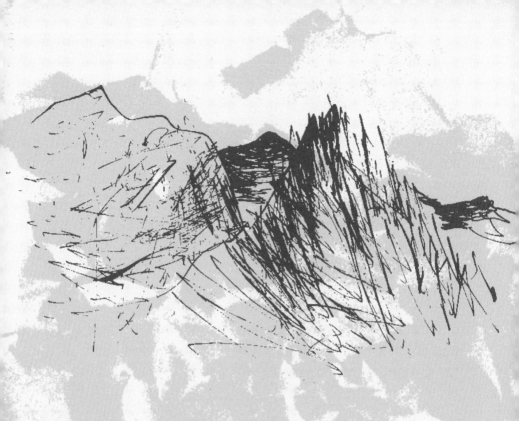

Always the Mountains

DAVID ROTHENBERG

The University of Georgia Press ATHENS & LONDON

Published by the University of Georgia Press
Athens, Georgia 30602
© 2002 by David Rothenberg
All rights reserved
Set in Berkeley Old Style by Bookcomp, Inc.
Printed and bound by Thomson-Shore
The paper in this book meets the guidelines for
permanence and durability of the Committee on
Production Guidelines for Book Longevity of the
Council on Library Resources.

Printed in the United States of America
06 05 04 03 02 C 5 4 3 2 1

Library of Congress Cataloging-in-Publication Data
Rothenberg, David, 1962–
    Always the mountains / David Rothenberg.
        p. cm.
Includes bibliographical references and index.
ISBN 0-8203-2454-X (hardcover : alk. paper)
1. Human ecology—Philosophy. 2. Philosophy.
3. Nature conservation—Philosophy.
4. Environmental (Aesthetics) I. Title.
GF21 .R68 2002
304.2—dc21   2002006735

British Library Cataloging-in-Publication Data available

CONTENTS

What We'll Never Know of Nature

I am looking for the story of human confusion in the face of actual events. It's about how little we actually know about the natural world around us.

They always tell us to write about what we know, but I feel the need to write about what I don't know. What we don't know can hurt us, but it is also what allows us to go on living, wondering, not hoping that we will find the answer and thus some kind of peace, but that we can live forward into the questions and be able to survive and enjoy the fundamental uncertainty that grounds human existence.

We will never know if we are part of nature, or apart from nature. Humanity comes from nature, but we step back to reflect on nature. The moment we start to wonder who we are and why we are here, we retreat from the process, not satisfied to live inside the flow. Not only do we think, but we change the face of our environment in order to live in it.

Once we build cities we then can escape the cities and are moved to tears by the raw natural power of the wildness far from our heavy omnipresent structures. Then we want nature once more and strive to go back to it, and imagine what it would mean to live back with it, and think how many ways our culture has pulled us away.

But one cannot return to nature before inventing nature. And if it is a good invention it will always be just beyond our reach.

Everything else alive is safely part of nature. We have pulled ourselves up out of nature and wonder why it is that we, we alone, must work so hard to find our way back. Then when we're back there we find nothing that wants us.

The human tragedy may be just this: to realize the world does not need us, that only we elevate our own importance so much in order to seem significant.

This all may seem abstract, and if it does, then you know why I need my story. In the essays that follow, I try to evoke what matters as much as explain it. I try to situate the masters in new places, and seek the significance of my own experience poised somewhere between philosophy and literature, betwixt beauty and reason.

The philosopher Martin Heidegger said all we had to do was sing. You might have heard other things about him, good and bad, but remember he did say that the Earth needs humanity in order to sing it into existence, to give it word, name, not substance but story. Much as I too want to sing I can't quite believe that. The world is wonderful because it doesn't need me at all, except perhaps to save it from the sum total of human mistake.

Is just to be here a mistake? If we are part of nature, then each species is opportunistic, doing the best it can, rarely holding back with any sort of prudence. There's not enough self-hatred in me to call our species a cancer on the planet, growing black, deformed, and ugly until we kill our host, but I don't mind being a weed, flourishing due to stamina if not ingenuity. We've spread far from our native savanna habitat, and there are too many of us to want to go back.

Sing: *The Earth needs us!* Do *something* to save the planet from ourselves. Earth goes on beyond eons of destruction. Time takes no prisoners, doesn't even care about *life,* because it can start it all over again. We want the world the way we want the world. *We* are a better species if we go against the grain of species, and think for more than just ourselves. Nature does not tell us to do that. We expand our circle of care: no more slavery, no more cruelty to animals, but more concern for the world that surrounds, that envelops us as we flow out into it.

I want to go in there, I want to expand, but I do so with trepidation. There is something about this direction I do not believe. Because to imagine we are nature seems to reduce the scale of the unknown, and the unknown is where I want to be, and I will only be there if I do not know where I am. Not to be too comfortable on the edge inside of nature and out, but holding my own in the wind so that I can be always reshaping the edge of the wave, the contour of the ridge, touching that cloud that perhaps looks like a mountain but in the end is still just a cloud.

Always the Mountains

ONE

Ways toward Mountains

W hat exactly are we climbing when we speak the word 'mountain'? Are we naming a particular feature of the landscape, organizing a common experience of the land, or commenting on a quality within a nature that permeates all things? In the accounts that follow there are different ways of encountering mountains and different ways of describing them. The idea of mountain that emerges is one of several discrete and valid meanings, some of which encompass the others. What separates them is a change in the amount of emphasis given to the connection between the knower and the mountains, between humanity and nature.

Two legendary ancient texts set the stage for this beautiful confusion. Petrarch's fourteenth-century ascent of a mountain in southern France describes a desire to know a specific mountain that finds its greatest significance as an analogy to the human soul. A roughly contemporary Japanese Zen text reveals fluid mountains inseparable from our human selves. Following these, we shall speculate through memories and dreams to reach mountains, present everywhere, as a quality or category that gives a natural structure to our world as we construct it.

Why look at mountains in this way? Beginning with a basic form we think to be in nature, we show that it only exists in a nature that encompasses our recollections and dreams, as well as the Earth's physical form, within and without.

On April 26, 1336, Petrarch ascended to the summit of Mount Ventoux near Avignon. His description of the ascent, written in a letter to his friend and confessor, the monk Dionysius in Paris, is famous for being the first modern account we have of a European climbing a high summit for pure pleasure alone. Petrarch intends to see more of the world by climbing the mountain. But when it comes time to recount the events, he entitles the letter "Concerning Some Personal Problems."[1] The problem, Petrarch comes to realize, is that his very desire to pay attention to nature is a distraction from the true purpose of humankind—contemplation of the soul. Petrarch goes out into nature but finds only himself, for he has not learned how to *see* outside the bounds of his inquiring mind.

Petrarch has lived in the vicinity of Mount Ventoux, the "Windy Summit," for years, but does not feel he knows it until he ascends to the summit. "My only motive was the wish to see what so great an elevation had to offer," he writes. To offer? What can a mountain *offer* us? This will be an important way to approach mountains—to ask them for something, and try to receive what they give. Petrarch decides that to participate in the offering of the mountain means climbing to its summit and looking out from it upon the world:

> The mountain is a very steep and almost inaccessible mass of stony soil.
> But, as the poet has well said, "Remorseless toil conquers all."

The goal presents itself as imposing, but Petrarch is initially optimistic. He knows he will make it, yet the route he chooses is slow and circuitous. His companions, namely his brother and two servants, take a more direct route up the ridge, while he tries an "easy, roundabout route through winding valleys." But he soon corrects himself—there is a moral problem. He is only trying to avoid the exertion of the ascent, but "no human ingenuity can alter the nature of things, or cause anything to reach a height by going down." He walks with an Aristotelian notion of nature—that it is *the way things are,* which cannot be altered or subverted.

Petrarch rapidly realizes the root of his frustration: an attempt to go against this nature. Getting tired after a few hours of unnatural route choice, he sits down, begins to leave nature, and simply lets his thoughts drift from the material task at hand to the distant privileges of the human, that is, the ability to separate oneself from the immediate so as to be able to reflect upon it:

> After being frequently misled in this way, I finally sat down in a valley and transferred my winged thoughts from things corporeal to the immaterial, addressing myself as follows:—"what thou hast repeatedly experienced today in the ascent of this mountain, happens to thee, as to many, in the journey toward the blessed life. But this is not so readily perceived by men, since the motions of the body are obvious and external while those of the soul are invisible and hidden."

In his weariness his thoughts drift to the inner mountains of the spiritual realm, so difficult to climb, and—in his account—so separate from the corporeal mountains of our world. Why must they be so distant? For, upon finally reaching the summit of the immediate mountain at hand, Petrarch, for a moment, is transfixed by its prominence:

> At first, owing to the unaccustomed quality of the air and the effect of the great sweep of view spread out before me, I stood like one dazed. I beheld the clouds under our feet, and what I had read of Athos and Olympus seemed less incredible as I myself witnessed the same things from a mountain of less fame.

Here Petrarch is at the verge of breaking with the authority of his time. His own experience of the mountain's offering seems so powerful that it challenges the life and presence of what he has read, that is, it confronts the strength of myth and religion with an authority of experience equally strong. This is a power from a nature whose meaning is somewhat different from the 'way things are'. And Petrarch recognizes this, but only for a moment. The spiritual realm rapidly calls him back.

He catches himself, and reproaches his mind for thinking that experience could be more intense than authority; at the time, such sentiment seemed close to blasphemy. The worried Petrarch reaches into his rucksack for a book, which just happens to be St. Augustine's *Confessions*. He opens it, apparently at random, to the tenth book. He reads to his brother:

> And men go about to wonder at the heights of the mountains, and the mighty waves of the sea, and the wide sweep of rivers, and the circuit of the ocean, and the revolution of the stars, *but they themselves they consider not.*

He angrily closes the book and admonishes himself for not realizing long ago that there is "nothing wonderful except the soul, which, when great itself, finds nothing great outside itself. Then, in truth, I was satisfied I had seen enough of the mountain."

Nothing great outside itself—Petrarch has opposed the true excellence of the soul to the apparent vastness of nature. It is this view that was honed into authority during the Middle Ages, and he is at the verge of escaping it by being able to look with wonder at the world around him. That is why Petrarch is sometimes called the first modern man, one who stood on the wall between authority and experience.

But are we not still standing on the edge, having passed through the Enlightenment, which taught us that nature is an objective to be recorded and investigated while the human mind is an independent mystery apart from it? Though people in our time are not afraid of our wonder in the face of mountains, we still tend to consider our faces as very separate from these mountain faces.

The sun sets and the mountain shadows lengthen; Petrarch and his party descend from the mountain. But what have they seen? The tendency of the human mind toward closure—and distancing—from the world around us. The great human soul becomes closed to any natural soul and builds its tendency to exploration of nature upon this fallacy. *Thus it cannot hope to discover anything but itself, wherever it goes.*

Petrarch returns to his village of Malaucêne, eager to transcribe his discovery of the greatness of the soul before he forgets it. Is it, rather, the richness of the contact with nature that is to be preserved, regardless of the moralistic conclusions derived from it? He is at the edge, and proved he could glance toward the horizon. But what he knew kept him back.

How often have we had similar experiences today—adrift in the virtue of the natural world, yet unable to escape our own cultured selves? How easy it is to simply decide we are more important. But this quickness is one of our limitations. There should be a way to penetrate our own experience of mountains, of nature, that allows us to question them directly as we question the objects of reason. There should be ways we can question ourselves and mountains at the same time, using our language to speak through them, to move with them, not to move over them or to conquer them. It is in a Japanese text, nearly one hundred years older than Petrarch's attempt, that we find a different, initially paradoxical description of the mountains, a description that brings them into fullness of being only through our speaking of them and our identifying with them.

The *Sansuikyō, or Mountains and Rivers Sutra,* is the twenty-ninth book of the *Shōbōgenzō,* the collection of writings of the Japanese Zen master Dōgen (1200–1253). It was given as a lecture in the hour of the rat (12–2 A.M.) on November 3, 1240, at the monastery Kannon Dori Kosho Horinji to an audience of monks and students.[2] It takes the form, not of the recounting of a journey, but of a commentary on several notions from Ch'an literature, the original source material for Zen. Dōgen tries to teach us to assess the mountains and rivers so that we can see them *for what they are.*

The present mountains and rivers are revealed to be actualizations—material forms—of the words of the ancient Buddhas. But the tone of the text is not so much descriptive as imperative: Dōgen is telling us what to do. The mountains present a certain value and must be related to in a particular way. They are perfect in themselves and so must be respected. Through their persistent presence, we can access the powers of nature that spring from them:

> Because the virtues of the mountain are high and broad, the power to ride the clouds is always penetrated from the mountains; and the ability to follow the wind is inevitably liberated from the mountains.

High and broad: qualities we observe of the mountains, what we use to define the mountains. And yet why are these qualities called *virtues*? They are values in themselves that show the mountains are able to be what they are. Through attending them, we reach nature: we can follow it, we can float upon it. This power should not be thought of as exploitative: we do not so much tame nature as we are tempered by it, if we attend to its values. We do not necessarily climb the mountains, but direct our intention toward them, and listen to them.

> The blue mountains are constantly walking. The stone woman gives birth to a child in the night. The mountains lack none of their proper virtues, hence, they are constantly at rest and constantly walking. We must devote ourselves to a detailed study of this virtue of walking. The walking of the mountains is *like* that of men: do not doubt that the mountains walk simply because they do not appear to walk like humans. . . . He who doubts that the mountains walk does not yet understand his own walking. It is not that he does not walk, but that he does not yet understand, has not made clear, his walking. He who would understand his own walking must also understand the walking of the blue mountains. The blue mountains are neither sentient nor insentient. Therefore, we can have no doubts about these blue mountains walking.

The mountains are alive. They give birth, and create life. This life, this movement, this walking, is *not* different from the movement we as humans engage in. If we cannot see it, it is only because we are not perfect, we do not understand; we walk, but do not understand our own walking. If we did, we would see how it is like the walking of the mountains, though they do not *appear* to walk as we do. It is this vision of the common walking that advances our understanding. But we refuse to believe it—it is we who are lacking in virtues, we who are imperfect.

This much is akin to Petrarch's views, but he does not make the next leap: the mountains *are* perfect, beyond the limitations of the soul. They are perfect because they can calmly be at motion and at rest. Nature has no dialectic, for it alone contains both states; it is only we who need to identify the opposites, we who are driven by reason away from the fact that nature has already reconciled them. Is it *our* nature to be separated from nature in this way, and to be hidden from that which we seek? Petrarch says that it is our fortune to know the spiritual virtues. But the logic of Dōgen says there are neither sentient nor insentient beings until we choose to make the distinction. Even within ourselves the distinction is not an actual one but only something we apply with analysis. Thus the mountains are, like our Selves, at motion, and at rest. We cannot doubt or uphold one at the expense of the other. That, too, is only the forced result of our tendency toward choice. Yet it is the "walking of the blue mountains, the walking of the self," that we should carefully investigate. Because, as Plato points out, the meaning of 'wisdom' is *"touching the motion or stream of things."*[3] The true may emerge only from a gentle grasp on the moving world that surrounds us.

But the text continues, well aware that we common people doubt the statement "the blue mountains walk" and are surprised by ideas of "flowing mountains." Dōgen is quick to point out the difference between the enlightened and the rest of us. We will quickly stop at the inadequacy of our perception and name these statements games of language, without realizing that what we may have come across is an inability to identify with certain beings of our world that cannot be said to be living or inert, aware or nonconscious. The paradox in words points out a path into the depth of the world.

The message of the *Mountains and Rivers Sutra* is that we must *try to understand,* even when words push against one another like the plates in a geologic fault. These words in their swells and ebbs point toward a recognition of something in mountains that is in us also. We must not try to break this cloud, but ride it. It is this wind we should follow, a current toward an understanding *with* nature.

> Sticking to words and sticking to phrases is not the speech of liberation. There is [speech] which is free from such realms: it is "the blue mountains constantly walking," "the East Mountain moving over the water." We should give this detailed investigation.

Here is the central wisdom of the text: that the words, which *hint at* something that seems *beyond explanation,* are the ones we should concentrate upon. For the speech of liberation will be transformative. It takes us beyond ourselves and to the stream. In the next sections, I will try to transform my own reflections and memories of mountains into words that aim at the same effect.

Dōgen reports that the mountains have been home to great sages through the centuries, people who have made the mountains "their own chambers, their own body and mind." Through contact with these sages, the mountains have reached their present actualization. And he remarks that no one has met any wise ones who have become actualized, en-realed to the point of perfection, but only the actual realness of the mountains remains. The mountain sages are no more; there is only the sageness of the summits themselves. So to understand what the word 'mountain' implies, we must go beyond its signification, of a certain rise of the Earth, to its sense, which can be present everywhere:

> As for mountains, there are mountains hidden in jewels; there are mountains hidden in marshes, mountains hidden in the sky; there are mountains hidden in mountains. There is a study of mountains hidden in hiddenness.

Looking for these hidden mountains, one is led to consider to what extent we can identify them or identify *with* them. We strain to consider what it would mean to have mountains walk—we stretch our belief in the implications of language, not its mere capacity to signify.

That is where knowing nature yearns through poetry: this is where a philosophy of nature must lie.

So how are we to walk with the mountains? And to whom will it matter? The pragmatic questions of our time beat against still lingering mysteries. Just look at the mountain, feel it as it comes into view, or—as you walk toward it or upon it—consider everything about our apprehension of it. We may easily see the shape as the result of movement, it seems to testify toward a dynamic Earth, whose geologic upheavals have led to this end. But, rather than through history, we must constitute the reality of the mountain through our sensation of its presence, and not as some kind of remnant or result apart from this.

Once, on a bus in Boulder, Colorado, I saw above the window, in a space normally reserved for advertisements, a poem by David Ignatow. It read simply: *"I wish I could look at a mountain for what it is and not as a comment on my life."* Through the windows of the bus were the slab sandstone peaks of the Flatirons, and the knowledge that the snowy Rockies lay up and invisible behind them. I wonder now how much of Ignatow's sentiment is the same as my chastisement of Petrarch, seeing that all he can get out of the mountain is self-reproachment for being lured sinfully away by the corporeal beauty of nature. Sure, look at the mountain for what it is. But is that even enough? I don't think that explains how the mountains could walk. We must make another step and look at our lives as comments on the mountain, a binding that may begin as invisible but one we should strive to see. The mountains, we remember, are hidden everywhere. To see them, we need to learn the quality that brings forth the idea and the presence of *mountain*.

So what qualities can we investigate, if not those of the solid, the big, the imposing, the silent, the now-fixed result of past processes of earthly metamorphosis at the scale of geological time? We have been asked to consider the mountains as moving, to move us away from an idea of them as fixed objects. The moving *processes* of them continue today, and only a limited vision sees them as fixed. Clouds move around and are formed through their presence. Waters flow swiftly down only because the mountain is there. Our walking changes as we ascend them—shortness of breath, exertion, effort to ascend to a point where our vision is extended, moved outward to a horizon beyond that visible from the hidden place of sea level. The only way a mountain is encountered is through motion. When they suddenly appear after a long journey across the plains, our eyes reach upward, try to scale the depth, imagine and place their height. The presence of the mountain means the horizon is closer—the edge of our field of view wraps toward us as the previously invisible distance now can be seen. Yet mountains also contain illusion: they may seem bigger and closer or farther and less massive than they actually are. And yet, sometimes cloud formations appear in the low sky that seem to be like mountains. Why? How can condensed water equal the solidity of rugged ground? The way they connect the ground to the open sky seems to imply an upward extension of the Earth, they make us wish the land yearned toward the air within our horizon. Somehow we too yearn for this connection, for it is clear that through mountains we are extended, we are made greater by our ability to know them—this Dōgen knew. But it also includes a danger, if the knowledge of mountains is subverted into conquest.

And yet, you may find what follows to be overly subjective, ostensibly the result of personal encounters with mountains and their nature. Can this reveal anything absolute about them, or is it merely another simple choice left by Western introversion? I am inspired to this method by a message from Dōgen: it is the self that immediately leads to selflessness.[4] And this selflessness is also described as something that is intimate and close to us. Through presenting my own limited experiences I hope to reveal some of the infinitude of mountain possibility.

Last night I dreamed of mountains. We were skiing up toward a summit, on a familiar trail. Suddenly a lake appears and bars our path. A guard stands by. "Don't worry," he announces, "the snow is melting, the runoff is tremendously swift—we're holding it back, but soon we will release it, the path will again open." Shortly the water gushes forth—I remember the image of a liquid, temporally perceived glacier, streams of water and ice breaking by. On what is left of the path, it is possible to continue, knowing that we had just witnessed an event impossible in external nature, yet somehow credible within my internal perception of what it is that mountains have to offer. As the dreamclimb continues a ghost town is reached, crumbling, with a small museum of mountains. What is inside? Beyond, the snow is gone, it is all some kind of sandy pinnacle. We climb slowly, weighted by the dunes. In the end, on the purest of summits, I remember: it is now like a staircase in a tower, the view only emerges sporadically, as from windows at the four directions.

There were glimpses of geology, of the Earth moving. There was a room for the preserving of ideas of mountains, but it was unclear what was in it. I suspect all the images from the dream are to be contained in the museum. Though the peak was somehow pure and open, like a desert, the final ascent was likened to the climbing of a staircase. Whatever was seen was only offered through windows in enclosing walls. *Whatever visions we reach are by something bounded.* These visions—the opening, and yet only through closing—will recur in other dreams about mountains. They have not yet been exhausted, in the fragmentary way we have reached them.

What is the unfinished quality of mountains? In speaking of them we are led to scramble up, there is no end, no summit, for it is the ascending that is the mountain. The summit does not mark the end to this rising but only makes it possible. How the top seems besides the point! Unfinished, rising, pointless like philosophy—simply another kind of walking across the Earth.

I sometimes have another, recurring dream of a wall atop a mountain. The wall contains a gate, someone stands by the gate. Passing through the gate, beyond the wall, is a route to a place higher than the mountain, somewhere above the summit of the mountain. And there is always something that prevents me from going to this place.

Perhaps this is because I see some lack of logic in its existence, that I know that a mountain peak should be seen as the summit of something, that to go from it to a higher place is somehow unnatural. Or maybe I am simply blurring together archetypal images of our understanding of the world, in a place where they do not fit. Let us try to connect these basic images of 'mountain' and 'wall'. Our idea of mountain must emerge as the way it gathers up, from a base, to a summit, revealing the world from some kind of higher vantage. But yes: mountains everywhere, hidden in everything. I confront my dream-mountain with a wall at its apex, something I cannot pass through. It may be just the gate to the understanding of the idea of mountain that is closed for me, or maybe I am seeing human life as a confrontation with walls and the attempt to pass through them, superimposing this kind of being over a landscape brought to presence by mountain. I could be reenacting a feeling I get while contemplating mountains, or climbing them, or even living with them, *that all I do with them is present to them a wall.*

This I return to again and again. Because I still do not know how to pass through the gate, rather than merely ask questions about the other side.

Another dream I am unable to escape reaches back to my childhood expectations of mountains: that somewhere, perhaps very close to here, was a mountain higher than any presently known, but invisible to those who have not learned to see it. This too is a recurring idea, well known from René Daumal's *Mount Analogue*,[5] a surrealist French novel of 1944 that recounts the journey to a mountain emerging out of the South Seas, higher than any presently known to humanity, which must exist simply because we think it; simply because the dream of the highest mountain recurs over and over again, even after our reputed measurement of Everest as the highest point on Earth.

Daumal's mountain is the result of what he calls *analogical* thinking; it stands for something else. Might it also be the highest mountain of spiritual enlightenment that is portrayed, whose summit must exist though no one has found it? What we want to say is that real mountains are analogical to this also and are inseparable from our notions of ascent toward anything. The idea of climbing upward comes from the Earth. There can be no "ascent toward the blessed life" without real mountains.

The mountains of dreams may also be analogies, though perhaps they show most clearly how any mountain is the constitution of ideas of mountains, and that any idea of mountain can be an analogy. It is a tool of interpretation that has at its origin a shape of the Earth, one that profoundly affects living beings who come in contact with it.

My own particular dream of the hitherto unknown highest summit placed it somewhere, I believe, in the Great Plains. It was the highest mountain in the continental United States, something over eighteen thousand feet, and I would ascend a particular route up its cliff face, over and over again. I can still visualize the particularities of the route, and even now it is accessible in my dreams. The summit is very flat and broad, and unlike the mountain with a wall, this one is not an apex but a broad upland, an opening to various experiences that more often than not emerge in the rest of the dream. The difficulty of this mountain is reaching it. But once on its summit, there are no barriers but untellable vistas over an extended, flat horizon. Here is a mountain that rises us above the surrounding land, opening up new possibilities. In its great height it is a little boy's wish, a place higher than anywhere known by anyone else! And its existence, albeit only in dreams, reflects a wish common to many—the desire to ascend.

The three dreams illustrate conflicting aspects within ideas of mountain. There is an imaginary journey through mountain processes that has at its climax only limited vision through human, rectilinear constructs. There is an apex, a point, which presents only a barrier and moves us to focus on a way to cross it. And there is a mountain that lets us view things from above, whose summit is warm and inviting though all routes to it may be torturous. And these are mountains that could exist everywhere, or nowhere.

The French phenomenologist Maurice Merleau-Ponty sought to identify what it is that allows us to perceive certain entities as unities, in their immediate presence before reflection. Are the parts of a thing only bound together through the association of their interrelatedness during movement? No, says Merleau-Ponty, for how could we see as things aspects we have not seen in motion? "The mountain must present in its actual appearance some characteristic which gives ground for recognizing it as a thing," he writes.[6] It is this quality that we have been searching for, and Merleau-Ponty's very perplexity at its existence suggests that there *is* a kind of movement, a process, a "walking" that mountains do manifest, in their very state of being, as Dōgen knew. The quality of mountains lies within the mountains—we have not the power nor the need to impose it. Recognizing this quality and its source ties ourselves and our perception to nature, in such a way that we will find it more primary to speak of mountain as quality than mountain as object.

And the quality is not something simply with us as we think and look. "To perceive," writes Merleau-Ponty, "is not to remember."[7] But it is to recognize the activities of our consciousness as a connection to the outside world. This is why we can search through our dreams for clues to the meanings of the mountain quality. This is why we should be receptive to the natural qualities that are there as they permeate our Selves.

Arne Naess has written of the eminence of mountains as something beyond the fact that they are very large. He suggests that "the smaller we come to feel ourselves compared to the mountain, the nearer we come to participating in its greatness."[8] But with this humility comes the moment of identifying the qualities of mountains as present in many things. The qualities are accessible to us when we approach the wider Self of deep ecology,[9] or the selflessness of Dōgen's Zen. And so it is that nature is what makes it possible for us to dream, to plan, and to envision change. But when we glimpse its range of variation and see just how wide its categories permeate, we cannot make the mistake of retreating into ourselves and, turning the analogy wholly upon itself, retreating from the world as it is offered to us.

TWO

The Return of the Sublime

There's a small mountain behind my house, just under fifteen hundred feet high. That's not so big by any standard, and it takes about an hour to climb to the top. They call it Bull Hill. Or, in moments of greater historical grandeur, Mount Taurus. Whichever name you prefer, the view from this local summit sweeps up and down the course of the Hudson River. Across the water are the plummeting hills of Crow's Nest and Storm King, and far to the north are the looming, ancient peaks of the Catskills. Right in front bends the river around its narrowest point. The stalwart walls of West Point shine impervious and warlike ahead. To the left, far beyond a faint haze and the widening of the river into a bay, are the distant peaks of Manhattan. Those that still stand.

The sky is piercing blue, the wind is strong, the snow has melted, dry leaves toss in the air. The surge of nature goes on, just another winter is through, never mind record snow or shattering cold or torrential floods. The mountain's still here, much the same as it was a hundred and fifty years ago when Americans began to chart its beauty.

Americans? Charting? What do we have to do with a beauty that has been etched out of the world over thousands of years? Nature lives and forgives, we humans learn to see it anew all the time. I have on my wall an old etching from the 1840s by W. H. Bartlett, entitled "Crow-Nest from Bull Hill." It's a record of the exact same view, a document from the middle of the last century. I recognize at once the hills and the rivercourse, the curves and the bends. A few old military buildings where today a grand edifice lies. There are sailboats on the river, as there might very well be today. But it is in the mountains themselves that I perceive the most difference between that image of yesterday and my view today.

In the print, the cliff of Crow's Nest is etched in precise, searing, but violent strokes that cut vertically down to the dark river before it. The whole mountain is a looming grayish brown. It looks ominous, dangerous, perilously steep. It could be a thousand or ten thousand feet in height, in the image one cannot tell. The view is carefully framed with gnarled, twisted and dead trees, such that it looks like the viewpoint has been hacked violently out of a lush forest. There is a strange light-green bird on one of the dead tree boughs. It looks like some kind of tropical kingfisher, certainly nothing really found around here.

There are clouds building behind that dark cliff wall, as if a storm might brew up in a few hours or a few minutes. This landscape is a careful blend of the pristine and the perilous, the picturesque and the sublime.

The sublime is an overwhelming beauty that comes at us so strong that we are nearly afraid. It was the goal of the rhapsodizers of landscape in word and image, poetry and song, in the heart of the Romantic age of the last century to stir us into excitement through works of art that presented the world as more than it really seemed to be, in the mundane contact with water and trees, wind and air. "Sublime" is a diffuse word today, meaning really good, wonderful, the best that there is. But it is no longer this specific and looming kind of spectacular aesthetic, where nature is drawn or described as more intense than it could possibly be.

Today it is more popular to discredit the sublime. Look, as I'm saying here, at this fantastic and surreal image of the view from the hill behind my house! Did it really look so wonderful back then? The cliff in that picture is surely impressive, but I know today there's a road across its face, and there's no way a road could be built across that cliff in the etching, it's far too steep. Were these artists *lying,* trying to deceive the public into believing that their landscape was more stirring than it could possibly be?

It is popular today to use our critical eyes to point out that nature as we see it is a social construction, an idea put together by society to build a myth that makes sense of the world that surrounds. Nineteenth-century America wanted a grand and noble nature in its backyard, so painted and drew it so it could be admired by all. The artists of the Hudson River School ignored the rough edges and squalor of the noisy, dirty riverfront life and promulgated the image of a pristine rural world not too far from the heaving city at the river's mouth. Look at Thomas Cole's painting of Kaaterskill Falls. It surges more spectacularly than any real spring runoff, and the view seems to be seen from a point high above the trees. This rather modest waterfall was once, due to its proximity to New York, as popular an attraction as Niagara is today. Not far was the now-charred Mountain House, also painted wildly by Cole, with wind whipping up over the escarpment, an anchorage amidst nature's fury. It all seems abandoned and tame today, yet the ghosts of searching feet and studied exclamations still haunt the trees. Was the artist teasing us, luring us along, or have we forgotten how to see?

The sublime has been under attack as long as it has been around. "The sublime," wrote philosopher Immanuel Kant, "is the absolutely great." That didn't stop him from announcing that the beautiful was better, because it was the goal of pure contemplation separate from the easy spectacularity of the powerful, the wild. We recoil from the sublime and choose instead the pretty, the complete. Niagara Falls is only magnificent because we are so tiny, it's a question of scale. In itself, it is just water falling over a cliff.

Kant was trying to discredit the sublime at the end of the eighteenth century, long before it caught the sway of millions of onlookers. What was he so worried about? This pull of sensation away from the pure safety of the human mind, out into nature itself was a straight challenge to his vision of the great miracle of the human mind, contained within itself. We just imagine vastness out there. It just looks big because we are small. We only enjoy the majesty and forcefulness of the wild when we know we are actually safe enough to contemplate it. The sublime is the absolutely great, but there is something better: the human mind. How's that for hubris?

Now today we all know they turned off Niagara Falls for awhile to do some repairs on the rock, to make the flow more smooth, more beautiful. Then they turned the water back on. Are we any more in control of the situation? The surge of the Colorado River down the inner recesses of the Grand Canyon is carefully regulated by dams above and below this sacred national treasure. Today they start artificial floods to keep the ecology going. Do we not own nature, and make it appear how ever we want? Don't we only let it impress us when we want it to?

The sublime is more than this. It is not a game. It's not something we can turn on and off, or keep within our clutches. It's a way of reaching out to the world where nature takes over, where we show our intelligence by learning to participate in things far greater than what we will ever know. But we have to face it, we have to learn to see. We cannot talk ourselves out of being impressed, out of loving the sheer, shouting beauty of the world. History should not lead us to belittle it, and we cannot let the ready availability of so much information turn off experience.

I don't believe W. H. Bartlett and Thomas Cole were lying when they presented the mountains as grand as they could. I don't think it was propaganda for an imaginary wild America that never was. I believe they were teaching us to see, and we need to learn this now as much as ever. It's not so much a question of saving nature as learning what it means to witness the wild that surrounds us in all its many ways of lying in wait.

While walking down toward Yosemite Valley one day in the early 1870s, John Muir happened upon two traveling artists who were hoping to run into him. Toting a letter of introduction, they had come in search of landscapes suitable for painting. All they had found were mountain vistas bare and scoured, foreground, middle ground, and background alike. Where could they find a truly sublime landscape, something worth glorifying, recording? Muir guided them east toward the Sierra Crest. After two days' walk they came to a suitable view. "At last," said one of the artists, "here is a typical alpine landscape."

This is the classic tale where the sublime is maligned. The wandering painters, easels in hand, searched far and wide through the beautiful wilds for a vista worth immortalizing. Why not instead look anywhere, why not turn the gaze on any aspect of nature and depict its amazement, depth, and intricacy? We must not forget how to see. We can learn to probe the infinities of anything.

Muir himself left the artists to their sketching in that high Sierra bowl, and headed straight into the landscape they were studying, ascending hitherto unclimbed peaks, inhabiting the view in the making, crawling deep inside the painting and going straight up to the top of the very peaks they were reducing to paint, not without real perils along the way. At one point he's trapped on a rock wall, his knees shaking like a sewing machine, and he's at the verge of a fatal fall. Gaining composure, he finds a way up, and then feels that vast sense of relief that any of us feel after a brush with death. Once safe, we can revel in the memory, but want at once to try again. Risk, confrontation, gauging our scale against the world. That's the sublime, a poise in nature we can touch, nothing painted, nothing written, nothing framed.

Anyone who's been to the tops of mountains knows that no picture can encapsulate the views one finds there. Everything is clear only in the distance, just background, not foreground. As a kid I would dutifully take my camera on all such journeys and hikes, and I would exclusively photograph mountains, no people, no clues as to why or how or with whom I had got there. People didn't appreciate my pictures, as I reeled off the names and altitudes of summits and explained how their locations connected. I was excited by the pictures because they excited my own memories. As early written books were once only triggers for telling stories, these images suggested to me the awesomeness of what had been seen, and the promise of future journeys. They were not meant to contain anything important of nature, just to remind me of how much is out there.

So it's not the frame or composition that defines the sublime landscape we can expect to find out there in the world as much as the ability to see the truly wild in what can so easily seem tame. Forget the cliff face, stare at the newspaper as the train whistles past the Palisades. It's all just a view out the window, time mulled over between home and work. Why even bother noticing?

Because to notice is to reach out to a home in the world, not in the mind. It's the only way to grab on to the little that's left of contact with a world that's still more-than-human, that will always be just a bit beyond our reach. We have to enjoy that, to keep longing, to keep changing, and never to destroy what we transform. The idea of the sublime can help, if we don't explain it away, if we don't trivialize it, if we learn to see it in both the strangest and most obvious of places.

When I lived in the city, going to parks always made me sad. The nature there seemed so bounded, so surrounded by the walls of human construction, of concrete and steel. Nature seemed so picturesque and under control. On the other hand, I loved the sunset from the Brooklyn Promenade, light glinting on the water's surface, boats disappearing out the harbor to other countries, other climes, the spires of Wall Street like a struggling castle, across the murky river, surrounded by the sky. But the sky has to be there, the expanse, the unfillable, dwarfing human folly and creation. Without that spaciousness, human construction seems so much, so total, filling every possible space. In the city too long and it's easy to forget what time of year it is, how warm or how cold. The Earth, like Kant's sublime, becomes quickly just another idea, to be debated or embraced or dismissed.

But it's supposed to be a feeling that bowls you over, to which you can't possibly say no. To wake you up from your slumber, to charge you with a beauty too extreme not to notice. Teddy Roosevelt insisted that the Grand Canyon should be left as it is, while one-time Secretary of the Interior James Watt asked to be taken away because he was bored with the place. "Many people come, looking, looking," said one of the Sherpa guides in a Nepal I visited a long time ago, "some people come, see."

In our postliterate culture we gauge how much we know by how much information we know how to look up, not how much we can recite or retain. Why visit the Canyon when I can download all the information I need about it from the Internet? Never mind the latest hype, but there have long been photos, paintings, views, facts, maps, routes, all claiming to represent the experience of walking through the awesome place. There's still no plausible reason to get bored. Some visitors, anyway, have noted that the canyon has been built too close to the road.

There is less need to see when what we're supposed to be comes so carefully packaged. There's a famous photograph of a woman at the brink of Yellowstone Falls, wearing a scarf with the same picture of the Falls wrapped right around her head. Now it's fine to wear the images of our travels, conquests, and beliefs any way we want, but we should not think them captured just for being labeled. "This car climbed Mt. Washington" says a bumper sticker you can find throughout northern New England. Then what did the people inside do?

The sublime has been called a purely aesthetic response to nature, separate from science, hard work, or real experience. It has been embraced and dismissed for centuries, and seems these days to generally appear out of fashion, a vestige of Romanticism with a capital R, unrealistic and an exaggeration of life. Look at the true landscape, the critics cry, from the top of your hill! It's gentle and humanized, crisscrossed by roads. The economy doesn't demand the wild, and the land is protected only by the grace of rich people who escape here from the city and enjoy it whenever they can, fully in contrast to the whir and business of the buzzing urban home. The love of country, of green nature, exists only together with firsthand knowledge of a way of life that seems far from the charms of the Earth.

How true, this dichotomy. Some would soften it, imagine green cities or post-rural high-tech villages. But the extremes of contrast are the essence of human life. They contain within them the sublime as well. You won't see it all if you ask for moderation in all things. Forget the balance of nature—there's a political myth if there ever was one. In the tumult, in the change, in the rough weather, you'll find the sublime and you might get struck down. If you live to tell of it, there will be something worth telling.

This is no argument just for danger, no call to take risks if you want to win. It is a call to embrace the unknown, not to reduce it to knowledge by knowing where to look the answers up. The challenge is not to search far and wide for the most spectacular experiences, the most severe places, but to see as the Hudson River painters did the daring in the immediate landscapes of home, to probe the depths of today's experience, to stare the sun in the eye as it slinks past the hills, to try for some vague appreciation of the way the snow melts, the cry of the prehistoric woodpecker as he swoops through the trees, looking like the descendant of dinosaurs that he is, ready to drill more holes in some dead wood. How red his crest is, against the cold-gray, leafless forest! There, gone once more. Probably won't see another bird like that for years, elusive as they are. What else, what else, keep looking. Realize there's always enough to see.

"I won't abandon nature to run after an image of it; however sublime a man might be, he's not God." Denis Diderot writes this in a review of the art of Claude-Joseph Vernet in the Salon of 1767, an exhibition he organized to present the finest paintings in Paris. But he is resisting, he does not want to look at a painted scene, and instead alights for the country to see the real thing—the very landscape the artwork purports to present. He's arguing with his traveling companion, the venerable Abbé Gua de Malves, who urges him to reconsider. Art *can* teach us how to see so much more in the world. "All right, but if you'd spent more time with the artist, perhaps he'd have taught you to see in nature what you don't see now."

Art has always guided us toward different forms of experience. That's the best way it teaches. A whole generation of environmentalists grew up on Sierra Club picture books of this country's threatened wild places. Ansel Adams's images of California mountains are more ubiquitous than tourists' own memories of Yosemite Valley. When I was there once, ostensibly birdwatching, I counted thirty-six different species of Winnebagos. Traffic, crowds, people craning toward the absolute beauty hidden somewhere there. But the Adams images are still carefully constructed, pure. I'll only find them in books, on cards. And those Sierra Club books, why are they a thing of the past? The public has become worn of them. The latest in the genre, from Earth Island books, is called *Clearcut*, featuring not beauty but hundreds of pages of landscapes ravaged by the timber industry across North America. That is the hard-hitting environmentalist picture book today.

Diderot's essay already hits on this paradox more than two hundred years ago. He's supposed to be reviewing the paintings of Vernet, but he's writing about them as if he'd plunged straight into the landscapes they depict, marveling at how perfectly everything is arranged. So perfect, in fact, that it would be impossible to commit any of the perfection to canvas: "Oh nature, how grand you are! Oh nature, how imposing, majestic, and beautiful you are! Such were the words that emerged from the depths of my soul, but how could I convey to you the variety of delicious sensations that accompanied these words as I repeated them over and over to myself?" Experience of the sublime can only be suggested, never replaced. Diderot admits his ruse in the end, it is art he has been extolling, not nature. But it is art that has sent him longing for the wild, a wild that makes sense, organized as a picture but somehow just beyond the limits of the picture.

The work that is genuinely sublime teaches you to see things a whole new way. A landscape painting can be faulted if the perception of its place becomes too easy, too familiar, nowadays a media image more than a true discovery. Even Ruskin wrote that you have to work to see what is most wonderful in the world outside: "Though Nature is constantly beautiful, she does not exhibit her highest powers of beauty constantly, for then they would satiate us and pall upon the senses. It is necessary to their appreciation that they should be rarely shown. Her finest touches are things which must be watched for; her most perfect passages are the most evanescent."

Do not drive to the summit of the mountain, for you'll miss the effort of the view. Walk up, walk on, even if the trail be muddy and the snow deep. Yesterday I crisscrossed the slopes of the Bull, looking for the exact spot where Bartlett's engraving was set from. Each vantage looked a little different than the one I had memorized from the wall. I scrutinized the slopes of Crow's Nest, trying not to think about the radio tower now on its summit and the fact that it's all in the U.S. Military Academy reservation, off limits to mere citizen bystanders and explorers. Too much "unexploded ordnance." How perilous might that cliff be imagined to be? I remembered Bartlett's firm, vertical crag strokes, and I saw the bare trees against the white snow like cross hatching, scratches one after another reaching down, plummeting to the melting icebergs on the spring river. Not so farfetched—it's looming, deep.

The bend of the river to the south seems perfect, more picturesque than sublime. *More* so even than the painting, as it is supposed to be. The work seems strained trying to encompass this arc, this long bend in the river through ranges of further hills. It's a cream haze day, not from deathly air but from the rapid melt of the winter light. Things will grow again here soon, the greenness will fill in the views.

But you know, out beyond General Anthony's Nose and the invisible Bear Mountain Bridge, the hills look larger than life in this early spring air. They rise up, ridges, one after the other, higher than they could possibly be. Lift the eyes higher, catch sight of the clouds. They are wispy, like brush strokes, the blue is crisper than any surface could be.

What would it mean to make such a landscape, or even claim to know it? If it is not ours, whose is it? Watching it become larger and larger makes it all the more like home.

I locate a brittle copy of Ruskin's *True and Beautiful,* over a hundred years old, in a used bookstore in a small upstate town. Amazed that in all my reading of the lore of mountains and the appeal of nature, no one has ever steered me in the direction of this text. The pages themselves seem a piece of the earth, crisp to the touch, ready to crumble in my hands. "The great mountains," he writes, "lift the lowlands on their sides. . . . The spirit of the hills is action; that of the lowlands, repose; and between these two there is to be found every variety of motion and of rest; from the inactive plain, sleeping like the firmament, with cities for stars, to the fiery peaks, which, with heaving bosoms and exulting limbs, with the clouds drifting like hair from their bright foreheads, lift up their Titan hands to Heaven, saying, 'I live forever!' "

Heaving bosoms! Those risqué palpitations of the land, the sensuous curves of the forest. Making it all look human, but to love or to control it? I'm drawn in by the pure engagement with the place, with the lack of embarrassment, the absence of science, the language empty of the apologetic laments of environmentalist whining. I am cynical, I admit; I've been worrying about the Earth for years. All my concern and assemblage of information seems to approach nothing but an educated despair.

As part of living with the world in a different way I want to see the world a different way. There is a route to this way in the daring of Romanticism, once you can get past the nihilistic lover's-leap aspect of young couples hurling themselves off cliffs in tandem to be torn into commingled bits on the savage rocks below. Pure love of nature should not lead to insane idealization of the object or extreme hyperbole. But look, such language is definitely fun.

"What we need," says my friend Nils Faarlund, who leads journeys across the Norwegian icecaps of traditionally minded outdoorspeople who must make their own backpacks and clothing, using no modern synthetic materials, only wool, cotton, leather and wood, "is *deep* Romanticism." The real thing. Heading straight to the core of experience. Art and ideas of art can help us get there.

Faarlund looked up from his books on a cold winter night, so cold that we could barely step outside before our eyelashes would freeze shut at the weight of the minus-forty windchill and the sheer presence of the icy air. He told me about one of the most beautiful places in the world, in danger of being defiled with a huge hydroelectric project on the west coast of Norway. There's a peak just south of Stryn with a long path of stone paths to the summit, many miles above the fjord. A crazy doctor in the last century wanted to build an asylum for tubercular patients so far above the waters—as if they'd ever be able to climb up there safely under their own steam! As if the Mountain wasn't Magic enough without a spa for recovery built on its top. He started work on a castle; all that's left is a solid, round turret. You can sleep there if you can find it. There's food all set. Take what you want. Pay when you leave.

But none of that is the point, save to set the stage for the attraction, the answer, the *view,* something you can see all around but that sees through you from all sides. Let it see you before you see it, the mountains all around rising up not into the clouds but into the whiteness of ice, the huge expanse of a giant icecap the size of Rhode Island reaching around the clutches of rock and wind. Such a thing probably once covered Rhode Island, a long time ago. It is not sharp and jagged but round and inviting, however cold and desolate it may be. And from its tongues come the cliffs, plummeting thousands of feet down to the blue-green ocean. Water cascading everywhere in long chutes, disappearing into the air as the height it must fall is so great. This is the real thing, the landscape larger than life. If I couldn't breathe before, now I'm cured. The hospital might have been a good idea after all. Any sickness dissolves in the raw pleasure of nature. This, by far, is the most beautiful place I have been.

When I was there, I did not think to use the word sublime. I did not know what it meant, or if I did, I would have found it mannered, distant, of another time. Yet the landscape itself seemed of another time, so far from the world people usually consider home. Because so few of us live in such places, they can remain valuable to all. It is not enough to know that they exist to hold on to this value. Nor is it enough to go there and tell tales of it when you come home. What would be enough is to see the world as so magnificent anywhere you go, to be so attuned to the way the world appears so as to find the sublime everywhere.

When I hiked in Nepal twenty years ago, I counted the days before I would get my first view of Mount Everest. When I saw it for the first time, I was amazed that it did not stand out so much from the ranges of mountains cutting the horizon in almost all directions. Another windswept dark pyramid, with plumes of clouds forming off the top. Didn't look higher than anything else, really, just somewhat obscured by closer and more ready peaks. Who would believe this was the highest mountain in the world? What did I expect? More drama, more certainty, more of a lone, decided mountain like Fuji or Rainier, a giant you could be sure of. Something obviously right there, too big, in place. The sublime.

Too easy to be overwhelmed by mountains, yet sometimes they simply rise, larger than they are, more present, more necessary and essential, inhabited by our wishes for them. The sublime decides when to reveal itself to us. It is not my purpose to go after the accuracy or value of ways of portraying nature, but to wonder how we're ever going to be able to see the utmost and most wonderful ways of the world if we try to dismiss the sublime, that lure of the absolutely great, the beauty tainted with danger that reveals what we humans actually are: where we stand, how far we have to go, and where we must stop.

The sublime, perhaps until now an aesthetic category, can at last become a way to value the world. Love of nature, Ruskin goes on, has been long derided as something requiring a kind of faithlessness in the hereafter, too much attention to the mundane details here at hand. But now the tide has turned. Love of nature has been alternately embraced and derided as a religious, pagan kind of celebration. There is no need to deride religion or to fault experience. We never just see the world, though, but learn carefully what's worth paying attention to. No reason to hide from the world in ideas that close off, but try instead to take in all that extremes can offer to us.

The more I consider that the extreme imagery of Romantic artists might be right, or at least honest, the more my home landscape begins to change. Today there is a richly colored hue of snowmelt fog, and it is gray, red, purple, the incendiary colors of a century ago, breathing softly down on the matching hues of brick and wood on the houses up and down the street. As Dōgen said way back in the thirteenth century,

"The mountains walk just like you walk. If you don't see it, you cannot walk." Each day they are different places, dancing, changing, waking us up. I want to remember all of this. I want to see things like this wherever I go.

I will talk to no one on my travels, look nothing up. I'll spend all my energy learning to see.

A hundred and fifty years ago John Ruskin could sincerely write a whole treatise on clouds just by looking at them. "It is a strange thing," he begins, "how little in general people know about the sky." Not because they don't need to, but because they do not take the time. It's simple: no one looks up. "Who saw the dance of the dead clouds when the sunlight left them last night?" Apathy, indifference. Don't look at pictures, look at life. But be careful, what needs to be seen does not simply appear. It must be sought after, only after careful attunement. Nature's most sublime touches are the quickest to pass. The most spectacular part of the spectacular is the part that is easiest to miss.

Last night Comet Hyakutake appeared in the night sky, just between the Big Dipper and the searing glow of a corner streetlight. Never mind the brightness of human life, the mysterious space cloud could still be seen. This is the brightest comet in twenty years. I may never see another object in the sky as anomalous as this. Still, it's so easy to ignore. To attach no significance whatsoever to this strange sky happening. Classically, it would be sublime if it were distant, awesome, and vast. Today I would emphasize the *separation* between our regular life and this strange, far object. The tragedy is that it is so hard to be affected. The sublime answer is to work to take it in.

The original sublime was mostly an aesthetic principle, a theory to explain why we are moved by the terrific and the terrible, the thundering and the huge—things that before the eighteenth century were usually shunned by human company. Edmund Burke worried carefully about identifying just those things that were sublime, as opposed to those that were merely pleasant or beautiful: "Among colours, such as are soft, or cheerful, are unfit to produce grand images. An immense mountain covered with a shining green turf, is nothing in this respect, to one dark and gloomy; the cloudy sky is more grand than the blue; and night more sublime and solemn than day." Such pronouncements of taste are not what I'm talking about here. I want a return to the beguiling power of the sublime, not some definitive statement about what it is and isn't, some checklist of feeling. Those eighteenth-century tastemakers sought full engagement with the presence of the world. That's what we need again.

But the sublime cannot be brought back so innocently. It was never just for the cultured elite, as the philosophers wished, something that the most educated could learn to love. No, it is something that tempts all of us, senses we are usually taught to discount. Connections between experiences that we are supposed to ignore, or to which no significance should be attached. That's right, keep moving straight ahead, pay no attention to the sounds behind the curtain of purpose, the tracks of the train, the car windows, the obstacles or alternatives on the path from point A to point B. Ignore anything that stands in the way of the job getting done.

The sublime is the pull toward astonishment at the world. Just to look at the sky and shout "blue!" or to feel the impending greenness of the grass growing up. The glow of the sun—that's right, stare into it—and the thickening rush of the mud sloughing off the mountains and stopping the road. "Mud!" "Mush!" Traffic stopped, the mountains moving. The comet hurtling toward earth and then away into the distance. It has to matter if we are to want to save anything about this planet and the life that is on it.

I'm not denouncing information or the need to catch facts. The complexity of what we know (or think we know) today is far greater than in the time the idea of the sublime was formulated. So much so that we are taught again and again that our experience cannot be trusted, that the structure of the world lies hidden, that things are seldom what they seem and we are not to trust what we see. There becomes too much to remember, too much to look up, too much to keep track of as the raw light of the world shines on our eyes and then passes through us without the register of even a blink. For who has time to look? There is so much to remember, and so much to forget.

Indeed, some of the best works of art in our time deal with the juxtaposition of past memories in order that we may see the possibilities inherent in the world anew. I think, for example, of the French director Chris Marker's film *Sans Soleil,* or *Sunless,* which takes the form of a voiceover narrative of a woman reading letters sent to her from all over the world by a traveler friend. He visits Japan, the Cape Verde Islands, the deserts of North Africa, and then connects what he sees to images of home and elsewhere. What is remarkable is that the traveler is a filmmaker, and he has filmed everywhere he has been. When he sees something that reminds him of somewhere else, he has the image on file. He can segue right from one memory to another, and the result is a seamless, dynamic picture of memory in motion. Not just any memory or collection of films of places visited, but an exact, attentive, questioning mind that has taken the effort to notice smiles, whispers, incongruities and similarities between home and the world.

You leave the cinema, look up from the film and then see the world as a richer, more engaging place. This film was made in 1983, but it prefigures the immediate accessibility of images that we now associate with the swirl of online images. New technologies promise the immediate link between any place and any other, but they are still preliminary, they don't quite work yet. But *Sans Soleil* seems sublime because of the immensity of images cataloged there, and the beautiful trajectory that links every one to every other. A traveler on the move: writing, watching. He is a filmmaker, he does keep his distance. More seen than spoken to. But this man is not aloof from his memories. He wants to be as faithful to them as possible, and that is why he presents his journey as a careful stream from one recollection to the next, asking as many questions in his letters as offering descriptions. So if we listen to him and watch his pictures, we see the world anew.

Burke writes of how Milton portrays Satan: "In images of a tower, an archangel, the sun rising through mists, or in an eclipse, the ruin of monarchs, and the revolution of kingdoms. The mind is hurried out of itself, by a crowd of great and confused images, which affect because they are crowded and confused. Separate them, and you lose much of the greatness . . . join them, and you infallibly lose the clearness. The images raised by poetry are always of this obscure kind." Precise obscurity, that's where the sublime lies. When you find sense and exactness in the world that has no easy explanation, that's when you latch onto it. Art that directs you to this kind of experience is the path to the sublimity of the world, not of work; the poetry that holds this whole place together.

So the sublime should not become merely a quality some art has and some lacks. It should not be some places and not others. It may be awakened by differing works, or inspired by visits to certain locales, but it should emerge as a way of assessing the world—graspable anywhere, at any time. If you can see enough, remember enough, and want it enough.

For there is vastness anywhere you choose to look for it. The classical sublime is no longer just to be found in the works of nature; in fact, it has been among the towering edifices of civilization for thousands of years. David Nye has written an entire book, *American Technological Sublime,* to show how our country's great bridges, dams, and skyscrapers have always projected an awesome symbol of human power, giving tangible evidence of the march of progress. But progress toward what? What goal do these edifices point toward? More, better, taller, bigger—not enough, not convincing.

Wherever we are going, the place should include greater attention to the wonders of the world. *That* it exists, that we can both change and know so much of it and still know and command so little. To have hope and humility at the same time, while not sinking into moderation in all things. Thrill at the immensity of what can be both made and found. Dare to find the remarkable in the familiar, the faraway at home, and comfort at the ends of the earth.

If you want to find the Kaaterskill Falls today, no sign will guide you. The authorities have taken them all away. The ladders are gone, the ropes have been removed. But there's an endless network of old abandoned paths that will lead you there if you know where to look. After all, this waterfall was far more popular than Niagara in its day, as accessible as it was from the metropolis. There are two abandoned railroad grades that lead to it. Every road to it is eroded, worn down by weather and the pounding of feet into mud.

It's hard to find the right angle to get the best view of it, scrambling around the edge of the crumbling cliff, looking for overlooks that have long since broken off and bashed into bits a few hundred feet below. Impossible of course to find the vantage from which Thomas Cole set his quite composed painting—that place must have been some imaginary nest in the sky. But we too can extrapolate and imagine the draw of the place to thousands who journeyed for miles. There is a special drama to the spot, as branches are brushed aside to frame the best view. A narrow cascade plummeting through a deep hole in the late-season snow, a frozen hundred-foot icicle where the blue ice is melded with the red dirt of the old Catskill Hills. Like any place when carefully observed, it looks like nowhere else.

But it inspires some of the same wishes as any waterfall. This is the right place to go, the perfect edge off which to jump. Or if you don't want to let yourself go, this could be the perfect place to cast off your identity. Throw away your wallet, your cards, your identification, and turn away. Then become someone new.

On January 10, 1996, at 6 P.M. in Grand Central Station, it looked like the beginning of the next war. Perhaps there was a coup in the government, or maybe some untold disaster had just struck. There were hundreds of people crammed into the great hall of the Station, so many that it was nearly impossible to move. Was it instead a rock concert? The arrival of a great religious leader? No, people were just trying to get home. Their eyes were transfixed by the big board above the ticket counters. Was this the racetrack? The stock exchange plummeting? No, the effects of the previous day's blizzard had struck; just a trickling list of the few trains that would be limping home out of the city. Where usually there would be twenty trains listed for a line over the evenings hours, filling the boards, here they were mostly empty. Only *four* trains were planned on each line, no more than one an hour. And some of these carried the legend "delayed" or even "canceled."

But when a track number was posted, the scene in the crowd turned crazy. People would applaud and cheer, and then, from my vantage point, surprisingly clear, at the top of the western steps, I could watch individuals scattered throughout the crowd push and shove toward the narrow doors at the specified gate. "Twenty-seven! Twenty-seven! Coming through, please, let me by, gotta catch that train, only chance to get home, hope I'll make it, never seen anything like this, can you believe it, ouch, coming through, let me through, gotta get through," and the crowd itself became pulsating, alive, surging with the very possibility that there would be a *way out,* one slim chance of leaving the city that night after a day of immobilizing, ever-falling snow and piled up drifts covering invisible automobiles and nature speaking up, laying a firm hand down and making any traffic at all an impossibility. Silent streets, city muffled, no chance of escape. A humanized place with the machines shut down, nothing but people amazed at the silence brought on by a white world blanketed by nothing but frozen water. What a world! What possibilities! Why can't this happen all the time? If so, we'd manage it, control it, plow on despite it. The mechanized city turns off. The human city begins. Remember what this is like. Keep this joy and this energy alive when it's 95° in the shade just a few global-warming months from now.

I did finally make it home to the hills. The next day, I am slogging, snowshoed, through eight-foot drifts toward the summit of Slide Mountain, modest but highest in the Catskill range, most ancient ones of the Northeast. The normally easy trail is a genuine effort as the snow is so still and so deep. It is still hard to travel through it as it was hard to travel through the city in its sluggishness. The difficulty is what makes it wonderful, having to fight to move through the silent white heaviness. Glimpsed through the trees are the staid curves of these mountains, made more pronounced by the snow. These are the kinds of mountain shapes that, were they in Scotland like the peak Suilven, no sheep would go near them. There is a certain brooding sinisterity to these hulking shapes, so dark and silent and imprecise. Where is the summit? Who can tell? They are covered in thick, snow-filled trees. Long ridges, round rises, so many trailless ones yet so close to town. Step to the wilderness from the city, fight your way out of the crowd, better to join it again when it's time to find a place in the fold. Thousands of people, then nobody. These spaces, these stories are right next to one another. The sublime is to be able to move between them, to hold the crowd in your mind, and then let everyone out the door. Like walking down Broadway with a Walkman playing the sounds of the Amazon jungle, we hold the extremes of experience inside our minds, and can pull them out at will. The mind holds on to all the edges. The sublime is outside, and inside.

THREE

Dare I Kill the Snake?

FROM AHIMSA TO DEEP ECOLOGY

In 1894 Mohandas Gandhi asked the following question in a letter to Raychandbhai Mehta, the famous Jain teacher: "If a snake is about to bite me, should I allow myself to be bitten, or should I kill it, supposing that to be the only way in which I can save myself?"

This is the classic kind of question used to test the firmness of a person's environmental ethics. After all that is said about concern for the equal rights of all species to blossom and flourish, when push comes to shove, will we not always choose self-interest if we are mortally in danger? Or even if we are not mortally in danger? It might be wrong to kill animals, but we do it nevertheless, more out of desire than out of necessity.

This sort of challenge is used to cast environmental ethics into the rubbish heap of high and mighty ideals that no one in real conflicts could hope to adhere to.

An ethic can be something reasonable and programmatic, telling us what to do, or it can be more like the tenets of a religion—a collection of ideals to aspire to, knowing they demand more purity than most of us are able to muster.

Jainism is probably the least known of the world's major religions, and it is also the most inherently ecological. The idea of not harming any living beings at all is a compelling image of pious ecological concern: wearing masks around the mouth so that no insects will be breathed in by mistake, treading lightly so that no ant will be inadvertently or maliciously crushed, refusing to eat any living creature and spurning those foods that contain a preponderance of bacteria, such as figs, or presumably fig newtons.

This image is of course only a first caricature of a deep and complex tradition. Someone from within this tradition will still need to decide whether to kill that attacking snake. And saying that the snake has as equal a right as we do to survive may not be the most serious way of respecting it. Before I tell you what Raychandbhai said to Gandhi, it is important to understand why the snake is more than an individual, more than just a single being.

There is nothing wrong with revering animals enough so that we would want to stay out of their way. But snakes and humans, cats and mice, are more than individuals who mind their own business. As long as we are considered independent entities with our own agendas, we will have purposes that will conflict. Only when we look past our own narrow interests will we realize that the shadowy, deeper parts of nature may be as worthy of respect as are identifiable individuals.

Does this mean we need to think less of ourselves and forget our own interests to worry about the greater concerns of the world that includes us all? The deep-ecology perspective says no. This view of human-natural relations is not opposed to animal rights, but it tends to look beyond unshared goals to find a perspective wide enough to include all of us, animal, vegetable, and mineral alike. First named by Arne Naess in 1973, it reflects a tendency that had been around for many years, expanding the Hindu concept of *atman* to address the present ecological crisis, trying desperately not to lose the focus on the singular person, so basic to Western thought.

It sounds like a tall order of compromise indeed. Deep ecology still begins with the individual, not with society, asking how each of us might best find a rightful place in the natural world. Personal fulfillment begins with a single goal: Self-realization, with a capital S, to remind us that it is not the selfish ego that is to be enhanced but a self that expands outward from our narrow wants to the needs of the Earth as a whole.

But there should not be a Great Self in which we lose our individuality, dissolving at the end into the cosmos like the specks of dust that many religions have told us we are. No—expanding the range of our concern should only make our individuality richer, more compassionate, more profound. We will save the old-growth forests because we need to experience them to fully live; we need to build and harvest wood in a way that respects the need for these trees to be above the limits of our use of the Earth. We gain more personally by leaving such ancient ones alone than by killing them to build houses that will last but a fraction of their living, growing age. Find some other trees, take them only if we are ready and prepared to replace them efficiently and gracefully.

The approach of deep ecology is most appreciated by those who feel an intuitive need to expand their own identity outward toward the Earth and who have never known how to articulate this feeling. More logically minded environmentalists sometimes try to counter this intuition. They ask: how can you amplify yourself to include a tree? Those who have felt it say it is obvious you have not had the opportunity, or the openness, else you would know it is possible to admit that "this forest is part of myself." Still, the critics protest: how can a mere self save the world?

It is here, I believe, deep ecology has much to learn from Jainism, the religion so admired for its severe stance in favor of other living beings beyond the human ones. Padmanabh Jaini writes, "*Himsa* has ordinarily been understood in India as harm done to others; for Jainas, however, it refers primarily to injuring *oneself*."[1] Harming animals is wrong because it demands passions that grip us in the bondage of everyday life. The killing of other beings is shunned as part of the path to the most profound kind of nonviolence, learning to see the full realm of yourself as a place in which the hurting of others becomes impossible to conceive.

This is compatible with the notion of animal rights, but it requires a wider and fuller concern for all of us as part of a universal ecology, a grand complexity we can reach upward to know. In the connections between things comes the solution to the inevitable conflicts. You will never do any action for anyone but the largest possible you.

So what did Raychandbai say back to Gandhi? "I hesitate to advise that you should let the snake bite you. Nevertheless how can it be right for you, if you have realized that your own body is perishable, to kill a creature that clings to its own life with great attachment? . . . Anyone who desires spiritual welfare should let their own body perish in such circumstances. If a person lacks a noble character, I might advise them to kill the snake, but we should wish that *neither you nor I will even dream of being such a person.*"[2]

Forsake the body for a future place. That snake is not ready for such renunciation, so he must be allowed to consume you. You have learned enough to make the choice. So you may let go.

But have we no work to complete here on Earth? Can we forsake the planet we have neglected for so long?

What would I do in that situation myself? Kill the snake if I could and did not feel it was yet my time to die. Perhaps that reveals me as someone who has not yet achieved noble character, a lifetime practice of aspiration, especially if your ultimate goal includes the quitting of samsara for a better place.

Or think of American desert ranger Edward Abbey, discovering that his trailer in Arches National Monument is infested with rattlesnakes. He too hesitates to fire his .45. In *Desert Solitaire* he writes, "I have personal convictions to uphold. Ideals, you might say. I'm a humanist. I would rather kill a *man* than a snake."[3] What does he do? Trap a gopher snake, sworn enemy of rattlers across the sagebrush, and train him to keep guard over Abbey's home. If there is to be killing of snakes, let other snakes do it. An ecological way to watch death? Or a one-step-removed way to kill? There is no way to avoid the death of ourselves and of others here on this earth, but we must be mindful of it, not let it go by without taking a stand.

I still want to save this place while I am here, and that means I can continue to consider the vision of Jains stepping smoothly in and around nature as a virtuous ideal, so important because for most of us it will always be out of reach, like the idea that a single self can encompass the cares of an imperiled planet. The challenge is to be able to act with conviction once these pure, seemingly inaccessible thoughts are inside us.

We wish to tread lightly on this planet, but we still leave a trace much more difficult to erase than most other species. As a species, humanity needs to leave a mark in order to realize our selves and ideals. Whatever we wish, that mark will still be left. There will be killing: some will live, some will die. It's not always the best who survive.

Should we all retreat from death, kill nothing but vegetables, rise morally into vegetarianism? It is a fine and noble path, but I would not insist that we all follow it. As long as we kill each other to survive, we who feel a part of the more-than-human world as much as the human realm must not shun *regret,* but instead learn to take it most seriously and share in the suffering that we inflict. It is part of being human, an inevitable part, to suffer and to cause suffering. Dare I kill the snake? Dare I identify with the snake? Dare I take the life of the snake as seriously as I take my own?

We thrive on life. We will have to take some others to continue our own. I do not know whether it is right to say we should apologize before pulling peppers off plants or wrenching carrots from the earth. It may be enough to begin by becoming mindful of the violence humanity participates in here, such that we may see through the tunnel of tragedy to the bright light of peace, available to those who are truly ready to be attentive toward the world and all the richness it offers.

FOUR

Contact! Contact!

UP KATAHDIN WITH THOREAU

The *wild* is more than a named place, an area to demarcate. It is a quality that beguiles us, a tendency we both flee and seek. It is the unruly, what won't be kept down, that crazy love, that path that no one advises us to take—it's against the rules, it's too far, too fast, beyond order, irreconcilable with what we are told is right.

The wild refers to many things. In wildness is the preservation of the world, says our canonized curmudgeon Thoreau. He did not say "wilderness." He did not mean wilderness. He meant the breaking of rules, the ostracized life in the midst of his peers. Walden Pond is a mile from downtown Concord, and a train runs close to the far shore today just like it did back in Henry David's time. That nearness is the wild in it. To buck civilization right in its midst. He said the wild is all that interests us in literature. That's where he lures us away from losing ourselves in nature to finding a deep surge of nature far inside us, what he named as the soul force behind creativity. Poet Philip Booth echoes the sentiment: "Whether we live and write in sight of Mt. Rainier or in midtown Manhattan, no matter where we experience being in place, we immerse in our deepest selves when we begin to write. It's from instinctive memory, from the wilderness of the imagination, from a mindfulness forever wild, that Art starts."[1]

Once again, Thoreau found the wild close by to the tame, and pledged allegiance to it as much in his bucking of authority than in any spurning of culture's ways. It is probably on the summit of Maine's Mount Katahdin that his writing, usually ornate, mannered, nearly Victorian, approaches a free wildness that approaches the timeless, animistic sense of wild wanderers from many cultures. He is here describing the windswept, barren summit upon which almost no visible plant grows, rising high above dense forests:

> This was that Earth of which we have heard, made out of Chaos and Old Night. Here was no man's garden, but the unhandselled globe. It was not lawn, nor pasture, nor mead, nor woodland, nor lea, nor arable, nor wasteland. It was the fresh and natural surface of the planet Earth, as it was made forever and ever,—to be the dwelling of man, we say,—so Nature made it, and man may use it if he can. Man was not to be associated with it. It was Matter, vast, terrific,—not his Mother Earth that we have heard of, nor for him to tread on, or be buried in,—no, it were being too familiar even to let his bones lie there—the home this [sic] of Necessity and Fate.[2]

He savors the alone-ness of the surrounding place, an enveloping world of raw natural phenomena. Reaching through appearance, Thoreau has grasped out for the Earth, and is groping for the language to say this. His cranky style fails him, his ruminations on nature as tonic have no place. He is in the elements here, and it nearly makes him speechless. Go there yourself, you will feel what he means.

The wild barrens of such a mountain are chillingly inhuman, while at the same time touching us deep inside our own human selves, as a weight in the gut somehow proves that the wild within belongs here, and will not be whatever home we choose.

> And yet we have not seen pure Nature, unless we have seen her thus vast, and drear, and inhuman, though in the midst of cities.[3]

The wild is only lasting if it is still within reach from amidst the metropolis. So to see the pure, we must have memory to rely on. Turbulent nature is a foil to the city, yet we need to be in the grid to glimpse its magnitude in opposition to the place where we are. The perfection of the silent mountain is only exalted by those who have come from the mess and noise of the centrum of civilization. It is a sublime vision, great in its vast difference from the scale and sense where we stand.

There is sublimity here out my own urban window. It is spring; the sky is a remarkable blue, beneath my window the concrete city plummets over choked highways to the East River below, strangely sparkling like a visitation of wilderness, waves, ferries, the monument of liberty, the haze of Jersey beyond. The sparkle of traffic, cars careening around the tip of Manhattan. An apparently all-inclusive and consuming city—how hard it is right now to write about anything else! To the west, the great Wall of money, that Street where fortunes rise and plummet. Just past, the twin peaks of World Trade. Metal boxes, amazing structures, towers rising up. (Who would imagine that in a few short years they would be down, exploded, reduced to rubble as memories? There goes another kind of sublime, the sublime of loss.)

Mount Katahdin is about five times as high as each of them, with more summits along the knife-edge ridge. If I see clouds in the distance I fantasize that they are ranges of light, snowy summits that I might reach in a long day's walk across the great swamps and bayous at the edge of the self-proclaimed center of the world. Seattle and Portland each have volcanoes on the near horizons, gigantic sentinels that make human ingenuity appear minute beside the immensity of nature. These mountains rise up to fill the need for a recollection of wildness from a world bounded by the human struggle. This is why the realms above the timberline make us feel free. At least it has always made me feel free. I am happiest as the trees fall away, as the wind whips up, and the vistas explode on all sides as I have climbed upward into the lonely openness.

I applaud Thoreau as he reaches for wildness, as he ascends to the most powerful, thunderous, and exotic of any of the places he visited on his travels. Katahdin is the sentinel of wildness, the greatest of eastern mountains. Not big by any world standard, being scarcely as high as Denver. We take our mountains where we find them; size ain't everything. See how much Wordsworth had to say about the savage hills of the Lake District! They are enough—such ripples in the Earth are sufficient to inspire unending reverie. They are beyond the human, they take work to reach, they are worth the effort.

> The tops of mountains are among the unfinished parts of the globe, whither it is a slight insult to the gods to climb and pry into their secrets, and try their effect on our humanity. Only daring and insolent men, perchance, go there.[4]

The summits of mountains, unfinished? Is it up to us to finish them, or to learn to revel in the incomplete? The human project was described by Aristotle as the completion in ends of what nature offers as beginnings, but he was a flatlander himself. Perhaps if he had lived to see what the *polis* has become, he might occasionally need to flee to unfinished high points if only to gain a sense of perspective. We haven't made everything, we still don't know how things came to be made the way they are. The cool, crisp highlands are the natural place for philosophy, where the air is thin enough to be fillable with logic and reason. We can try to explain, or we can be carried away. Thoreau, in this incantation, this moving prayer, this wild commentary, does both. It's the roughest place he goes, this tableland and way up to the summit of Maine's highest peak. Why is he comfortable? Why is it here that he touches the Earth?

Let me explain out of my own recollection how mountain becomes myth. When the child was a child, he read the book, pored over pictures, built up the romance. I can appreciate the sense of Katahdin as awesome and Great Summit as I first learned of it from a handsome edition of Thoreau's *Maine Woods,* illustrated with the turn-of-the-century photography of Herbert Gleason. I received as a gift a copy of this work when I was twelve years old, and today it remains solid, though well-aged, with a hint of sun fade to the left side, by the binding. It has sat by the window a long time, catching the rays, taking in the brightness. I have a near photographic memory of reading slowly through the pages, and poring over the illustrations, wondering how much the landscape has changed since those early and wild days of the northern country. I fantasized on the *batteaux*, those elongated Quebecois lakeboats that so impressed Henry David. More pointed and angular than a canoe, they seem to reflect an external, European geometry more than the silent sweep of the more native craft through the still or windy waters. Yet these were working boats, tools of the fur trade, a practical, not an idealistic, invention. And Thoreau was a pragmatist; he appreciated the commerce of the wild as much as its romance.

The whole book promised a vast forest of still possible adventure, and I soon discovered firsthand that the landscape up there still looked much the same as it did at the turn of the last century. Staying with my parents and brother, the family spent a few weeks at one of the last of the old resort camps (now closed) just beneath the Katahdin massif. It was gray and stormy for days, and the mountains could be as tremendous as I wished to imagine them, rising only into the solid bank of clouds that rimmed the lake in. Doublehead, North Brother, Barren, Mount O-J-I. The summits' names are explicit, simple, severe, echoing the sense of a still present frontier.

For days we looked up in vain, the gray mist of the rough field of rocks . . . The weather was not right for an ascent of Katahdin. Sometimes in the late evening the peak would appear, glowing in an orange, uneasy light. I had discovered alpenglow.

The day we chose at last to head for the summit was as gray as any other. Walking toward the foot of the Abol Slide, I was as full of anticipation as Thoreau, and as ready to imagine the huge mass of mountain as a great symbol for all that the earth offers as inhuman, beyond the pale, more than us and what we will ever become. We can eliminate mountains, but we cannot really move them. If we pay attention, they move us.

On the trail, in the thin forest under the portentous clouds, the first hazard is crossed on the path. A downed hornet hive, lying on the trail, surprises me as I walk right into it. Now as a child I was inexplicably scared of bees and wasps, not particularly allergic, but cowering in fear, of something. This moment, in my thirteenth year, was the moment this fear ended. Because I was surrounded by hornets, particularly sinister-looking black-and-white ones, all over my arms and legs. I was confronting my demons, swatting at them everywhere, killing them with my bare hands, running, dashing down the trail as they followed with vengeance.

The clouds had slipped lower, the rain was around us. Multiply stung and somewhat feverish, there was no choice but to return. The mountain remained an unreached place of the country, and so became an even larger symbol around which to dream.

Three years later another attempt was made. This time the approach began further from the mountain—two weeks away. Beginning at the last outpost before the longest roadless section on the whole Appalachian Trail, in the town of Monson. Where fifteen cent ice cream cones could be got at a general store that doubled as the justice of the peace. Where the youth hostel was an old Lutheran church now filled with rows of huge brass beds. We headed straight up the Chairback range, laden with overstuffed packs, struggling upward through a torrential rain. On this muddy, sopping journey, every time we came near a mountain, the black clouds would descend, and we would be soaking wet. The only views were from the valleys and the marshes, looking up at the solemn wooded summits, made strangely inaccessible by the unplanned patterns of the weather.

Some of this land was much wilder now than in the days of Thoreau, more remote than in the heyday of Maine tourism following his call to the people of leisure of the last century. Gulf Hagas, the former "Grand Canyon of the East," and once a major tourist attraction for vacationers in the old fishing and hunting camps on the shores of the northern lakes, was now a hidden gorge, with its intricate network of old nature paths now almost impossible to navigate. Back then this area was the most accessible wilderness to the large centers of American population. Now it lies forgotten as it is easier to fly west to Yellowstone or Vail. The nation seems smaller, so the local attraction returns to wildness.

As it returns to remoteness it also has returned to resource. All this country is owned by paper companies, who are desperately trying to make clearcutting of the evergreen forest into something profitable. I remember on the trip how we would be traipsing down the muddy, moose-imprinted Appalachian Trail, frequently consulting the guidebook to imagine where we were. Then suddenly, in the midst of a documented wilderness, we would cross a completely unmarked, wide, packed-down gravel road. A highway out of nowhere!

These new logging roads have been cut throughout the forest. The hikers' maps can't keep up with the rapid transformation of the landscape. (What did we expect, that words would be the most accurate guide to the shifting landscape?) Of course, a hundred years ago the hillsides were far more ravaged than they are today. They have recovered in a sense, and might again, when the cutting stops.

The wildest land may also be the least protected land, where the ethics of the frontier survives. There is something tame about a park, where rules hold, where things are forbidden. We are not completely free. In the free country, the forces of use and appreciation vie for the determination of value of the place. People want to make a living off the earth, as well as enjoy it. This is the current battle around the northern forests. If completely protected, does it then become a museum where humanity can only be a visitor?

Thoreau realizes on the climb up Katahdin that he treads upon an earth that was not made for him or his ilk, a land of Titans, the clouded tablelands of sublimity above the cliff falling down to the timid plains of humanity. "Five thousand feet," as Nietzsche would have said, "above men and time."

And yet there is a need for the visit, the place serves a purpose, and affects him. He is leaping past the veil of explanation, and the Earth is touching him. "Contact!" he implores, as the stark country makes a deep impression upon him. It is the country for philosophy. We need raw wildness in order to learn how to think.

Coming across that logging road at the age of fifteen as I thought I was walking through the wilderness shattered my vision of the wild place. It shouldn't be there, it disturbs the gestalt, it was not what I expected. The trail itself was mowed over, and we had to walk for mile after mile on a new, ugly road that appeared on none of our maps. It was a complete and utter insult to the wish that we really were crossing the wildest portion of the whole Appalachian Trail.

Now it is twenty-five years later, and I feel that I *should* hold a more balanced perspective. Oh well, maybe I've been in the city too long. Perhaps I'm aging into conservatism. Thoreau's reverie on Katahdin is that of a visitor, someone distanced from the place, using it to clear his mind and soul from the wasteland of civilization. Breathing in the mountain air turns his own writing style toward the pure, the direct, the apprehension of wild experience. He sheds the shackles of culture as he learns to let go. We should all have the chance for this experience, so this land is so preserved, part of the large rectangular green area on the map, Baxter State Park.

But what of the rest of the North Woods? Who is it for, who knows best how it should be managed into the future? The lovers of wilderness hope it will be a huge national park of the East, untouched by roadbuilders, vacation home developers, or paper companies. Enough is enough, the forests have submitted to enough abuse for the time being. Then the green spot on the map would increase, and those of us living far away would rest easy knowing a beautiful and philosophically important place has been set aside for all of us to choose to relive Thoreau's experience, in the mind or on foot, whenever we want to.

On the other hand, what of the people who live in these woods, make their livelihood here, and are close to the land in a practical sense, not the sublime one? They may have less time to reflect on its beauty, but they make their culture amidst this wild nature. Often they are the people who want to keep cutting, and keep developing. Maine is an impoverished state, and it is unclear how to improve its economic condition. Is it enough to be "Vacationland, USA"? Is Thoreau's summit climb toward truth simply part of the holiday mentality?

What traditions are worth saving? There has always been a pragmatic lore of the woodsman tacitly opposed to the romanticized sense
of tonic described by a Thoreau. One hopes that both will be able to
survive: a local culture of the forest, and a place worth visiting by those
of us who by fate live far away from our beloved mountains. There is
a chance for commonality, embracing different senses of what is fun.

Certainly we need better forestry practices, we need an enlightened sense of development, which will neither keep the poor beaten
down nor desecrate the landscape in the name of instant profit. No
romantic wants to let out the battle cry of "compromise!" so we will
all have to pool our different kinds of love for the mountain, and the
uncertain land that surrounds it on all sides.

I'm wondering about all this now, but nothing was farther from my
concern as our party slowly approached the mountain through weeks
of questionable weather. With each rainstorm the mosquito invasion
retaliated, and my love of nature was questioned again. No matter how
much Ole Woodsman's Fly Dope I applied to my ragged green felt
crusher hat, the beasts returned again for another chance at my blood.
(At least the stuff kept people away, though.)

You may smile and write this off as just another part of the "Mainely
Maine" experience, but I know that back then, haggard, exhausted,
underfed, underweight in the prime of adolescence I wanted more than
once to burst into tears, collapse onto the trail and scream, "I give up,
I'm yours, take my blood, please." The insects seem poised to win. Now
I look back, and the whole episode seems but a small tribulation—we
both win. There's enough blood for all, parasite and host.

Can we love and curse the black fly, midge, and no-see-um all at
the same time? I am reminded of the Dalai Lama visiting Vermont,
interviewed by Bill Moyers on TV, swatting away flies as he spoke.
"What," said Bill, "about the mosquito? How do we show compas-
sion there?" "Hmmm, good question," His Holiness ruminated. "First
mosquito . . . no problem. Bite. Second mosquito . . . brush away.
Third mosquito, . . ." as he grinned a wide Tibetan grin, "splat!"

I'm not sure if this anecdote is about patience or frustration, but it does bring a little realism into the abstract kind of love of nature. There is killing in nature, things are taken and consumed. Is the humane approach simply to think twice when we do this, or to feel a little guilty? Must we explain our position, or be content with benign hypocrisy?

Such stories of inconvenience are sometimes left out of tales that embrace the wonder of being returned to the world of the wild. And that is all right, I suppose, but we still should be encouraged to remember everything. Take no pictures, make expression of the journey more work: write, draw, think, memorize, keep technology out of it. Let the mind and the body retain what has happened.

Back to my teenage trip, after two weeks, we reached the campsite at the base of Katahdin. The Great Mountain loomed above us, too close to actually be visible. This time, I thought, nothing could stop us. We would reach the summit the next day.

Yet as luck, or the fated plan, would have it, a rare hurricane had ascended into inland Maine. Most unusual. Heavy rains, wind, downed trees, dark skies, and impassable conditions. In this regulated wilderness, the mountain was deemed "closed." Unfit for ascent, out of bounds, off limits. We wandering pilgrims waited for days under plastic tarps, amusing ourselves by building balanced matchstick sculptures atop polyethylene canteen bottles, an art form that can take years of aborted mountain climbs to master.

The mountain closed? Close a mountain? What would our forefather Henry D. have thought? In his musings he felt such a mountain was inherently closed to the human way of being, but then thought that we needed to go there to discover it. It is doubtful he could have foreseen the need for regulation in the mountains that society now requires. The Maine woods are by now a scene of dichotomy—on one side, the bounded and watched-over park, on the other, the reckless lumber lands. Which then is more wild?

After two failed attempts to climb Katahdin, the mountain had achieved a kind of legendary status in my own internal mythology. Something about this place was keeping me from reaching the summit until I was ready. Each year it seemed a looming possibility, another journey, another fated disaster. Naaah, let's not go, let's put it off, let's keep the myth alive.

This is how a mountain becomes a symbol and its qualities become larger than life. The idea of the mountain situates itself inside us, and from the hum of the city we close our eyes, breathe in the air, and imagine the summit. Then hold the memory in a special place to guide the anticipation of the climb.

In college I finally organized a trip there in the autumn, during the height of the blazing colors bringing on the white hope of winter. It was a long drive, a cold camp, and the morning seemed stormy. Once again a sign at the trailhead announced that the peak was closed for the day. Gales were expected in the afternoon, there had been snow, the path was icy.

This time we had to ignore the warning, transgress the law. I had been waiting too many years. This time we had chosen Thoreau's own route, a longer path, up through waterfalls and onto a green sloping ridge. Thoreau Falls. An honorific place of rushing water, or a historic upset? His reputation falls, he falls from grace. The man seems a contradiction, an anachronism, a dated, lonely rhapsodizer of the near and familiar. Will we let history get away with this?

I repeat, up toward Katahdin Thoreau is at his best. He was on the climb of what the native Penobscots called the "Greatest Mountain." None of them cared much for the ascent, as they probably had better things to do. But for the lonely white man who chooses to go up there, there awaits not an empty nature but a pure one.

Up the falls, into the spruces and pines. The views emerge, red and green seas of color in between blue-black lakes heading clear to the Canadian border. The higher one gets, the more that seems that this is not just the greatest, but the only mountain for miles. The place where the sun first shines at dawn in the whole United States, highest up, furthest east, the beginning of the American day. That was true for Thoreau and is still true today.

No trees, just wind, rock, and for us a light coat of rime ice and snow. The wind was beginning to gust, up from the glacial valleys onto the open headland. The only danger seemed in the future, in the imagination, or in the secure memory of this mountain as a sacred and personally inaccessible place.

Beyond the ridge the trail emerges on the open tableland, and the landscape approaches the harsh and the strange. Too high and windy for trees, too stark for most creatures, only the ancient green map lichen seems to be comfortable living here, as it has for thousands of years. Henry D. found it inhuman up this far and fought the urge to turn back, but I have always felt happiest in such places, able to think most clearly, most at home, most at one with my idea of nature.

What clarity did I find this time? Some kind of expulsion of all the detritus I had brought with me from the city, a necessary and opposite pole to the bustle of ordinary life. And yet this is ordinary life too, ancient life of things growing slowly on glacial granite, enduring across generation after human generation. What can be said? Any prose becomes purple, the mountain denies language, as it encompasses all possible views of it. A thousand views of Katahdin each season, a hundred visitors a day in the height of summer. Each takes home a memory, each has ascended somewhere else inside themselves.

Thoreau let himself out on a limb, and I guess he is still right. We touch the Earth in such places, and we learn in an instant the experience of the release from the civilized, the bond with the wild. He and I reach the summit, a hundred forty years apart, and we feel the same sensations and releases:

> I stand in awe of my body, this matter to which I am bound has become so strange to me. I fear not spirits, ghosts, of which I am one—
> *that* my body might—but I fear bodies, I tremble to meet them. What is this Titan that has taken possession of me? Talk of mysteries—Think of our life in nature—daily to be shown matter, to come in contact with it—rocks, trees, wind on our cheeks! the *solid* earth! the *actual* world! the *common sense! Contact! Contact! Who* are we? *where* are we?[5]

Disorientation, question, then reality. A candid Thoreau admits he *fears* the earth, that his solitary life may have made his own body seem a stranger. But up where the air is thin, the ground is close and direct.

He knows now he is more than mind. And we know the mountain is more than memory.

Every mountain has its chronicler, every landscape its literature, every human her home, whether lived or imagined. *Contact* those who will need it, who will live it, who will save it, who will understand how to reconcile its place and purpose when put against our conflicted civilization. This is it, Henry D. and I have come home, we are united by experience. The practical reason of breaking the rules, civilly disobeying the authorities to climb the mountain, to accept blithely the risk. At the summit I met a ranger, and smiled apologetically. "Isn't it beautiful?" I suggested to her. "Isn't the mountain always open whether we wish it or not?"

It's there now as the first summer storm brews over the East River. It's there as I unplug the phone. It's there as the skyscrapers are swallowed by clouds. The mountain looms inside us. And the wild will win in the end.

FIVE

Will the Real Chief Seattle Please Speak Up?

Every part of the earth is sacred. . . . All things are interconnected. What happens to the earth happens to the sons and daughters of the earth. . . . Man did not weave the web of life, he is merely a strand in it. Whatever he does to the web, he does to himself. . . . Where is the thicket? Gone. Where is the eagle? Gone. What is it to say goodbye to the swift pony and the hunt? *The end of living and the beginning of survival.*

These chilling fragments come from the famous speech of Chief Seattle, probably the single best-known summation of the ideas of the environmental movement. It is familiar all across the globe, appearing in countless talks, epigrams, and quote books. It is said to be compulsory for German schoolchildren to memorize it, and in Scandinavia there are "Chief Seattle Clubs" dedicated to its message. At the museum beneath Mount Rushmore, there once was (and perhaps still is) an interactive diorama with the disembodied head of an Indian that glows red when you press the button, and the solemn words came out, in a soothing, serious voice, impossible to forget.

The words of Seattle are profound, inspiring, and the stuff of a truly spiritual document. They touch people in the way religious texts are meant to, deep inside the heart, straight down to the feet and the hallowed ground beneath. Wherever you are. For the words teach us that all ground can be seen and felt as hallowed ground, and admonish us that our kind is wont to forget this simple and important fact.

This speech has been passed down to us over a long, convoluted journey lasting more than a century.[1] The voyage has many of the qualities of an oral tradition, in that we are not quite sure who said what along the long path these words have taken. They continue to be changed, adjusted, rearranged the way all good stories do as they are told and retold again. So whose words are they?

Here's the lowdown. In 1854 Seattle (more correctly, Seathl) made his speech to Isaac Stevens, Commissioner of Indian Affairs for the new Washington Territories, expressing his wish to cede his land peacefully to the government while affirming deep reservations and sadness for the fate of the land and the differences between his culture and ours. Seathl spoke in Lushootseed, his native tongue, and his speech was translated by Dr. Henry Smith, a young physician who knew the language. Smith realized the speech was something special and that the gravity of its message was certainly watered-down in translation. He is said to have visited Seathl many times over the next several decades to discuss the speech, so he could get it down as accurately as possible in English.

Thirty-three years later this event had already passed into history. Smith published his version of the speech in the *Seattle Sunday Star* in 1887. The style is ornate, Victorian, typical of the way English was supposed to be written in the time, more by people like Smith than Seathl.

For about eighty years the speech lay hidden in obscurity. The late William Arrowsmith, professor of classics at the University of Texas, discovered Smith's article and decided to re-edit it. He was either trying for a more authentic Seathl-like style of writing closer to the way natives would have spoken, or else he was modernizing the words to fit the rebellious spirit of the 1960s. You may read and decide for yourself. He published his "translation" in *Arion* in 1969.

Arrowsmith read his speech at a large student gathering on the very first Earth Day, April 1970. Thousands were listening. Among them was Ted Perry, a young film professor who had been hired by the Southern Baptist Television Commission to write a script for a film called *Home* about pollution and the state of the planet. He immediately had an idea: adapt the words of Seathl for our own time, taking the solemnity and grace of Seathl's way of responding to crisis and apply them to the environmental problems America was now facing. A bit of a historical fiction, for the original speech is more about the folly of claiming to own the land and the white man's lack of respect for ancestral ground than it is about the poisoning of the planet by human indifference. Perry proposed to take Seathl, bring him into our world, and imagine, "What would he say?"

He had no idea how successful his script would be. Once it was shown on network television, the words spread like wildfire around the world. Eighteen thousand people wrote in for copies of the speech. The Southern Baptists sent out a flyer with the text, claiming it really *was* a speech given by Chief Seathl. This is where either the lie or the myth began.

Environmental Action magazine published the text in November 1972, this time claiming it was not a speech but a *letter* from Seathl to President Franklin Pierce! Shortly afterward Northwest Orient Airlines' magazine *Passages* published the "letter," again with no reference to Perry. The speech was published in the *Catholic Herald* in Britain and spread further around the globe by the World Council of Churches. Monsignor Bruce Kent called the speech "almost a Fifth Gospel."

In 1991 illustrator Susan Jeffers brought out a children's book, *Brother Eagle, Sister Sky: A Message from Chief Seattle,* which sold over 400,000 copies and is found in elementary schools across the country. Her Chief Seattle is a distinguished-looking elder in a headdress with buffalo horns. Indians ride ponies through the prairies, and stand in tears before clearcuts. Never mind that Chief Seathl lived in the forests of Puget Sound and never saw a buffalo in his life. He would never have ridden a pony.

In the multicultural 1990s one can't get away with this kind of historical inaccuracy. The story of the fabrication of the speech of Chief Seattle made the front page of the *New York Times* in April 1992— famous Indian speech turns out to be a fraud! But is it a forgery or a case of the malleability of oral history?

Ted Perry, now a professor at a small college in New England, is deeply apologetic. He never intended to write something that would become canonized in the lore of ecological thought: "I didn't want to say 'based' on Chief Seattle. I told the film's producer I was influenced by and inspired by Bill Arrowsmith's reading of his version at the Earth Day rally. But the producer decided that it would seem more authentic to take the written by-line off. The film then says *researched* by Ted Perry—*words* of Chief Seattle."

The most significant thing, it seems, about the Chief Seattle speech is just how widely known it is, how powerful the words are, and how the story and the idea have just sort of spread around. People want to hear someone from the destroyed culture speak up and say, "This is what is different, this is what is the same." It's larger than life, and can't be stopped.

Putting these powerful admonishing words into the mouth of an Indian Chief out of the distant past somehow seems safer than actually saying we want to speak about the Earth ourselves. We want to speak poetically, we want to say the Earth is sacred. But we are afraid of laughter, retribution. If it's a noble Indian, some respected distant person, then it's somehow more trustworthy and indisputable. What would happen if people would quote these words without mentioning Chief Seattle? Do you need to bring in the chief to make the message carry more weight, or can any of us just ask, "How can you buy and sell the air?" as an American today? A Chief besieged by the government. The underdog giving up or making a final plea. Would it be better to write some other speech that would spread just as widely, without appropriating the authority of another time and another culture? Why not accept that these sentiments come from *our* time and our culture?

Nevertheless, in the Chief Seattle speech there are a few real differences between different versions. The real Chief Seathl emphasized a real difference between the God of the red man and the God of the white. "Our God," he said in conclusion, "is not your God." Ted Perry veiled almost all the overt references to God in his script version, in an effort to appeal to a secular America. But then the Southern Baptist producers added this conclusion: "One thing we know. Our God is the same God. This earth is precious to Him. Even the white man cannot be exempt from the common destiny. We may be brothers after all. We shall see." These words have been repeated in most of the versions of the speech promoted by Christian groups and also appear in the version at the Spokane Expo of 1974. Yet they seem diametrically opposed to sentiments expressed in all earlier versions of the speech.

Today the hazy history of the Chief Seattle speech is often taken up by those who want to discredit the rhetoric of environmentalism. Enemies will cite this confusing tale and say, "Look, this just proves that environmentalism is a myth, you people are making up these ideas!" But that's just the point. We have made up this myth. We are the people who need this speech, this message. And it is not going to go away. It may well be with us for a thousand years. It will continue to inspire, like any good religious text. And as the years go by its authorship will be even less conclusive, even farther from memory and actual happening. That's how a text becomes sacred. That's when we know it will not only survive, but live.

Excerpts from Three Versions of Chief Seattle's Speech

Version of Henry Smith, who heard Seattle speak in 1854 in his native tongue, Lushootseed, and then recorded it in print in 1887, after visiting Seattle several times to discuss its meaning

Your God seems to us to be partial.
He came to the white man.
We never saw Him.
We never even heard His voice:
he gave the white man laws
but He had no word for His red children
whose teeming millions filled this vast continent
as the stars fill the firmament.
No, we are two distinct races
and must ever remain so.
There is little in common between us.
the ashes of our ancestors are sacred
and their final resting place is hallowed ground,
while you wander away from the tombs
of your fathers seemingly without regret.

Version of William Arrowsmith, who dug up Smith's little-known newspaper article and published a version in 1969, which he later read on the first Earth Day at the University of Texas, 1970

Your God is prejudiced.
He came to the white man.
We never saw him,
never even heard his voice.
He gave the white man laws,
but he had no word for his red children
whose numbers once filled this land
as the stars filled the sky.
No, we are two separate races,

and we must stay separate.
There is little in common between us.
To us the ashes of our fathers are sacred.
Their graves are holy ground.
But you are wanderers,
you leave your fathers' graves behind you,
and you do not care.

Version of Ted Perry, who wrote his adaptation in 1970 as a narration for a film on the environmental crisis made by the Southern Baptist Television Commission

The white man's god gave him dominion over the beasts, the wood, and
   the red man,
for some special purpose, but that destiny is a mystery to the red man.
We might understand it if we knew what it was the white man dreams,
what hopes he describes to his children on long winter nights,
what visions he burns onto their eyes so that they will wish for tomorrow.
The white man's dreams are hidden from us.
And because they are hidden, we will go our own way.
. . . .
And because they are hidden, we will go our own way.
The white man does not understand.
One portion of land is the same to him as the next,
for he is a wanderer who comes in the night
and borrows from the land whatever he needs.
The earth is not his brother, but his enemy,
and when he has won the struggle,
he moves on.
He leaves his fathers' graves behind, and he does not care.
He kidnaps the earth from his children.
And he does not care.

Smith, 1887

Every part of this country is sacred to my people.
Every hill-side, every valley,
every plain and grove
has been hallowed
by some fond memory
or sad experience of my tribe.
Even the rocks
that seem to lie dumb
as they swelter in the sun along the silent seashore
in solemn grandeur
thrill with memories of past events
connected with the fate of my people,
and the very dust under your feet
responds more lovingly to our footsteps than to yours,
because it is the ashes of our ancestors,
and our bare feet are conscious of the sympathetic touch,
for the soil is rich with the life of our kindred.

Arrowsmith, 1969

Every part of this earth is sacred to my people.
Every hillside,
every valley,
every clearing and wood,
is holy in the memory and experience of my people.
Even those unspeaking stones along the shore
are loud with the events and
memories in the life of my people.
The ground beneath your feet responds
more lovingly to our steps than yours,
because it is the ashes of our grandfathers.
Our bare feet know the kindred touch.
The earth is rich with the lives of our kin.

Perry, 1970

Every part of this earth is sacred to my people.
Every shining pine needle,
every tender shore,
every vapor in the dark woods,
every clearing, and
every humming insect
are holy
in the memory and experience of my people.
The sap which courses through the trees
carries the memories of the red man.
The white man's dead forget the country of their birth
when they walk among the stars. . . .
We are a part of the earth and it is a part of us.
The perfumed flowers are our sisters;
the deer, the horse, the great condor,
these are our brother.
The rocky crests,
the juices in the meadows,
the body heat of the pony,
and man all belong to the same family.

SIX

Melt the Snowflake at Once!

HENRY BUGBEE'S HISTORY OF WONDER

The Walk from Philosophy to Poetry

I first took down the name of Henry Bugbee when I noticed how many American philosophers wrote that he was the one whose writing spurred them to take up philosophy. Bugbee's name comes up time and again in *Falling in Love with Wisdom,* a collection of essays in which philosophers tell their own stories. The mutual recommendations were enough to encourage me to take a trip down from my cabin in Maine to the Harvard library to pick up a copy of *Inward Morning* and see for myself what the excitement was all about. Immediately I understood that here was a uniquely American voice in philosophy, one that inspires us not to follow or agree with him but to engage in our own moving reflection that does not stand still. Bugbee, like Thoreau, needs to be walking in order to be thinking:

> During my years of graduate study before the war I studied philosophy in the classroom and at a desk, but my philosophy took place mainly on foot. It was truly peripatetic, engendered not merely while walking, but *through* walking that was essentially a *meditation of the place.* And the balance in which I weighed the ideas I was studying was always that established in the experience of walking in the place. I weighed everything by the measure of the silent presence of things, clarified in the racing clouds, clarified by the cry of hawks, solidified in the

presence of rocks, spelled syllable by syllable by waters of manifold voice, and consolidated in the act of taking steps, each step a meditation steeped in reality.[1]

Ideas come as we move through the world. They come out of a need to question things that happen to you. To ask the meaning of them as we move around and through them. This is not simply literature, telling a good story with resonances of meaning, but it relates to literature as long as it is written beautifully. Philosophy for Bugbee is like poetry for William Carlos Williams, "a structure built upon your own ground."[2] The central question then becomes: how is it different from poetry, or from literature? This is the distinction that Bugbee will wrestle with throughout his work, and it is a conflict that still goes on at the borders of philosophy, as maverick thinkers want to go deep and also be clear, to reach a wider public and still be true to the inquiring stance of the discipline.

Bugbee is impressed when one day he hears Williams read his poetry to an audience: "Relax! Relax!" the good doctor comforts the crowd. "Do not try to make something of it. . . . Take it as it comes." Poetry is no more than poetry. Philosophy is no more than philosophy. It changes nothing, perhaps because it attends so carefully to all that is already changing.

Bugbee writes in aphorisms. They are not Wittgensteinian aphorisms of cool detachment and careful convolution. They are pithy calls to wake up! To pay attention to all the wonders that are around. Admitting wonder brings so much more reality to any walking, waking life. He worries what all this meditative reflection will do for his career. He does not want to join ranks with the existentialists and the phenomenologists. He will not become a continental philosopher, unless they will let him pick this American island as his continent, no land of deep history and the mass rush to enlightenment. Bugbee finds his answers, not in the march of history, but in the clarity of the wild walk home and away from home into the frost-covered hills and back down to the warmth of the hearth.

He looks to Zen techniques for sudden shocks out of our slumber:

"*What would you say right now?* A snowflake on a burning stove."[3] Is it enough to ask and to ask again? Or need we interpret such tales, through years of meditation, or careful analysis?

I can see why Bugbee has so many secret admirers. He is one of our few countrymen who demands that philosophy hold on to the sense of astonishment that begets it, that astonishment at the color, taste, and richness of the world that wafts on right under our noses, so easy to ignore, so simple to forget. His philosophy arrives in moments, in twists of fate and sudden tales. I can see why he so admires Williams, the poet of everyday life, the doctor who made his patients recover through word and image. But there remains a difference between philosophy and poetry. It is not that one seeks to explain, while the other evokes. It is that the former must ask and ask, and keep asking, until our very sense of perplexity becomes exact, complete, not solvable, but a place to contemplate and inhabit through *wonder,* a positive word, a state of grace, an excited way of loving the world.

Meanwhile, poetry captures brief moments of our being, and renders them unforgettable. One should not try to "make something" of the poem, but philosophy exists to be challenged. The challenge should be in the spirit of wonder, not of picayune unmasking. "You have no idea what kind of people study philosophy," cautions the Oxford don in Philip Kerr's Wittgensteinan thriller, *A Philosophical Investigation.*[4] He quotes Keats: "They are the kind who pull off angels' wings."

Sure, philosophers deserve the bad rap. There's a whole school of philosophy of music that asserts that music is not "about" anything but itself. There are schools of linguistic philosophy that proclaim that if we can't say something unambiguously then it shouldn't be said at all. And too many have been afraid of poets and other disreputables because we all "lie too much."

Well, what worth is the truth if it cannot handle the rich ambiguity of reality? Show me a perfect triangle and I'll show you a shape that has no place in our rough, beautiful, tactile, and imperfect world.

The snowflake melts before we can study it. There is no thought-out answer to anything that can hope to stop time. The objects of our contemplation move out of view just as soon as we see them. And yet, and yet . . . We imagine there can be an explanation, that we can add to the wonder. What is the difference between philosophy and literature? The writer answers: "Does the dawn of a new day have any purpose?" The philosopher: "Why do you want to know?" The answer can be an image, or another in a series of endless questions.

One of my graduate-school professors thought that the following question should be asked to all candidates who would teach aesthetics: "What is it about a cello that moves us so?" Enough philosophers of music would answer that this is not an appropriate question to be asked, citing historical evidence that music is about music and nothing else, that what is moving or sullen is of no philosophic consequence. The scientist would want to mention pitch, vibration, correlating them to the dimensions and frequency of the human body. The watcher might notice the similarity between the scale and shape of the instrument and the form of a woman. Once I heard a somewhat radical piece of music where the cellist confronts the instrument and stops to ask "who *are* you?"

The writer would tell a story that would evoke the answer. The philosopher would make generalizations about humanity as a whole, making use of the royal "we" and assuming at least at some level that we are all one in agreement.

Despite his fine rhetorical gifts, Bugbee remains a philosopher. He wants to embrace us all with his own thoughts: "We must see to it! We worry. We hurry along. We translate necessity into anxiety and effort, trying to take charge. We are swimmers flailing the water to keep from going down."[5] He is making judgments about the global "we." Who is this great group? All of us? Modern Americans? Anyone who can read the words? All humanity, for all time? Philosophy usually doesn't want to make such distinctions, but instead wants to embrace any and all of its readers in a collective but unidentified group.

One moment we understand, the next we may be lost. One moment we are lifted gratefully along the gentle stream, another we are stranded, gasping and writhing, estranged from the element in which it is given to us to live. The stream comes upon us laden with the twofold aspect of responsibility: *the demand and the capacity to respond;* if we swim with necessity we discover power.[6]

Bugbee likes the metaphor of swimming, because moving in the water we cannot forget that the world is thick and in deep flux all around us. See, I want to be a philosopher too. I mention the "we" to give weight to any pronouncement I say. The poet might say "I" instead, the fiction writer might transmute it into a story and claim nothing but the tale itself.

You might say Bugbee's resonant popularity links his method to existentialism. He says "we" but he wants you, the reader, to replace it with "I." You too will be able to experience these things, and can bring the philosophy to life in a way that logic always resists. *Delve into experience. Articulate it so it will become more of the same, more of itself.*

Essence before Existence?

The popularity of Bugbee's *Inward Morning* might have something to do with the popularity of existentialism as a genre spanning the gulf between philosophy and literature. To embrace existence is to admit that life is a tumult of suffering but realize it is wonderful all the same. Still, it can take a lot of suffering to get the point of wonder. Sisyphus rolls his boulder up the endless mountain *forever* before he starts to enjoy it, and smile during the push. An unforgettable image, but perhaps not all that much fun. It's still an acceptance of traditional religious guilt. Or look at Meursault in Camus's *The Stranger.* He has to kill an Arab for no particular reason, live a life utterly devoid of emotion, be put on trial and convicted and be stuck on death row and finally, the night before his execution, he realizes his life has actually been pretty good. Awaiting an inevitable but senseless death, he is finally happy and at peace.

More troubling, but great stories. Literature, not philosophy. Oh? They are both philosophy to the extent that they perfectly convey inexplicable answers to those nagging questions. No analysis can take their crystal qualities away. Literature plays and dances in the faces of the hard questions. It laughs at death, smiles at suffering. Philosophy must continue to worry.

Bugbee passes closest to classic existentialism with his experienced tale of the drowning man. Along the North Fork of the Trinity River in northern California, Bugbee saw a man swept into the furious current of the raging stream. Swollen after a storm, the river seemed sure to devour the frightened man. But he grabbed for a willow branch, and held on with all his strength. Pulling himself against all odds up on the muddy bank, he seemed safe but shaken when Bugbee reached him:

> Slowly he raised his head and we looked into each other's eyes. I lifted out both hands and helped him to his feet. Not a word passed between us. As nearly as I can relive the matter, the compassion I felt with this man gave way into awe and respect for what I witnessed in him. He seemed absolutely clear. In that steady gaze of his I met reality point blank, filtered and distilled as the purity of a man. . . .
>
> Some ten or fifteen minutes later, as we lay on the warm sand having a smoke beside the pool, I noticed that this young man had commenced to tremble, and I trembled with him. We had returned to our ordinary estate, and I cannot recall anything unusual about him or the subsequent conversations we had.[7]

So this drowning man knew fear, and he acted, saved himself, and reached a higher state of wonder and the sense of being alive. But the wonder is not only registered in he who suffers but in he who reaches out; Bugbee touches the survivor and meets reality right there, a surge so much greater and more definite than the ceaseless questioning of the musing philosopher. And then, even more remarkable, past the shared trembling, the orgasmic partnership of endurance and empathy, the greatest realization: this was an ordinary man, it could have been any of us who met danger and wanted not to die but to live. The moment fades. We have to write it down. The questions remain.

The eyes lock with the stare into his eyes, the drowning man being carried away by the cascades. The difficulty is to hold onto this closeness, to feel as connected to another, in the thick of any ordinary encounter. Do not wait until something special happens to you before you learn how full of wonder the world is.

What will you refuse to give up *right now*? The master cannot live a day without silence. The writer cannot live a day without the rush of a filigree of words. The philosopher cannot live a day without wonder.

But the problem with existentialism as a life philosophy, beyond its detached morbidity, can be brought home by recalling Václav Havel's remarks in a speech to the U.S. Congress. "It's time," he proclaimed, "to put essence before existence," *reversing* Sartre's famous embrace of existence before essence. The problem with those guys, Havel seems to imply, is that their free love of experience led to bad politics. Totalitarian communists or fascists all. They experienced too much and felt no responsibility after a time. That is why their movement became bankrupt. Sooner or later we must own up to the truth: all the best questions have no easy answers.

Bugbee knows this. It is never enough for him to exist, but to experience. And in experience comes responsibility. Not "with" experience, but in it. We are required to respond. Nothing happens to us passively, without effort. We look, we listen, we direct our senses, we open them up, and things happen. To me or you. To anyone, whether they care to read this or not.

"What time is it?" they would ask Yogi Berra. He would also answer: "You mean right now?" The baseball star had a knack for zenning the question. Time moves. Nothing we can say about something that happened can hold true, as the world moves on. You just have to wonder about this. It's amazing we can do anything at all, that we can say anything at all.

The sky opens up and the snow melts to a freezing rain. Are these observations warm or cool? Words come flowing out, but the totality evades them. There is no whole picture to be formed out of the cascade of strong insights. This is why Bugbee is stuck with aphorisms, non-plussed by the dream of a whole held together with logic or cement: "For five years I have been writing in an exploratory way, gradually forced to recognize that this was the case and I must accept it, along with its professional consequences. . . . It has been a precarious business."[8] His best insights are often the quickest, single captures out of experience around which he has left enough space so their weight will sink in.

"What is the difference between belief and discovery?" The writer: "I'll make you trust the unbelievable story." The philosopher: "I will teach you to discover your own unbelievable truth." The master: "What was your original face before your parents were born?"

Out in the high woods there was less than an inch of snow on the ground, not a leaf left on the trees, and the long gentle ridges had hardly been traveled upon as the paths rose up slowly past the distant pond to easy views to the west and the east. A tame but open country. Cold but not too cold to be out of doors; at first it's easier to stay in, then stifling to stay in, obviously clearer in the waning winter light: it was the shortest day of the year.

The return was a white-blue walk into the orange sunset. Another easy image. Another exact crispness. Another day in the woods that are not the wilderness, that might have once been the wilderness but only in a time that no one cared to love it and celebrate it, instead dreaming of its civilized possibility.

"I learned from the mountain but then I forgot to learn from humankind," said Bugbee. From the mountains he learned that "things say themselves, univocally, *unisonously*,"[9] a fact he found to be of "infinite significance." But there were no people in this world of singing things. A philosopher in this world would only take things in, and seek out experience, but would have no need to act.

Never mind the snowflake. Put your *hand* on the burning stove, and remember just what it feels like forever. You won't need to do it again and you won't be sorry you did it just once.

What Use Have We for the Wild?

> It can give the lie to it. It can extend, now and then, its elemental emissaries to shores, to suburbs, to the folks downriver, to throngs in airports, to the breadbasket of America, to swaying buildings and empty streets. In pelting downpours, the reach of sky, the weathering willynilly impartial to all, the crawling of ants, the cry of gulls and caw of crows, the rankness of weeds, the silence of snow. . . . Our very dreams might suggest the hidden bulk of the wild which is immolated by our day. And the culture *contrary* to the wild may prove after all, though cloying, to be made of feeble stuff; able to pass itself off only in our waking sleep; some pantomime of life, a common dream, mumbled in unison by an endless crowd.[10]

It is he who lives in the wilderness who forgets the wilderness. The mountain dreamer in the city does not forget, the suburbanite looking for a parking place by the mall, the freeway commuter motionless in a traffic of chrome, sunshades, and mobile phones. The San Gabriels rise over the L.A. smog, the Hudson Highlands are a storied reverie barely visible from the skyscrapers of Manhattan; from Chicago, forgetaboutit, could take you days to reach the realm of trees.

But in any city the wilderness looms in the back of everyone's memory, or imagination, another possibility, another way out, another invented home. But Bugbee knew this wilderness is architecture, not nature. What we want of it is our time's creation, no hint of an original home or primal whiff of the savanna.

I myself have lived for months on end among canyons of concrete, barely seeing the richness of life, and have cried when thrust into a forest of trees. We are adaptable creatures and can be tossed into many strange environments, but at the same time it is amazing how little we forget.

Yet these are the times of doubt and scrutiny. We are taught not to trust our feelings, not to be sure of the primacy of anything, because we are bombarded by images, creatures of culture, never fully restful at home anywhere. Unexamined life, worthless but happy. The questions, they never go, they're so easy they ask themselves, and no one can stop them unless we choose not to wonder. And wonder, Bugbee reminds us, as any good philosopher reminds us, ought to bring us closer to reality if it is to bring us anywhere at all.

> Could we ever understand ourselves in the image of the rocklike island or the stronghold, impervious to what surrounds us, living a life of inner containment, perduring incorruptible in solid singleness, or reigning over ourselves to secure constant excellence and tranquillity within the island of ourselves?[11]

No one is an island. We are not ourselves if we imagine we are alone. All decisions are made in tandem with the world. "Humans," writes David Abram, "are tuned for relationship." Do not go into the wilderness to be alone, or to find yourself alone, but to connect with the world. A world that fans out from the arena of other people into the peacock spread of the universe. Be attentive to all of it.

Restoration and the Return

But the world melts down, its beauties fade away in the glass and gray of exacted civilization. What can we recover? Is there anything original that we want? The old ways became the new ways, so there is no point to nostalgia.

Bugbee saw all these problems with looking back, and he anticipated today's environmental movement toward restoration, remaking the wild right in our midst, and he cast it in a certain optimistically spiritual light that I think still gives it a greater meaning than any naive attempt to *construct* wildness:

> It was in the fall of '41, October and November, while late autumn prevailed throughout the northern Canadian Rockies, restoring everything in that vast region to a native wildness. Some part of each day or night,

for forty days, flurries of snow were flying. The aspens and larches took on a yellow so vivid, so pure, so trembling in the air, as to fairly cry out that they were as they were, limitlessly. And it was there in attending to this wilderness, with unremitting alertness and attentiveness, yes, even as I slept, that I knew myself to have been instructed for life. . . . Philosophy is not a making of a home for the mind out of reality. It is more like learning to leave things be: restoration in the wilderness, here and now.[12]

Not just ecological restoration, but restoration of something larger, some sense of life and experience, recovery of an openness to wonder. Because it's easy to lose.

I know the lostness he means. So many recent times when I don't want to look out the window, when I won't go outside, when I seek solace in things, the owning of objects when I know inside that they are meaningless. No need to go on when I've already produced things out of experience. I have closed down, I am blasé, no longer open. If philosophy can help me it will have to *restore* wonder. Not only through beautiful words, but in words that inspire wonder.

Philosophy works like the voice-over commentaries you hear in certain films, particularly those speculating works with cascades of images, marked by a single speaking commentary that questions the meaning of the happenings that are observed, albeit at a distance. Earlier I mentioned Chris Marker's *Sans Soleil.* In this 1983 film, a woman is reading letters she has received from a friend who travels to Africa and Japan, a filmmaker who is describing his work to her as the images come over the screen. As the traveler looks up at a place and remarks how it resembles some other place, he can note that down, and he has the film footage to prove it, to demonstrate it, to construct a story. The running commentary seems to me to be philosophy in action, the recording of the happenings around as we move, and the struggle to make sense of it all:

I remember the month of January in Tokyo, or rather I remember the images I filmed of the month of January in Tokyo. They have substituted themselves for my memory, they *are* my memory. I wonder how people remember things who don't film, don't photograph, don't tape. How has mankind managed to remember! I know, it wrote the Bible. The new Bible will be an eternal magnetic tape of a Time that will have to reread itself constantly just to know it existed. . . . The memory of a precise color in the street bounces back on another country, another distance, another music, endlessly.[13]

Marker is amazed by the links within his own repository of images collected from all over the world, all moods and places and times. He is amazed by the way the future rapidly becomes the past, and we attempt to document our place in time any which way we can. His film is a catalog of wonders, and you leave it seeing the world a new way. It works as philosophy should, to awaken our senses, and builds on the tradition of Bugbee's journalistic form.

This is how philosophy must change the world. Not by giving us reasons to opt for clearer logic, less ambiguous communication, but to celebrate the magic in the very way we see. Wonder itself is what we must restore, and it can be witnessed anywhere, from the wilderness to the city. Nature can awaken it. Time can awaken it. Everything that happens to us can be filled with significance.

I decide it is time to end this essay while reaching a moist snowy meadow deep in the Catskills. Down the valley is a view up the rounded peaks of Wittenberg, Cornell, and Slide, and on the ground are tentative tracks of baby bears that have woken up to play in the snow. In the sudden cold the streams have frozen into thin topographic rings of brittle ice, which crackles easily as you step on it through to the rushing water below. A warm mist rises, the temperature will change. Daylight is brief, the slopes soon darken. *What must I do so as not to forget this place?*

The day before I was in Atlanta, trapped in a cement hotel like so many others in my profession. The fog was so thick some planes circled the airport for hours before a glimpse of the landing lights could coax them down. This mist made the new downtown even more surreal than usual. No one is meant to go outside among these banks and malls, as the buildings are all connected by winding walkways, many stories above the ground. The street has been declared dead, closed off, inhospitable and not to be tread upon. Taking the risk to walk outside at night, I gave a homeless man the remains of my Indian dinner, in a styrofoam box. He said he lived in an old warehouse at the edge of the downtown redevelopment district. "Downtown," he mentioned, "you will not find a high class of people. Out in the suburbs, you know, beyond the ring, that's where the better people live."

The city is changed into cold, empty structures. People flee to be far from its center but then not too far. In the wilderness, even farther beyond the ring, glimmers of wind and sky make it seem that restoration might be possible.

The snowflake is already gone. The snow never fell. It is cold and dark some place while it is warm and gray somewhere else. What temperature is it *right now*? There is no right answer, but always a ream of questions. Henry Bugbee taught us how to notice, how to ask. He has set us all on the track of the history of wonder.

SEVEN

Who Is the Lone Ranger?

EDWARD ABBEY AS PHILOSOPHER

Anyone who sets out to write some examining words about
Edward Abbey is asking for trouble. It's like preparing to
fight with an angry dog over a small table scrap, both
of you trapped in a tiny room. Except with Abbey the room has no
boundaries that you can see—it's not the desert spreading out in all
directions, but the myriad canyons and ridges where literature and
philosophy grind against each other to form the mountains of our intellectual hope and possibility. For he has always asked the questions
the best writers ask: How to unravel the greatest mysteries? How to
attack the most important questions rigorously and still leave room
for spontaneous beauty?

But he wants his dinner. I want mine. He doesn't want to be pushed
out of the running. Abbey loathed critics, nature writers, anyone else
who might encroach on his turf. Here's how he stared us down:

> What a gutless pack of invertebrates you mostly are. What a fawn-
> ing groveling writhing genteel array of . . . gutless fence-straddling
> castrated neutered craven equivocating vapid insipid timorous high-
> minded low-bellied spineless cool hip cowardly moral jellyfish!
> Banana slugs of literature![1]

Who was he talking about? Everyone else but himself. Sure, all real
writers have a healthy animosity toward the critics who can make or

break their reputation. Abbey lived out in the heart of the world, but he so craved attention from the heart of commerce. Why wouldn't the East Coast literary establishment ever welcome him in? He wanted to be known as a novelist and fictioneer; they saw him as a regionalist: chronicler of a little-known and faraway essential core of America's presence. But Abbey needed the critics and baited them along. He also needed philosophy, and I believe he used it in the way it should be used: outside the textbooks, far from the classroom, as a guide to transmute the experiences of a full and genuine life.

Abbey's oft-ignored experience in philosophy informed his various reflections, real or imagined. For philosophy is not the same as literature, as we have all been told: it's supposed to make us angry, to perplex us, to leave us with more questions than answers. What Abbey does with it is to make it literature in the end, so the results are also beautiful and, at their best, impossible to forget.

Abbey is an idol to many of us reluctant academics because he turned away from the institutions that spawned him. When they invited him to their inner sanctum, he walked. Not many remember that Abbey was a graduate student in philosophy at the University of New Mexico. Here is a thinly fictionalized scene from a meeting of his master's thesis committee, with the aged professors grilling Abbey's alter ego Henry Lightcap about the progress of his research:

"And another question, Lightcap: Do you really want to be a professor of philosophy?"

" . . . I certainly want to be a philosopher, sir, and live *la vie philosophique* goddamnit."

Henry reflected. A fork in his road of life had most suddenly appeared dead ahead. To the right, the right way, a broad and shining highway led upward beyond the master of arts toward the Ph.D.— the tenured leisurely life of overpaid underworked professorhood. A respectable life. Anyone who is paid much for doing little is regarded with obligatory admiration. To the left a dingy path littered with beer cans and used toilet paper led downward in darkness to a life of shame, of part-time and seasonal work and unemployment compensation, of domestic strife, jug wine, uncertainty, shady deals, naive realism, stud poker, furtive philanderings, skeptical nominalism, pickup trucks, a gross and unalambicated nineteenth-century eight-ball materialism. He called his shot. I will not tell a lie. Looking at his three Inquisitors looking at him, he answered them collectively:

"Not really," he said.[2]

I have always wanted to tack this quote up on my office door. Sure, we can fight back. It can be hard to work honorably as a professor, teaching and talking, writing and reflecting. But I and many others have always felt the pull of the other way, the dangerous track of the loner, where you must go if you truly have the creative talents Abbey fought for and cultivated. There is so much more philosophy out beyond the bounds or the rules!

Yet Abbey was never without his regrets for the road not taken. He was not one to be easily satisfied with any one outcome or another. I would say this is because he studied enough philosophy to get hooked on the idea that dilemma is worth more than solution, that *both* the bird in the hand and the bird in the bush are worth more being out there than choosing one over the other. Abbey was *addicted* to philosophical conundra, and the love of uncertainty (which philosophy can give you) is probably what kept the man out of any club that would have someone like him for a member. Like Socrates, he said just those things that would make him unpopular, while teaching the rest of us a thing or two. Only he died long before his time, and our loss grows deeper with each thinking year.

I must confess that I speak from philosophy with more than a tinge of ambivalence. I never wanted to become a philosopher. I got into it through love of the Earth, through an apprenticeship with Norwegian coyote ecosopher Arne Naess, who told me I was too deep within it all to escape. But I tried, maybe am still trying, went through the same rite of passage Abbey ran from, and still remain in the fold. For the moment. Why am I telling you this? Only to work it out for myself, to basically admit that philosophy and the wilderness are not so much strangers as necessary partners. Now if I am honest and think all the way back, it was in *Desert Solitaire,* read when I was twelve on a family trip into the desert, that I first heard of philosophy and tried to figure out what in hell the man was talking about. More than twenty years later I realize the genius of a man who made real sense out of the timeless and impossible obsessions, brought them into a language that is both deep and understandable to all of us.

And he lures us in by twisting our expectations, keeping his reflection always just a false-peak beyond the familiar viewpoint. For right from the intro, *Desert Solitaire* is expressly "not primarily a book about the desert. . . . I have tried to create a world of words in which the desert figures more as medium than as material. Not imitation but evocation has been the goal."[3] The old extrapolator is using nature for his own purposes just like every other human throughout history. He is making the desert into the stark landscape of his own dreams and doubts, constantly urging us not to follow him, insisting it can't be done, that the landscapes he has loved are no more. This guidebook instructs us to find our own roads, and make sure they are ours and ours alone.

For when he announces on page one that "this is the most beautiful place on earth" he immediately softens the pronouncement with the admission that "there are many such places." His litany includes places rural and urban, all localities that have mattered to him in his wanderings. My students in Newark are particularly intrigued by his enamorings of Hoboken. I tell them that when I read this as a teenager the word *Hoboken* became like a magic incantation, some kind of legendary place. I knew it was a seedy river town in Jersey, but if Abbey loved it, there must be something to the place. Later I learned he wrote most of *Solitaire* there, living with one of his early wives. And when I finally went to Hoboken I learned what he was talking about: if we become sensitized to the inspiring qualities of place, any place, any home we deem serious enough to try out, then the immediacy of any view can lure us toward philosophy. Abbey looked across at Manhattan and saw the end. In the desert he could run from it, but so much for the beauties of death: "Looking back at it from this desert perspective, you've got to admit that Wolf Hole, Arizona, can never have so rich a death."[4] But he had to return to the desert, if only because there was so much more space to fill with the most stark kind of questions:

> What do the coyotes mean when they yodel at the moon? What are the dolphins trying so patiently to tell us? Precisely what did those two enraptured gopher snakes have in mind when they came gliding toward my eyes over the naked sandstone? . . . They do not sweat and whine about their condition. They do not lie awake in the dark and weep for their sins.[5]

No remorse. No mercy. The strength of philosophy can be measured by one's confidence in sticking with the questions and not rushing on to answers. Abbey is always in hot pursuit of raw experience, never attainable, always some place beyond where the mind might no longer wonder. He could not be satisfied, and would never get enough of the trying *or* the groveling. Those living in pure experience have nothing to say about it. The writer must step back and invent his persona. We will never come close to knowing who he really is because he spent so much time trying to tell us, leaping between fiction and thinly disguised fact. But questioning can easily turn to defense. In the end a simple touch can win over an idea:

> Do I seem to write only of the surfaces of things? Yet, it seems to me that only surfaces are of ultimate importance—the touch of a child's hand in yours, the taste of an apple, the embrace of friend or lover, sunlight on rock and leaf, music, the feel of a girl's skin on the inside of her thigh, the bark of a tree, the plunge of clear water, the face of the wind.[6]

When Abbey gets serious, it is over the emotion and memory of fleeting immediacy. This catalog of images we all know is the surest answer to feelings of futility, since we know nothing beyond the human edges of a much deeper world. Phenomena, not noumena, like old Immanuel

Kant said as he proceeded to write thousands of pages on why he had given up trying to know anything about the core of reality. Abbey is wise to refute it thus, and any commentary upon such clarity trudges down into the muck.

But I see Abbey smiling way up above me in the arc of the irreducible vultures above in the autumn sky. He remains a philosopher. He answers the question, but the questions still haunt him. Because they will never go away he must go on asking, posing the big ones and returning with a joy in the mundane and the sudden. The bigger the question, the more he wants to laugh. I do not know whether or not this is an easy way out.

"Newcomb," I explain, "we've got to go back."

"But why?" he says. "Why? . . ."

"Because," I explain. The role of the Explainer has become a well-established one in recent times. "Because they need us. Because civilization needs us."

"What civilization?" he says.

"You said it. That's why they need us."

"But do we need them?"[7]

The dance of the philosophical dialogue is back, thousands of years after Plato. Philosophers always return to these dialogues for the back and forth, the living sense of the two sides of the best questions, hunting and pecking around the impervious answers. No explanation seems enough but we cannot be too afraid to try. Try as they might, philosophers have been unable to breathe much life into the dialogue form over the past two millennia. Literature, of course, has taken over: think of the philosophy debated in Dostoyevsky, even Shakespeare. But Abbey is the sparse talker, the cool, the breath of wind in the middle of the canyon heat. Who? Who. The end of the questions never matters as much as the *need* for the questions.

There is the love of questions, and then the need to make a difference in the struggling and bruised world. The impotence of philosophy seems inherent in its whole method, asking, twisting, playing around, never giving in. Abbey couldn't get enough of it, but as he watched his vision of the Great Southwest recede into the past, he knew it was time to take action. The action of a writer is of course to write, but a writer can concoct a fantasy of revenge against the way the world has become. That is the hook behind *The Monkey Wrench Gang,* his most popular novel, the invention of a band of rebels sworn to destroy the encroaching tools and artifacts of industrial civilization, the spirit of the megalopolis heading into the beautiful desert: billboards, bulldozers, power lines, and dams. These are our enemies, not people but the property and agents of blight on the landscape. It is time for the lovers of the desert to fight back. George Hayduke figured it out: "My job is to save the fucking wilderness. I don't know anything else worth saving."[8]

Wilderness matters most to Abbey, and that's not just because there's no people out there and he can finally be left alone in his perpetual curmudgeonhood. No, it is because this is where he feels enough openness to think, to fill the desert dryness with a culture of precision. He doesn't hear twanging guitars or lone plaintive flutes, but the harsh, entwined string tonalities of Webern and Schoenberg, a music just right for a place that is "both agonized and deeply still."[9] Wilderness is home for the renegade survivalist of ideas, hiding remorsefully from the dying centers of culture, at the same time endlessly craving attention from that culture. He could never really move away! Love of the word kept him in, craving approval from just those people most scared of his wildness, most content to keep it at bay in pretty words.

Enjoying this ambiguity rather than trying to break through it, I consider Abbey more successful as philosopher than polemicist. He liked open questions, he liked to twist the minds of those tribes who tried to claim him as one of their own. From wherever he stands, however alone he might seem, there is always someone a bit more lonelier than he, an alter ego or a challenge, a dream at least of a more detached observer always one step farther from civilization that he would dare to step.

This starts with the old Moon-Eyed horse in *Desert Solitaire,* a formerly tame beast who had found the wild life by choice and lived alone up a dry canyon. "That," thinks Abbey, "is the kind of horse I would like." He endeavors to tame him, to lure him in. Walks up the canyon alone with a canteen. Old Moon-Eye appears, suspicious and at the edge of twilight view. Abbey sweet-talks him, lures him with the faint promise of the benefits of culture: "Moon-Eye, how long since you've stuck that ugly face of yours into a bucket of barley and bran? Remember what alfalfa tastes like, old pardner?"[10] Careful cajoling long until the sun sets. Abbey wants a horse as independent as he is. But Moon-Eye will have none of it. He turns alone back into his desert tracks, thus earning the author's respect. Not a wild horse, but an independent horse. Still out there, making his own way.

And Abbey, too, making sure no group can have him. He does manage to achieve an inspirational effect many writers dream of, but few realize: he invents a fictional movement that then comes to life. The Monkey Wrench Gang's final dream is taking out the great Glen Canyon Scam and restoring the fabulous canyon to its original sacred state. It's a rousing adventure of true believers fighting for the public good, long before having to answer to the scourge of being labeled "eco-terrorists" and the like. But even they are not a safe society. Still more remote than the Gang is the mysterious Lone Ranger, who appears sporadically in the novel as the lonely savior about whom precious little can ever be told. There is always an outsider behind any of Abbey's revolutions, an extra spoke in the wheel of paradox. As strange and as necessary as the fact that Bonnie Abbzug will always remain the only Jewish gentile in southeast Utah.

True enough, Abbey's fable of monkeywrenching vigilantes became reality in the mid-1980s with the emergence of the Earth First! movement, determined to effect no compromise in their defense of Mother Earth. Some welcomed their rousing brand of political theater into the now stodgy, mainstream eco-movement, while others feared it was all too silly, if not outright destructive, in clearly malicious ways.

For my part I would say that Earth First! has been successful in the ways the Monkey Wrench Gang was successful: showing how fun it can be to fight back in the name of saving the wild, something that is so right to fight for, so important, and in so much danger. True to the fiction that begot it, real-life Earth Firsters were persecuted by the FBI and sent to jail for sentences upwards of ten years. Two supporters were nearly blown up in a questionable bomb explosion: immediately following the accident the FBI accused the victims of planning a violent act, whereas all their previous demonstrations were nonviolent! The feds clearly became scared of Earth First!, not the least because they advocated the destruction of private property in the name of public good. And as good as we want the public to be, private property remains this nation's most sacred ideal.

For Abbey's part, he seemed to have a mixed relation with Earth First! I have seen films of him mumbling eloquent words at various gatherings of would-be miscreant defenders of nature, and I'm sure he was flattered by all the real-life effect his imagination wrought. Still, he never seems all that comfortable out raising the crowd into a frenzy. Abbey remained foremost a writer—someone who sits safely behind a typewriter and lets his words take the risks for him, scaring off enemies and would-be friends, articulating with logic and emotion a convincing critique that is never easy to put down.

Abbey's final novel, rushed to completion as its author lay dying, brings the inevitable return of the Monkey Wrench Gang into the real Earth Firsted world of the late 1980s. Though I know I am in the minority here, I actually prefer it as a novel to the original, which seems to ramble on and on after a while. *Hayduke Lives!* is a series of character studies, working one by one through the members of the original gang as they contemplate how life has treated them in the years following the original ruckus. Abbey visits the Earth First! Round River Rendezvous and makes it sound like a rousing gathering of wild country philosophers, angry redneck mountaineers, and pagan new paradigmists, all ready to save the world. The protagonist is the lovely Norwegian maiden Erika, "last name unknown, representing the song of Norway, the mind of Arne Naess, . . . the beauty of Greta Garbo"[11] who speaks with a German accent throughout, mysteriously in love with former Mormon missionary Oral Hatch now turned FBI mole. (When I once showed these passages to Naess he was honored that his name was enough to articulate a character.) The plot is questionable but hilarious, the role of the original Gang in this gathering non-existent. The goal is to stop the giant GOLIATH earth-moving machine that grinds along the desert creating an instant superhighway in its wake. The Earth Firsters, led by fearless Erika ("Ze Eart' she first!") aim to make a giant blockade across the plateau to stop the machine from paving over paradise as it lumbers maliciously along. But what can they do? Have a good time, put on a show, get TV and radio to pay attention just as in real life, but ultimately they are dragged away by the cops and the machine still moves.

But wait! While Earth First! postures and talks and shouts and gathers, the Monkey Wrench Gang is getting the job done. No one knows where they are. No one remembers who they are. But they succeed in secret where the noisemakers are doomed to fail.

This is a powerful and typically cantankerous message for Abbey to cast forth to the activist group originally inspired by his fictional band of merry pranksters. They have become famous, in the newspapers and on television all across the land, and they have brought a wrenching humor to staid and confrontational environmentalism. But can they really stop the beast? The result is completely independent from the posturing. Leave no footprints. Leave no trace. Above all, never get caught. *No one must know your name.* That is a different strategy than that taken by Earth First!, who remain a protest theater group and lobbying faction in the eyes of the media. Stopping the encroachment of evil machinery is still best done in secret. The wild is preserved. No one hears about it. If anyone thanks you for your efforts, it will be nature, silent, unheralded, solemn, alive.

Philosophers have generally been uncomfortable with ecosabotage and have offered careful arguments against it.[12] Principles of nonviolence become of greater value than getting results. Your side always looks better if you take the moral high ground and do not resort to low and nasty tactics. But this all may be too cool for the real world, and Abbey may have been too real to stand on top of abstractions for all his days. He used philosophy to open up his vision, but when he took a stand, he went one step beyond frustration to an invisible pragmatism: get the job done, and make the action speak where the person behind it remains silent, someone whereof we can never speak.

There are always such persons one step beyond the action, one step beyond the known, part of the realm of mystery pervasive in Abbey's works. *The Monkey Wrench Gang* has a familiar but ghostly Lone Ranger, who helps out the Gang in key moments when you're not quite sure he's for real. He's back in *Hayduke Lives!* leaving the Reverend Bishop Love stranded with his soon-to-be second wife, pleasingly plump Ranger Dick. There is always someone watching from the sidelines, a character or plotline not quite visible to the reader or fellow journeyer with the old buzzard himself.

"Stop the car," cries the author at the end of *Solitaire*. "Let's go back."[13] They go on, and with sadness old Ed knows nothing will be the same when he returns. Nothing ever does stay the same, and that always saddens those who love the way things used to be. And lovers of wild places usually remember and rhapsodize those places as they were just one time and no other, before the stream of humanity descends upon them; first the writer, then those who read him and want to repeat the already impossible past.

This is what Jack Turner called "Muir's Mistake," for how could the Sierra Club's founder not realize that such an organized society would prevent the lone and complete wonder he felt and described in the midst of the great and incontrovertible Sierra Nevada?[14] Now that everyone goes there they are not likely to be any more surprised than on a walk through a city park. Abbey knew this; he specifically wanted no one to follow him. One early parable describes an overland journey through rutted Texas desert roads with one of his numerous wives, just after their wedding night. Far from the labeled highways, they pass a cryptic junction: "Hartung's Road. Take the Other." So adrift on the Other Path they go, until the brand-new Ford is unable to continue. The woman storms off, and they never speak again. A few years later there's a book out: *Abbey's Road*. The implication is clear. It's up to *us* to take the other. Don't follow Cactus Ed. He's always made sure he's none too appealing as role model or source of wisdom, high or low. Nope. Too many unpleasantries of character and persuasion: dirty old man even at the age of twenty-five (if that is possible), racist, ranting bigot, sexist, perennial curmudgeon at best. But at least he can laugh at himself throughout. And, most importantly, he can inspire a kind of individualism that does allow us to join up with his spirit at the core, even though we are told to follow our own restless tracks when the crossroads come.

The totem image of "Abbey's Road—Take the Other" lingers as a mixture of Zen koan and fearsome backwoods retreatism. Would you follow the named path or go the anonymous way the words point to? Depends on your self-confidence, your trust in the directions. I admire Abbey, so would I want to do what he says? True enough, his road has already been taken. The unknown calls out. We ought to find our own way. Perhaps steer clear of the vulture by a thousand miles. If the country is still big enough for us to do so.

Here Abbey is not so dissimilar from a man he must have admired just a bit, Arne Naess, philosopher at the foundation of the deep ecology movement, inspirateur to the Earth Firsters, tacit supporter for the goals of the Monkey Wrench Gang if not their methods. Well, Naess would probably prefer the Gang to the First, because they are taciturn, secret, impossible to trace, though their results be far-reaching. Polite and gentile, Naess wrote a careful philosophical analysis of Gandhism, showing it to be a consistent approach for conflict resolution.[15] Only after Rachel Carson's wake-up call to prevent a silent spring did Naess, a lifetime mountaineer, stop dumping garbage behind his mountain hideaway and realize that a thinker could do something serious to save the Earth.[16] But all the while, as a teacher and policymaker around education, Naess had encouraged several generations of students to find their own roads, never founding a coherent school or singular way of seeing things.   ·

With the recent popularity of deep ecology in the United States, there has been some tendency to idolize the man and his ideas, taking his ideas of equal value for all living things and putting the Earth first before human needs and aspirations as a kind of gospel. But he never asked for that! He would rather we all articulate, experience, or at least *live* our own philosophies. No cloning of the master's words, please. He and Abbey would have gotten along fine, and it's a pity they never met. But at least we have him somewhat personified in the spirit of Erika ("Down wiss empire up wiss spring!" in a once again obtusely generic foreign accent).

Yes, as much as he savaged the academy, Abbey always respected philosophy, elevated its ability to inspire into something more: laughter, and a tool for making sense of the straining surge of remembering. The world is changing, and yet what we found there remains impossible to forget. Those who remember too much are often faulted for "romanticizing" the past. Charles Bowden told me recently that this is why he believes the public turned slightly against Abbey in the end: "He kept going on and on about the decline of the West, while the West went on and kept changing."[17] Changing into a corrupt, developers' paradise with levels of strange evil that made even the full range of Abbey's complaint seem tame. Could he have anticipated Charlie Keating, a businessman more deeply sinister than any of the cartoon villains from the sketchbooks of Abbey?[18] The future will still grow darker before we can glimpse any light. Sure we have lost things of inestimable beauty. And we must not repeat the grave errors of the past. But we will not be given back the past, no matter how crisply we remember it.

Abbey did not fare well with the future. His novel about the end of the world was entitled *Good News!* A more useful environmental philosophy will dare to imagine the future. And will, paradoxically, find it even more romantic than the past. Bowden, perhaps the Abbey of our present generation (with a dash of William Burroughs thrown into the sauce), offers us this to look forward to:

> This is how the future comes to me, how I stumble down unmapped
> lanes and suddenly am in front of that cathouse where she waits
> unloved, the face of indeterminate colors, the lips smiling and the

eyes knowing far too much. . . . There will be no first hundred days for this future, there will be no five year plans. There will be no program. *Imagine the problem is that we cannot imagine a future where we possess less but are more. Imagine the problem is a future that terrifies us because we lose our machines but gain our feet and pounding hearts.*[19]

Bowden is seduced by the future in a whorehouse of his own devising. She is alive and enveloping and he's damn scared of her. And yet we strain for a chance at her and hope she will remember us, when her time has come. There is an alluring irony here, but also a chilling and powerful feminine spirit that is more serious than anything Abbey would ascribe to his female characters.

Abbey's women are part of the world of remorse—they usually lie in his past. He rhapsodizes them as part of the good old long-gone days that puff themselves up into phantoms in his rickety memory. They leave him and do not return. Abbey's writing became increasingly a chronicle of times that are no more, of a life spent and continually re-invented as either fact or fiction, often with little difference between. Abbey, Lightcap, the nameless and beak-nosed worn journalist in *Hayduke,* scribbling down all the passion and belief around him.

Now tell me, what philosopher really wants to fit in? How can a speculator, a dreamer, an artist of concepts ever find a home? You always ostracize yourself when you take on the sacred myths: money, progress, personal space, happiness, self-realization. Can we get to any of these places while trashing the world? Can selfishness ever be safely stopped? By who? *Who?* Who.

The philosopher is safely unpopularized with his litany of questions. He takes down notes to transform the facts. But they never hold water. He wants the water to flow through them, he wants the sand to outlast his words. He has questioned the human situation long enough to know that the world will get on fine without us, and not whip itself into irascible paradox and lazy impossibility.

Never afraid to be a hypocrite, at least Abbey is consistent: his fiction and his nonfiction, his private and public writings, all generally present the same unforgettable character amidst his friends, loves, and landscapes. There is no question that this indefatigable questioner was a great writer, of quotable aphorisms, careful descriptions, and rambling novelizations. I believe it all will hold up over time, and we will still laugh and cry with Abbey many years down the line. From philosophy he learned that the most important questions can never be answered, yet one can go far by asking and posing them over and over again.

His life was one answer, but his inspiration should serve to set us adrift. Do not imitate, never join up. Take what you want, and make your life and ideas your own. Philosophy dries when it loses its original spirit of wonder, but the desert comes alive when one's attention is attuned. The philosopher is trained never to be satisfied with one response as opposed to another, and it's clear than forms of restlessness kept Abbey moving forward and around all through his life. The Lone Ranger can never stay any one place too long before his identity gets out. He's got to ride out of the picture and leave only clues as to who he was or why he was here. The words are the clues, the writings his legacy. May we never figure out too much about that grizzly buzzard, Edward Abbey. Worry not, we vultures will never pick him clean.

EIGHT

From the Opaque to the Concrete

THE POETIC SIDE OF ARNE NAESS

From Movement to Philosophy

Most of the writing concerned with deep ecology tends to focus on the deep ecology *movement,* an international assemblage of theorists and activists intent on using environmentalism as a basis for a fundamental change in the way we live and understand the human place in nature. In this definition such a movement implicates people like Murray Bookchin, the late David Brower, and former vice president Al Gore, whether they like it or not. As a movement, deep ecology is an embracing, umbrella term to cover all those who believe ecological problems stand for deeper social, political, and ethical problems.

But the *philosophy* of deep ecology is something altogether different. This is, I believe, something much more specific than the movement, something less recognized, less well-understood.[1] Deep ecology as philosophy is the attempt to articulate a new relationship between humanity and nature, one that does not accept familiar divisions between the subjective and the objective, or between the natural and the human. Deep ecology as philosophy suggests that humanity is not only part of nature, but intertwined with nature, as idea and fact, connected to our surroundings in a way that our language is not prepared to let us speak. Our language and categories of thought are questioned in order that we may develop new ways to "speak the world into existence" (in Heidegger's words), changing logic, syntax, and conception. This is the most radical kind of ecological thinking, and this is the hardest to engage in or to explain.

Arne Naess's particular articulation of the philosophy of deep ecology depends on a human ability to directly apprehend the qualities of nature. This borrows from phenomenology but does not use the terminology of phenomenology. In this paper I intend to explore Naess's terminology of *concrete contents,* which builds on a rejection of Galileo's distinction between primary, secondary, and tertiary qualities and posits instead a way of understanding where we apprehend the qualities of things only through their relation with each other. Naess rejects the notion of 'quality' and comes up instead with the word 'contents' and calls these contents 'concrete' because they are directly apprehended reality, not structures invoked to explain reality.

Naess then sidesteps the phenomenological tradition, with its subject experiencing the world, and hints instead at a world that as a whole experiences itself, with no primary subjects or objects, but instead as a *web of relations.* I say "hints" because the philosophy of deep ecology has always, in its radical break with tradition, seemed by nature to be preliminary.[2] How to develop it further? I suggest that Naess is trying to push philosophy in a direction toward poetry, using a series of resonating examples from Italian writer Italo Calvino, a film by John Sayles, and Swedish poet Tomas Tranströmer. For philosophy to redefine itself, it sometimes needs to find inspiration outside its borders.

The Relational and the Real

Naess rides the train to the mountains—he sees birches smiling, firs weeping. He wants us to believe that these smiles and tears *come before* we see trees themselves, and are not a projection from human moods or glances. These emotional parts of reality he calls the *concrete contents* of reality. We see the world first as relations between us and it. Smiles and cries are actually there, they are the fabric of the world, the threads of nature and the foundations of the universe. He doesn't want to call them human appearances, but natural appearances. Not human experience but simply experience, the world experiencing itself in surges of emotion, sparkles of light. We need to wake up and perceive the world as alive, dancing upon itself, wondrous and self-aware.

With this idea of the content of reality as concrete, Naess is reaching for a name to mark out an area of existence, and giving it greater weight by saying it is real. In his drive to make up these phrases and hope they will stick, I see him striving for a peculiar kind of logical poetry, trying out a metaphor to see if it will catch on, a gentle jab to consider the pieces of experience and wonder what would happen if we were to put them back together another way.

It is my intention here to investigate what it would mean to see the world this other way—how the primacy of all qualities might make things recede and relations come into prominence, how it might be the birth of a less arrogant way of placing human beings into an equally experiencing surrounding, also a subject, not only an object. And the announcement that the emotions we sense there in nature are not mere projections, or whims of different perspectives, but an actuality that can't be denied.

Leave your left hand out in the cold winter air, keep the right one cozy inside a mitten. Then stick both inside a pot of room-temperature water. The left one feels warm. The right one feels cold. Is the *water* warm or cold? Galileo says neither warm nor cold. These are secondary qualities, subjective, in the hand of the beholder. To be distinguished from primary, objective qualities like volume and shape, what he would have called properties of the water and the pot itself, wholly contained and clear in the object.

Presocratic Protagoras has already disagreed, two thousand years earlier. According to Sextus Empiricus, he would have said the water is *both* warm and cold. "Water has all kinds of qualities, but a sensitive being is only able to experience a limited number of them."[3] We feel different aspects of the water in different relations to it, but the water still contains these different aspects since as water it is defined in terms of its relations with the world. Naess goes on to find support for this view in the following ancient Sanskrit formula: *sarvam dharmam nihsvabhavam* (every element is without self-existence). Things exist only linked to each other, caught in the web of the world.

But subjects and objects are primary categories in most of Western philosophy. When Naess tries to go beyond these divisions, he is led, like other philosophers of the twentieth century, to create his own language to describe the way he sees things. And all is not equal in this view: feelings of water as well as the rootedness of sense of place are contents of reality, because they are there in the sea we swim in or the place with which we identify. But there is a level of understanding that takes a step back from the immediacy of relating with the world: deciding how much land is worth in monetary terms, or discovering the chemical formula that constitutes soil or the cell structure of wood. These are *abstract structures,* once removed from the concrete relational contents of the nature that includes our ability to know it.

The implications of this view for tactical, pragmatic environmentalism are clear: if a defender of a mountain sees it as beneficent, glorious, sublime, then that value is *as primary* as the value of the mineral deposit that might lie beneath the summit, ready to be excavated and converted into cash, even though it is harder to quantify. Beauty in nature is not subjective (used by the "rational" as a pejorative term) and therefore impossible to dismiss as sentimentalism. The full range of qualities latent in the Earth come from there, belong there, and we should ensure that they stay there.

Phenomenology Minus the Subject

What is different in this world of concrete contents from the world as described or wished for by the phenomenologists? These are the philosophers, inspired by Husserl and Heidegger, who want to present to us things as they are meant to be seen, before any forms of theory or explanation. While a promising goal, their approach too often seems mired in obscure terminology, clearly representative of a very specific theory of just the type they want to strip away. And, it is always a human view that they see, not a world in itself, or seen *from* the things themselves. The things themselves are always seen from a human view—they remain inside the bounds of description, and phenomenology promises us that we *will* be able to explain things. It does not want to admit the unknown, or the unknowable, which is the ridge crest always one range beyond the vantage of any philosophy.

The truest, purest phenomenology is an exact delight in the reverberations of the environment around you. It throws its own terminology out the window, and instead might describe those who look at the sky and cannot help but shout, "Blue!" One who catches the afternoon winter light on a wall of a concrete building and is amazed by the tactile surface of light: "Orange!" "Gold!" The names are nothing but exclamations of wonder. Let the Earth see us before we see it, and the encounter will shake us to the core. There will be no things in themselves, only presences, light, shapes, movements now perceptible and strange.

To feel the freshness of the wind, the smile of the aspen, the tear of the willow, and not to denigrate these discoveries in the name of narrow human imagination. The emotions are of this world! We are here first to see them, and then to make sure they will still be seen for many generations to come. The philosopher of nature must learn to be a witness for wonder, and to teach others what is necessary to keep this wonder visible and free.

Now Arne Naess comes to these problems from the guarded perspective of the analytic philosopher. He is an expert in the invention and refinement of linguistic concepts, of names for the irascible and the fleeting. That leaf winked at us, didn't you see? Rather than delve into this experience, it is enough for Naess to *defend the fact that it is there.* This is the direction logic implores us. Argument leads to dialogues, and here is an excerpt from one of his written but unpublished dialogues:

A: The birch is smiling!

B: Not really smiling.

A: Yes, really smiling. I describe experienced reality as best as I can. I do not make inferences.

B: I propose a test. Ask why it smiles—does it answer?

A: No. But from 'x is really smiling' it does not follow that 'x answers or can answer questions'. Reality is not that simple. I describe contents, not abstract structures.[4]

A did not imagine the smile, but considers it a *concrete content* of reality. Where Naess differs from the phenomenologist is when he says *not* just a human reality, a human experience, but reality as a whole, the experience of the world, a fact that contains value, ephemeral but essential to be marked and noticed for its worth.

The phenomenologist still perceives the world from an aspect, seeing from somewhere, grasping a part of the universe, never a whole. Naess wants to claim something more: that the world-in-itself is attainable by the human being who listens, watches, learns from the feelings sensed out there, beyond the mind's narrow confines. It is not a mystic's oneness with the universe but a rousing sense of the Earth's importance, grasped by feeling its inanimate parts to be as emotional and sensate as we are.

I climb a mountain in the fresh snow and try to grasp what this would mean. Ascending into the woods, in crisp and cold morning sun, I see the branches straining to bear the weight of a cool but still heavy overnight snowfall. Dare I say they suffer? The burden is clear, but does it hurt them? The insight is poetic, not commonsensical, something Naess might not at first admit. The Romantic writes, "The birch laughed with the light easy laugh of all birches." This quote is from poet Henrik Wergeland, not from any scientist or systematizer. To avoid anthropocentrism we must maintain that the trees' laugh is not a human laugh, though it is a laugh nonetheless. This commonality is the kind of relation that keeps us tied to nature.

The kind of inspiration that Naess's world of concrete contents suggests to me is the notion that nature might be primarily constituted out of different categories than we presently admit. Why start with trees, then count them up into a forest, and then see the whole hillside blanketed with snow? Instead start with *laughter,* and see it on the sloping Earth everywhere, a first look before the objects coalesce apart from one another? *Expression* in the growth and fall of the universe, before things are demarcated and named. Seeing the sparkle when the light hits the white place, before we then decide it is a patch of newfallen snow. The wind as a song before it moves through the air, lifting flakes, forming clouds, transforming water into darkness and action.

The Earth is alive before we can stop it. Processes in the midst of change before we can freeze them. These contents of experience come first preceding humanization, first before anyone claims them or attaches them as qualities to things. This is no Platonic form of 'laughter' like a thing held invisibly behind the desert of the tactile. This is an emotion expressed not at the edge, but out from the core of possibility, touching us not uniquely but in the same way any other being might choose to grasp it.

You see it when you're out on a winter afternoon, the sun low, soon to disappear. Perhaps you are on a north slope and already in the shadow, gazing across the valley to a glowing mountain or hill. The light comes first, the reflective sheen of the Earth, before you see a mountain or a slope of trees. Why search to name, pick a piece of the land? Begin with light, grasp the particular hue, the crystal tone. We might call the winter light crisp, exact, hard-edged, overdefined, precise like the extra-sharp world seen through amber sunglasses, the kind worn by hunters and pilots to make sure their targets are clear. Whatever words we use to name this light seem like just ways the hues appear to us as we see them, just then, just there. But in the world of concrete contents, they are at least as real as any calculations we may come up with to explain why winter light is so much tighter, noting down wavelengths, showing the fine outlines produced by a sun low in the sky. The feel of the light is as primal as any other quality. It is originary, initial, the first ray that strikes us as the planet turns toward the sun at the start of the day.

From Philosophy to Poetry

Phenomenology wants to get philosophy back to the things themselves, but it does so still from the view of the subject. Naess wants to break qualities down to the relationships themselves. Whose terminology best suits the task? It is almost as if the moment these things are named and given categories, their fluidity is lost. Our philosophical language is so used to breaking things into parts that it is hard to use precise language to explain how the world flows together, where 'things' dissolve in a torrent of relationships in which we spin and are spun, dashed down and upstream, through the rocks and into the mud.

Poet William Carlos Williams demanded "no ideas but in things!" wishing poetry to be concrete in the same way Naess wants philosophy to be. But his disciple A. R. Ammons twisted the demands around, calling for "no things but in ideas! No ideas but in ideas! No things but in things!" A true attentiveness to relationship must dissolve demands into their opposites.

Must it as well dissolve philosophy into poetry? In general, I think not, but in the case of Arne Naess, I believe there is a yearning toward poetry that he has steadfastly resisted all his life. Naess is an associative thinker: he jumps from one rock to the next as nimbly as anyone as he tries to cross the stream of discourse en route to the other side: reaching fact from value, skepticism from cynicism, joy from doubt. He has always stood up for *intuition* as the foundation of his deep ecology, and prefers that the reader share his innate trust in a human place in nature rather than provide elaborate justification for why nature has value in itself, apart from the service to humanity. His ecophilosophy is an environmental ontology, not an environmental ethic.

Naess appeals to us to accept all perceived qualities in nature as concrete, but he doesn't always have the language to do so. "There is a certain kind of poetic philosophizing," he has told me, "that I detest." Yet his finest examples (like Kant's of the sublime: "bold, overhanging rocks, volcanoes, etc.") come from poetry, or expressive language and metaphor. It is my belief that the vision of a world of concrete contents can best be strengthened by reference to literature, art, and the poetic that may run through all of these. Following are a series of examples that I hope will enrich and explain the core of Naess's view with image, not argument. I believe this is the kind of deepening of ecology that Naess would welcome, not reject.

First is a recent literary essay by the late Italian writer Italo Calvino, "From the Opaque," which is phenomenology in action as an experiment with metaphors, placing the human observer at the edge of experience, poised between a mountain of precipitous memory and a deep seacliff of unknown chances:

> Obviously to describe the shape of the world the first thing to do is to establish my position, I don't mean my location but my orientation, because the world I am talking about differs from other possible worlds in this sense: that whatever the time of day or night one always knows where east and west are, and thus I shall begin by saying that I am looking southwards, which is the same as saying that I have my face towards the sea, which is the same as saying that I have my back to the mountain, because this is the position in which I usually surprise *that self that dwells within myself,* even when my external self is orientated in a completely different fashion. [5]

Now Naess is less concerned with this initial positioning, so sure is he that what he perceives of the natural world is actually part of that world, not part of his relation to that world. Here he does not differ so much from the natural scientist, or at least the traditional naturalist, observing living beings, drawing conclusions about them, sure about the concrete (if not objective) aspects of what is seen, felt, and heard. There is a certain human hubris he admits in ascertaining that he can know when the trees are smiling, the rocks crying, the birds conferring on the future of the planet.

David Abram calls this an awareness of the "more-than-human world," and he finds it part of most oral cultures of present and previous times.[6] Many cultures identify themselves as being part of groups and gatherings named from the animal world. Still, to me it involves a certain arrogance. I can call myself a member of the turtle clan, but is it fair if I haven't asked the turtles whether they'll accept me or not? I might want to be a turtle. I would like to be a turtle; I see the world differently if I imagine myself a turtle, but it is as much human metaphor as any other—this is part of knowing nature that the phenomenologists want to stress, to show how a human view on things need not be a human-centered view of things.

I remain divided on this point: it seems to be both arrogant and humble to feel that nature wants us. Is it more sensible to admit that nature does not care? In either case, it seems prudent to protect the world and its wildness, rather than destroy it without knowing what we kill.

Yet is it arrogance of humanism to imagine that we know how nature feels, that the wholes we observe—be they of living entities, inevitably mechanical "systems," or amorphous shapes of feeling that hold together in our field of view—are parts of the world as it actually is, apart from the human gaze? Naess tells me in *Is It Painful to Think?* that he is happy to speak of "experience" as long as the word "human" is not applied to it to narrow the word's relevance.[7] This is a clear divergence from traditional phenomenology. The vision of a world of concrete contents is as much a plea to step outside of the perspective that has been "handed" us and take the chance that we could actually see more.

The test, of course, is if this other way of seeing nature really looks different. I think Naess would smile at the trouble Calvino has with being more than a spectator as he writes his explanation of a world unfurling from the point where he can reckon exactly his geographical position, presumably anywhere on Earth. For how do we participate in a world we are incessantly looking at, describing, trying to frame within a window or a proscenium arch. Here's Calvino's struggle of nature with culture:

I've gone back to using metaphors that have to do with the theater. Although in my thoughts of that time I couldn't have associated the theater and its velvets with that world of grasses and winds, and although even now the image that the theater tends to bring to mind is of an interior that claims to contain within itself the exterior world, the piazza the fête the garden the wood the pier the war, is the exact opposite of what I am describing, that is *an exterior that excludes every kind of interior.*[8]

Calvino is after words out of doors, flung from the confines of paragraphs, streams of thought that first flutter in the breezes and then alight in the buoyancy of the air. In subject matter there is no division here between the natural and the human, but more between inside and outside, between the bounded conditions of literature, words on a page, held down in a book, carefully considered, bound and printed, and the open trace of philosophy, ideas on the world that cannot quite be set solidly in words. The first step then in deepening deep ecological philosophy is perhaps an instruction on how not to read it: throw out the idea. Choose to imagine how the new conception would change the appearance of the world.

What about the easy romanticizing of the world through language? Naess, and especially Calvino, here look beyond language creating the world to say it evokes the world in a powerful way different from logic, different from representation. To say humanity constructs our world through language is not, as Joel Kovel would have it, to irrevocably separate us from nature.[9] We live according to natural rhythms and constraints, being born, surviving, eating, and dying not so much differently from other animals, but we also reflect, and only admit that other humans reflect. So we are destined to understand only our own kind. This can be a relief or a sadness. Naess and Calvino take it as a challenge. They want to explore with words, and to look beyond the despair.

Know that language cannot yet describe the world of concrete contents. Think what could happen if it could. Perhaps the whole thing might look like this, the phrases that come out of Calvino when he discards the metaphors of the theater once again:

> . . . we are in *a world that stretches and twists like a lizard* so as to offer the largest possible surface area to the sun, opening up the fan of its suction-cup feet on a wall that's growing wary, its tail retreating with threadlike jerks from the imperceptible advance of the shade, eager to have the sunny coincide with the existence of the world . . .[10]

This to me is a wise picture of the world of concrete contents in full force, an Earth becoming an animal, moving slowly and methodically out into the light, a place envisioned not how it might look to a lizard, but *as* a lizard, say, a huge land iguana on the Galapagos Island of Fernandina, a huge volcanic caldera that erupts every few years still, where the large, ever-smiling beasts have no shortage of sun to identify with as the world.[11] The world is doing the slithering, meandering, maneuvering itself toward the light, swishing, leaving a trace, adjusting its angles into curves in this strange image, taking only the strange prisoners of memory and account, choosing to look like this, to remember like this, to test out this lizard picture as a new alternative to the many others that abound. It's not an obvious or clear picture, but it doesn't have to be to be right. For the universe must be somewhat opaque in order to catch our attentions. And we ourselves are then caught in the midst of the opacity:

> From the opaque, from the depths of the opaque I write, reconstructing the map of a sunniness that is only an unverifiable postulate for the computations of the memory, the geometrical location of the ego, of a self which the self needs to know that it is itself, the ego *whose only function is that the world may continually receive news of the existence of the world,* a contrivance at the service of the world for knowing if it exists.[12]

And this is an interesting justification for having a self; Heideggerian in the sense that we humans are here on the planet to "speak the Earth into Being." That is a literary calling, a purpose in the biosphere to speak up and give names to things that otherwise would be voiceless. This opaque and beautifully articulated phenomenology of Calvino is convincing in that it does not hold on too tightly to the notion of a self, it does not sound subject-centered but genuinely searches for a voice of the world.

The notion of the self has always been problematic for deep ecology in general, and for Arne Naess in particular. Enough weight is laid on the concept that the whole philosophical perspective has been criticized for being individually centered, impossibly distant from the nets of relation that make up the world, far, far from the home that tempers the hubris of individuals claiming their own paths through experience and into nature. The image of the deep ecologist, only encouraged by the literature, is of a solitary traveler contemplating the wilderness, identifying with the world of patterns she finds there, taking care not to feel part of the spectacular, but looking for commonality with the tiny and the overlooked instances of life. We become closer to nature when we identify with things radically inhuman, far from our immediate and bodily scale of experience. The gestalts of nature welcome us, for they are patterns that can include a human who cares to notice them.

But how far can the self go? Naess likes to add a capital S to imply a Self that is larger than the ego, still an enveloping identity where individuality is not lost. There isn't much of a picture of shared reality, but rather the solo participant in a world that embraces the thinker who also chooses to act, and recognizes their part in the biological and cultural ecology of relationships that defines us.

When Naess chooses to get more specific on just what counts as a gestalt and what does not, he unfortunately reverts to the style of philosophical writing that he learned as a young man: "A definite waterfall at a definite time, including its music with modifications due to winds, has gestalt character, but is neither a thing nor a state of affairs. But we may say that the content of reality is all that is the case." [13] This seems to be an allusion to Wittgenstein's *Tractatus* factual world of all that is the case. Naess's world is instead a place of grouped *impressions*, not an amalgamation of truths. There is a poetic quality to this observation, and that is why I have endeavored to point out similar thoughts so colorfully explored by Calvino above and Tranströmer below. Walking this way through nature you will step through a series of patterns, not looping Venn diagrams of set theory, but nets of relations, ordered places in which the human traveler also has a location and a part. The truth is never only the appearance that all who gaze on a natural gestalt can agree upon. The aspen quaking in the wind can be both happy and sad—what is important is that it contains within itself qualities that are both fleeting and deep. Poetry is true—to be open to it, the rules of experience must constantly be questioned.

Wittgenstein did not think human beings could see a color called reddish-green. Indeed, our very rules for how colors are to be measured on the spectrum or mixed in the palette of paint or light seems to indicate that these hues do not go gently together. Yet anyone who has walked through an autumn New England forest will know immediately that the woods can shimmer with the bright changeling color of reddish-green. Simply hold up a transitory turning maple or oak blade, and you will see at once an image of green becoming red, and the leaf as a whole speaks of red mixed with green more than anything else. It is a tone that exists clearly as a quality of something simple that we uncertainly try to describe, tossing out a question to our rules of the spectrum, to our sense of how the eye tends to demarcate such things. The content of this natural reality throws a monkey wrench into the neat theory of color wavelengths and scales.

So what then of the human and more-than-human shapes that we see looming in mountains and in rocks? These must also be taken more seriously than as simile:

In a famous painting by Kittelsen the mountain Andersnatten is presented as a huge troll. There are trees on the top of the mountain and the same holds for the troll. The trees are the hair of the troll. Those who rally find the presentation of the mountain as a troll meaningful and adequate—somehow. The conception of a troll clarifies what they experience when looking at the mountain. Asked for word characterizing the mountain and connecting it with a troll, people offer expressions like: *uncanny, mysterious.*[14]

The mountain after the painting is heretofore seen a new way. Is this way invented or discovered? There is a larger richness to nature if the troll is found there, not invented. There is a more outward arcing sense of humanity if the notion of "mountain" is a category of thought that includes the lean of ascent, the picture of trolls, as much as it names a feature of the landscape.[15] Perhaps the greatest richness is found not in saying the troll-mountain is out in nature, or in humanity, but in some ineffable but most real and honest gestalt connecting the two.

True relational thinking will need to dissolve the poles of the entities doing the relating. There will no longer be a humanity, or a nature, but a continuum of connection that is the primal asking force. In this way a particular *mood* can cast a bright or dark shadow across an observation of a movement or yearning that seems to be nature's, seems to be affected by ours, and is concretely belonging to no one, poised as it is as the link between who sees and who is seen:

> Suppose my pleasant work at a certain place requires me to repeatedly pass a mat of flowers of a certain kind. I notice that they turn toward the sun, pointing in a different direction as the sun moves. The process of identification with the flowers makes us see them as seeking and appreciating the rays and warmth of the sun, and being at work to satisfy a vital need. Being myself pleasantly at work, the total situation is that of working together.
>
> But suppose my work is unpleasant and hard. The usual way of talking is to say that the mat of flowers as part of reality is the same, but our subjective impressions and experiences are different because we feel different under the strain of the unpleasant work. We never escape from our world of subjective feelings, it is said, but science and common sense can teach us about objective reality, a reality where trees are neither joyful nor sad! *There is, I would say, both a common sense and a common lack of sense.*[16]

The flower is only knowable if we admit that it can be both joyful and sad, never a gray or colorless object. That would not be a flower. The qualities are primary, long before the object has been set aside with the grace of a name. For seeing, as artist Robert Irwin has written, "is forgetting the name of the thing one sees."[17] His work consists of building sculptures in the environment that subtly change the way we experience the space around us. His 1995 exhibit in New York consisted of a series of translucent cloth dividers, in between which the public could walk, seeing each other and the room between varying layers of half-invisible walls.[18] The piece made visitors more conscious of the way people walk through space, and the ways our world is divided in rectilinear ways. What is the name of what we see? Not an object, not space itself, but the way we walk among these names and among each other.

In the world of concrete contents our familiar ways of naming things will have little use. The qualities that present things will be so immediate and vibrant that they will overshadow the identities of the objects that hold them.

What Naess is asking for here is something beyond altruism, far past caring about nature for its own sake. Is it a sign of appreciation that we admit that the tree is *really* laughing? Not at all—it is a conceptual choice. It is a question of looking and thinking outward, not hoarding emotions for humanity or the sentient alone. It is about drinking *for* the water, thinking *for* the spirit, laughing for those who already laugh, but do not know it. The late Emmanuel Levinas speaks of the same condition, with his own choice of language:

> When one smells a flower, it is the smell that limits the finality of the act. To stroll is to enjoy the fresh air, not for the health but *for the air.* These are the nourishments characteristic of our existence in the world. It is an ecstatic existence—being outside oneself.[19]

This kind of phenomenology enjoys the world, potent with a *jouissance* of experience, not because the world presents itself as being useful in a kind of Heideggerian tool-presence, but because it is a place we can care about by identifying with, by loving it, conjuring our language into its terms and its emotions into ours. Naess, like Levinas, wants to loosen us into the world. Who then listens to the songs we sing of it?

The Truth of Fantasy

Consider the recent and remarkable film of Irish island life, *The Secret of Roan Inish,* directed by John Sayles. Known most for his eclectic and socialist-inspired tales of the American working class, here Sayles tackles a delicate if somewhat sentimental story of myth and magic by the blue waters of the Old Country. The frame of the story is familiar: the new generation has had to move the family off the pristine remote island home of Roan Inish, first to the mainland, then to the city. Little Fiona, age seven or so, can't take Dublin life, so she is sent back to Grandma and Grandpa, who dream of returning to the remote island, but can't imagine how to survive a life so hard. There is also the family tragedy to reckon with—Fiona's little brother, Jimmy, was lost in a storm when his cradle, with him in it, drifted wantonly out to sea.

Where is the magic of nature in this tale? (I'll admit it, I'm a sucker for sentimentality when it comes to myth and nature.) It turns out the birds and the seals took little Jimmy away, as punishment because the Kinnealy family had left the island. The animals wanted the people with them! They were angry that their human kin were leaving, and had to conspire to bring them back. Why? Turns out the whole family is part *seal,* as a great-great-grandmother was a *silkie*—half woman, half seal. The yearning of the sea runs deep in the family's blood. Every generation there is one *dark one* among the brothers and sisters. They are each a little distant, a little fishy, a little too quick to dive into the foaming icy waters and disappear—for hours, for days, for years.

The film is remarkable in the way we viewers are convinced that the animals are watching, that they too believe the myths, that they also yearn to be close to us and our world. And if the emotions of the more-than-human are told and retold across generations, the world of concrete contents tells us not necessarily that we must be sure these ancient tales are true, but that we need to realize the animals too need their stories—they imagine a way closer to humanity. Just as we talk to our dogs and cats, *they* try to talk to us, in their languages, understanding as much, or as little, as we do.

The point is not getting the message across, but the reach outward and the grasp for interspecies understanding, identifying with a smile, or a cry, wanting desperately to know what it means. The suspiciously intelligent whale song, and the chillingly human whelp of the coyote, what then is out there, our selves, our images, or something radically different that we are actually able to understand? The world of concrete contents suggests that the *song* comes first; the call linking howler and listener, performer and audience, speaker and spoken to. This is how things are connected. This is how we reach out to the mysteries that surround.

His Life and His Labyrinth

In the end, we witness the world as a real but changing foil to the way we see things. What about conflicts in experience? I have asked Naess about this in *Is It Painful to Think?*, and he maintains that the experience of a pristine lake is better than zooming across the lake on a speedboat. Why? His answer does express a distaste for the noise and the velocity in the still, open country.[20] But some people do need the whoosh of the machine to feel they are really living. How will Naess dissuade them? Their enjoyment and link to the place wastes too much energy. It destroys an inherent quality of the beautiful place as it enjoys. Naess has been chided often enough for dismissing the existence of conflict between opposing views. I believe he would say that his way of sensing, naming, and relating to nature is a view that is open to other forms of description and love, but only as long as those other forms do not destroy the context they inhabit. What is concrete in that context are just those qualities that must be recognized and preserved if the place is to retain any original identity at all. Perhaps that is why the birches are smiling—even when we choose to look away.

The concrete poetry of nature itself remains confusing. The rhythm and verse shift from moment to moment. But we are never alone in determining the qualities of what we see. We want to see structure, and decide it is there. When we're looking, the world offers order to us. We do not choose our habitat. It permits us to thrive inside it.

The end of Tomas Transtrōmer's long poem "The Gallery" provides an image that may stand for Arne Naess confronting the tangible world, looking for meaning with the step-by-step re-framing of a mystical logic:

> He stands full length in front of a mountain.
> It's more a snail shell than a mountain.
> It's more a house than a snail shell.
> It isn't a house but has many rooms.
> It's indistinct but overwhelming.
> He grows from it and it from him.
> It is his life, it is his labyrinth. [21]

A character tries to explain the shape of his world. First it's something he appears before. Then it curves around us, spiraling away. Then it seems like a home. Then it is no longer a home but it has many parts, impossible to pin down. Who belongs to whom when the world is finally understood? We'll never know. The poetic world of concrete contents can only be found if we attune ourselves to the sheer richness of real qualities that define themselves through relations to us. There will be no division between the human and the nonhuman, because relations will be the first level of facts that hold this world together. That's why it doesn't fall apart. That's why humanity is necessary to save it.

NINE

Get Out of Whatever Cage

*J*ohn Cage is most remembered as a composer of silent music, but his influence and experiments inspire across all contemporary arts and phi-losophies. His lives and works are a series of stories, bound between con-texts, from the city to the country, over all the world. Pieces follow each other, and chance encounters are celebrated. Defender of accident, champion of the happening, general anarchist, patron saint of the avant-garde, what did such a man want from nature? He placed his work in the context of our time, and so alluded to the limits of his world. In the end, his advocacy of chance operation admits that nothing is ever random. Nature stands behind everything he did.

My composing is actually unnecessary.
Music never stops.
It is we who turn away.
Again the world around.
Silence.
Sounds are only bubbles on its surface.
They burst to disappear.

I have come to the conclusion that much can be learned about music through devotion to the mushroom.

A man is walking delicately down the summer wooded road. It is north of Viitasaari, central Finland, nineteen years ago. He and I are supposed to meet in this sharp lighted place, where the sun won't set for a month. But we are each a day early. There is no one else here as we approach each other on the road. He's carrying a potted plant with long, drooping leaves. I carry nothing, and strive to remember the sound.

People grow into their rightful ages and hold the pose that we identify with them until they die. John Cage seemed a smiling, gently wry old man from at least age fifty to nearly eighty. All along he was either older or younger than himself, like the Tao, like the Flow, like the ineffable silence he was inspired to search for until he smiled the knowledge that it could not exist at all.

Silence. Three movements of it. 4'33" set aside on the program of time. This is what John Cage is most famous for, an insolent quiet. A composition entirely without musical sound is a defiant act, civil disobedience against musical convention, but it is not a joke. He wanted us to listen to the surroundings so the Earth might be saved.

Get out of whatever cage. Forget what hems you in. This is the message to all who need to escape the bounds of stifling limits. For Cage, this view comes after years of observation and question of one thing and one place: the imitation of *nature,* not in appearance, but in *manner of operation.*

The idea is stronger because it never came out of nowhere. Cage got it from art historian Ananda Coomaraswamy, who spoke in the early 1900s of *process* as what we can most learn from the world that surrounds. And the notion is much older than that: it is already there in Aristotle when he says our art completes the clues nature has left for us. This is an old and venerable message. Yet spoken by Cage it is part of the shock of the new.

(To write with nature, you think nature. And first throw away the barriers of language that you have been taught. In favor of space, isolated lines, emptiness before and after words.)

His inspiration speaks from music but beyond as infusion to all the other arts. This way his influence on our time has been at least as great as that of any other composer. He offers not just music to listen to but a method to conceive of the ecology of sound. The world holds together as vast composition, a symphony of the human noise and the unknown rustle of the Earth and its leaves.

"Everything in the world has its own spirit, and this spirit becomes audible by setting it into vibration." To express tranquillity in discourse is not the same as reflecting peace as art in sound.

Cage seduces those who follow him into the joy of randomness, and the chance of encounter in any unknown place with someone or something you might or just might not have met on the path of life's way. He resists the planned critique, favoring aphorism or anecdote. Yet to latch onto his method is the easiest way out. He wants you to accept the chance of finding the method that is most right to you, which you can honestly represent as key to the sensing of the world. I hear all these stories of him as the light between music and nature through the cry to all of us to "Listen!"—aware of each chorale of the world as we go.

(I want to write about him through fragments, which is the way he told stories about himself. Still, I cannot rest the way he could with randomness. I want there to be order here. I will look all around for whatever patterns may come, though once found, I intend to hold them. Cage might ask me to let go.)

Those who heard of his exploits imagined Cage to be an arrogant resister to the draft of convention. "Have you no sense of order, or tradition?" they might want to ask. Upon experiencing him, this view would change. Here was a man who projected discipline before all else. An order he found in the process of chance, in the systematic stripping away of all decision-making made on the basis of mere like or dislike.

Glimmers of the theme cross my page as I go. I take hold of the potted plant, we turn together and follow the trail back, talking of musical worlds near and far. On that path back from East to West, amidst the sounds of a language neither one of us knows. One singular choice for a life's path, at play with the century.

Deep into a chamber to shut out all sound. Inside the anechoic room at Harvard in 1952, set up for research into the physics of sound and its lack, Cage still heard two distinct but exactly clear rumblings inside him emanating into the room around. The high sound the whir of the body's nerves, the low one the thrum of the blood in motion. The body moves, and we will never find the coveted silence.

It was initially through mushrooms that Cage found his specific route to nature's ways. When he moved from New York City to the country in 1953, he began to explore the edibility of the surrounding fungi. It became a bit of an obsession. In 1962 Cage and a few friends founded the New York Mycological Society. He never saw this hobby as any kind of breather far away from music. As a matter of fact, the word mushroom comes just before music in the simpler of dictionaries.

At a reading in Kentucky in 1967, Wendell Berry introduced Cage to the writings of Henry David Thoreau.

From Norman O. Brown he learned the desire for "an environment which works so well we can run wild in it."

From Buckminster Fuller he learned what technology can do to the impossible.

He always took care to mention his friends.

In teaching he told students to use art to compose the environment: "Imagine that the music you are writing is not music but is social relationships, and then ask yourself if you would like to live in that kind of society that would be that kind of music."

So he admits us into his new country, formed by instructions that combine and dismember sound. There is a special kind of aesthetics then to judge the composed place: let it call forth a community, and put yourself inside it first as a listener and then as just one more sound. The music maker as anthropologist gone native, settling in to a sudden place in the unknown culture. The previous rules for music no longer hold. Cage smiles as he opens his window for me above the cats and plants in the Chelsea district of Manhattan. Cars honk hopelessly at each other below. "This," he says, "is all the music I need."

"The reason I am less interested in music is not only that I find environmental sounds and noises more useful aesthetically than the sounds produced by the world's musical cultures, but that, when you get right down to it, a composer is simply someone who tells other people what to do." Music as useful works, awakening us to each other and to the accidental exactness of the world.

On a quiz show in Milan, *Lascio o Raddopia,* Cage appeared for several weeks and became an Italian TV personality as he was poised to answer the two million five hundred and sixty thousand lire question. Mike Bongiorno announces: "We give you an envelope containing seven color photographs of mushrooms. You have to tell us: Which of them represents *poliporus frondosis*? Is it edible or not? Does it grow on the ground, or on trees?" A tense silence. Cage answers without hesitation: "It's photo number seven. It's an edible mushroom and it grows on wood." His first financial break. Bought him a Steinway and a station wagon.

Against the social vision, the triumph of the virtuoso. The old split between individual and community. "I became interested in writing difficult music, etudes, because of the world system which often seems to many of us hopeless. I thought that were a musician to give the example in public of doing the impossible that it might inspire someone who was struck by that performance to change the world."

Music performed all day and all night, even with no one to make or to hear it. Sounds and texts, *empty words,* where music is no universal language but a realm beyond language, where words can be sounds, and their meanings are far from their sense. These ecological pieces written in the seventies: *Branches, Inlets, Child of Tree.* This is the time Cage finally accepts improvisation. Before then it seemed to drag intention into the moment.

That awful pain before change. Something has to be done. Music so important because it has so little effect on the situation. Equally, art is no consequence of life. Existing so apart, it cannot be considered. This is neither philosophy nor poetry.

Cage as writer may admit more intention than as composer. Not because words encourage more ambiguity, but because they are more generally understood. He must try even harder to disperse them.

The final experiments, the lectures where content is replaced by the serial swirl of empty words. Where language is returned once more to sound, and there are ways still to shock those of us most jaded.

Absence of place in his work? So it may be at home everywhere? Don't be fooled. He always knew exactly where he was and how to respond to it, if not where he would be next.

I don't want to shock you into respect for John Cage. You might not yet know who he is, or feel he has much to do with any real kind of reverence for Earth. I can assure you he does. He taught us to hear the forest for the trees. And not to judge what belongs there over what does not.

I have long been troubled by Cage's misleading use of the *I Ching*. He used it solely to pick random numbers between one and sixty-four, spreading intention thin across his work. But the hexagrams are exact, describing a geometry of the world of relation-states. Each one implies a meaningful shift from harmony to dissonance, rise to rest. Score for the music of our changing human moods, sixty-four basic categories for ways we can attest to the whole. I asked him if he ever considered composing according to the wisdom of this book of changes. He said "no, but one certainly could."

I wish I was more willing to write with randomness. John would never wish me to. It might not be my way, and we must be true to the way that is our own. The random has had its chance. What we hear when we shut intention out is never devoid of plan.

John Cage wrote a piece called *Inlets* in 1977 based entirely on the gurgling sound of water flowing through twelve conch shells, played in tandem by three performers, each with four shells apiece. The score is a single written paragraph that asks the performers to try out sound and silence with different amounts of water inside the shells. So you ask: why not more instruction? What, no specification of the sound? There could of course be greater detail, but the liberation lies in asking the performer, and the audience, and the place, for just this much, and no more.

then again, not all his music is like this

Thoreau, from his *Week* on rivers:

> It were vain for me to endeavor to interpret the Silence. She cannot
> be done into English. For six thousand years men have translated
> her with what fidelity belonged to each, and still she is little better

than a sealed book. A man may run on confidently for a time, thinking he has her under his thumb, and shall one day exhaust her, but he too must at last be silent, and men remark only how brave a beginning he made; for when he at length dives into her, so fast is the disproportion of the told to the untold that the former will seem but the bubble on the surface where he disappeared. Nevertheless, we will go on, like those Chinese cliff swallows, feathering our nests with the froth which may one day be bread of life to such as dwell by the seashore.

A difference: Thoreau, transcending, moving toward the universal. And Cage, preparing the individual, allowing the universal to move toward you. And yet, and yet, wanting to transcend the self who likes and dislikes. They both, together, there, paring all down to the essentials, and then, *to celebrate life in all its wonder.*

witH

dEsire

you see cloud iN sky

Rain

foggY

Dew

mountAin stream

eVer

Inlet

Doing

or up and abouT

batH

the thOught of coming home

spRing

to bE not there but here

previous yeAr

where is the mUsic

The form here, christened by Cage *mesostic,* does not intrude on the sound. One need not judge the mix of words and shape, but only read through them slowly, pausing where appropriate, distilling sound out from sense. The words will touch shards of our memories, and they have been taken from everywhere: *Walden,* Wittgenstein, McLuhan, the morning news. It does not matter if our faculties have already been cut to pieces. We have heard too much, we know too much, we have forgotten how to tell what we should hold onto or ignore. No need to panic, this is only where we are.

Influence? How does a composer have influence? Here was one who wrote a philosophy of art through response to nature. He blew apart logic by not being afraid to let the sense of place into his ideas through sounds into instruction or into words. He made music into a way of perceiving the world, an openness to the happenings around that would tell us how to live. So maybe he alone made the radicalism behind contemporary music accessible to all. In no way does this mean he cast away discipline or assent to the details. (Although I thought it did mean this for years. Now I'm recovering.) Time and the details— what a man lost in the dark does remember:

"When others left for nearby lake, refused to leave. Arranged to meet on road at 4:00.   3:30 hurried back.   4:00 hurried. 6:30 lost.   Yelling, startled moose.   8:00 darkness, soaked sneakers; settled for the night on squirrel's midden. (Family of birds; wind in the trees, tree against tree; woodpecker.)   Fire. Roasted *L. aurantiacum.*   Thought about direction (no stars).   Where is north?   5:30 sky overcast.   6:00 aiming for solid dry spots, angry (7:00): full circle back again   Goal: walk in one direction.   *Mushrooms.*   9:00 heard horn.   Shouted.   Received reply!   Don Reichert and Rick Shaller picked me up.   *Friendship vs. nature* (distinguished between sounds and relationship of them: no sounds)"

Before music, men and women are men and women, and sound and silence are sound and silence. While studying music things are not so clear. After music things are themselves again. *Because we have now heard, and still survive.*

On commitment:
"There's the example of someone devoting himself to one square foot of Earth, hoping before his end of time to learn what he could about everything in that small plot. (Apparently at no point in time or space is the wall impenetrable. Push or not, and the door opens.) . . . We are as free as birds. Only the birds aren't free. We are as committed as birds, and identically."

So list the commitments:
"Many doors are now open (they open according to where we give our attention). Once through, looking back, no walls or doors are seen. Why was anyone for so long closed in? Sounds one hears are music. Mushrooms: we see them everywhere even when we're driving along in the night at sixty miles per hour. The same with world improvement: now that we hunt for signs of practical global anarchy, such signs appear wherever we look. Renunciation of competition. World-enlightenment. Not a victory, just something natural."

Two monks came to a stream. One began to cross the stream by walking on the surface of the water. The other became excited and called to him to come back. "What's the matter?" said the water-walker. The other said: "That's not the way to cross a stream. Follow me." He led him to a place where the river was shallow and they waded across.

Splash! Who wants an easy way over?

breaking the branches

If Zen was music how would it sound?

I walk from my place in Soho toward Cage's place in Chelsea, on one of the incipient spring afternoons, in the busy and sudden increasing heat, trying to keep track of the sounds. First the slam of my door into the street noises. A skateboard swerves by, chafing the pavement. The din of a whizzing motorcycle. A concerned delivery truck peals warning signals as it backs up. Screams inside a handball game. Smidgens of many languages not my own. (Baudelaire asked for anywhere, anywhere out of the world.) Someone humming walks by. Or is it me disguising my quest? Cars switching by at every street crossing. Pigeons making love high above. A crowd of onlisteners observe a woman taunting (or training?) a huge Great Dane. She says, "Mama!"—the dog breaks into a contorted howl. Jumping up. Repeatedly. Babies giggling in prams. A kitten lost on high. Brakes, horns, air on asphalt everywhere. It's too much, I've only gone a block, usually I ignore this great din, now it's overwhelming. *I try to separate the sounds of nature from human ones.* It is hopeless. Beyond the cheeping of sparrows we humans are now everywhere. Take me anywhere, anywhere out of this world. Underground, unfocused rumblings. The buildings shake. Who hears them? Another drunk bellows for more. I run into a drummer friend in from Pennsylvania. He tries to talk to me, but I am already taking in too much, the cacophony of the busy neighborhoods as the season changes. Leaves rustle in potted plants outside a brand-new store. I faintly hear someone bite into an ice cream just beside. I am asked the time, and wish that I didn't know. A man holds a small captured bird in his hands. It is a ruby-crowned kinglet, and it says nothing. I soon reach the familiar door. The booming, buzzing confusion is all around. I press the old buzzer. There will be no answer.

Then suddenly I walk down the road back in Finland, in the trees with a plant in hand. It's far from the Manhattan grid, and long away from the mushrooms of the present, distanced from the wash of fat sound. Memories are silent, they are as close to the pulse of the heart and the nerves we can get.

breaking the branches on the stage
> *breaking them according to a random but picked plan.*
It's all part of the show.
> > *This is the way the piece was meant to be.*
> *We have passed through the period of chance but this is not the end.*
This is our nature, the disappearance of sounds toward an unreachable silence,
> > *where humanity wishes a home*
> > *a symphony of the possible unfolds*

John Cage, 1912–1992. Listen in Peace.

TEN

Truth across the Divide

THE FRAGILITY OF CULTURAL IDENTITY

Inside the borders of my country, I have to close my eyes and shut my ears if I am to believe I am not at the center of the world. Though rumors persist that we are slipping in world economic competition, the image of the United States is stronger and more prevalent than ever. Back home the presence of other societies and ways of life comes and goes, always filtered through the simplifying tinge of American arrogance: We say we are the world; if not, we always claim to contain it.

The picture is all the more clearer the further away we are beyond its borders. Images of America penetrate every place that I travel. They are brighter, more blatant, bigger than they appear back home. There is little chance for escape, as the hunger for things and lifestyles American increases the farther one is beyond its borders. The global reach of one single culture was supposed to be like a village. Is it? Not really; imperialism is much cheaper. The electronic media knows this the best. It costs less than a hundred dollars to air an episode of any American television series in Bangkok or Dar es Salaam. A native production would cost at least thousands of dollars.[1] We will not be undersold.

The omnipresence of American cultural imagery is just the most blatant symbol of something much larger: a modern illusory mythology, an exciting vision of rich people leading dangerous but fun lives.

It is of course only one side of the coin, but it's the side that shines brightest from the farthest shores, beckoning, glowing with promise. The other side will not be televised.

What I want to present here is only the beginning of an antidote to the generic images that broadcast the allure of modernity without revealing its dangers. I will consider ways of talking and thinking that individuals can practice to foster direct encounters between different cultures that might mutually aid those on both sides of the reach from one world to another. "Cultural diversity!" is a popular cry these days. We don't want everyone to end up the same. Or do we? We also ask for universal respect for human and natural rights, along with racial and political freedom. How does this gel with awareness and tolerance of the world's differences? The answer lies in maintaining opportunities for diverse solutions to our common and particular problems. Any agreement of basic values should include the possibility for many ways of carrying these principles to practical fruition.

I am suspicious of attempts to preserve independent, primal societies apart in a museumlike existence while we admire and learn from them, all the while protecting them from the "threat" of our modern ways. They will find out about those ways. And they must be encouraged to learn as much about the modern world as possible, beyond the stereotypes dividing rich and poor. It is possible for an independent, minority culture to learn to confront the modern world and make its own decision about how to deal with the increasingly global nature of our shared and specific problems. Not to say: "Turn back! Save the values of your own ways of life!" but instead: "Watch out! You may know enough about who you are to save yourselves from the disturbances of the modern industry of promise, but it will not be easy."

Identity is a very fragile thing, and if you choose to open your eyes and ears to the world, you may be fast sucked into a center that cannot hold. It is a myth, and a myth of dissipation rather than one that holds communities together. Myths may always have a touch-and-go relationship to the truth, but here is one where concrete experience must be encouraged to challenge the clean white media sweep.

Scrutiny of the contact between cultures must come from both sides. The way people live on Earth has always been changing, and these days it is changing faster than ever, probably too fast for anyone's good. But it will keep changing, and the answer is not to halt this change but to direct it.

It is difficult to know just how to do this. My advice for how to temper cultural change comes from my own limited experience in individual encounters between people of different local worlds. Travelers may arrive alone, but they represent image and stereotype until they try to prove their hosts wrong. We must learn to separate what we expect to see and to feel from what actually happens in each strange and new place. Pay attention to what confounds expectation.

The imperialist traveler who has come thousands of miles immediately suggests a whole foreign life of leisure and excitement. "How much," one is often asked, "does a cup of tea cost in your country?" An instant gauge of prosperity, or of how much of a rip-off a place might be. And then, "Just what does it cost you to come all the way here, to this small valley?" How many hundred cups of tea? The sheer economics of it all. Money cannot explain too much. Just how much is it worth for me, an outsider, to visit this place and study this remote kind of music, this remote facet of a way of life so far from my own? It cannot be quantified. It is of intrinsic value that this cultural path be allowed to flourish, to exist, and above all discover its own way to evolve.

What can the visitor do to help? Andrew Harvey asked a similar question in nearby Ladakh and received this answer: "You cannot help Ladakh except by loving her, by understanding her heart." Harvey was working with a local poet, translating Ladakhi poems. The poet muses, "A few poets in England and America may read our work and say, 'These are beautiful.' That will not do much to halt the dying of my culture. But it will be a gesture against that death."[2]

The aesthetic reach for the distant and the other world. Is there more than romantic longing in this? Would we love such a place if it were not dying? Is death the only choice for a fragile culture? Can change be beautiful as well? The solution to this problem first requires the acceptance of evolution—nothing exactly remains the same. Once a culture becomes accessible to the global myth of the West, there is no innocent way back. So should begin a fight to discover the truth of the imposed future behind the mask of televised wealth. It is hard work to convince anyone that so polished an image is in any way false. Harvey describes a young Ladakhi, in a tee shirt printed with nonsense English, slicked back hair, yearning for some personal contact of the distant and sexy world he knows only from images:

> I will be your friend forever if you teach me how to disco! I do not like this country. Why should I like it? There are no films here, there are no good coffee-houses, there are no girls. . . . I like cities, very tall cities. What kind of life is this! I have to spend all the winter getting frozen in the hills trying to cheat the villagers out of bells and bowls and spoons and turquoise necklaces so I can come and cheat the old German ladies here [in Leh]. No one lives like this in America, do they?[3]

It is not enough to answer by admitting that there are many people who live in the same way in America or in Europe, so many who simply imagine a better life fueled by the superficial images of expectation. You could try to bring in philosophy, and ask, "Yes, but where will all these things get you? You have a right to try to get them, but will they help you become, or remain, who you are?"

We need to learn to ask the right kind of questions to dispel the arrogance of our arrival in the first place. If the study of philosophy has taught me anything it is this: How hard it is to phrase the right set of questions so that those who ask and those who answer will both be challenged by the changes they encourage. There is always a time in life when one's identity as an individual lost in the world carries more weight than one's place in a community, local or global. This is an exciting time, but it always ends. And then we are all left to wonder how we can best fit in. It is my belief that people seduced by the allure of modernity are not simultaneously willing to give up their grounding in a traditional, lasting way of life. The flashy, ever-changing culture of fashion versus the staid reality of art and behavioral patterns established long ago. So much choice, but so little reason to choose one choice over another.

Anthropologists have long debated the validity of descriptions that come from within or without a given culture. Who knows best about the structure of the way a people lives? Lévi-Strauss was arrogant enough to call the Bororo native self-classifications "a sinister farce." Nowadays people are less sure than ever whether they are inside or outside the constraints and opportunities of the rules that are supposed to contain and support them. And the rules themselves are constantly being challenged. As much as everyone faces the same ultimate challenges, we are part of a global humanity that must deal with the increasing awareness of absolute limits to our inhabitation of the planet: resource and population constraints, and the dream of universal humanitarian standards that respect some sanctity of the individual. And what if this individual comes from a society that does not think as highly of the individual as we do? There the debate must open.

Riding on a slow train route through Norway, I remark to the other passenger in my compartment that every village looks the same. What once was the main village street with an array of locally defined shops and services as been replaced by a glass and metal shiny mall building combining supermarket, hardware store, and post office. Each one looks identical, and every little town has one. Gone is the local diversity that marked this northern European nation, whose sparse population of four million supported hundreds of local dialects and cultural variations. I told him this made me sad, and he laughed, reminding me that it was useless to resist progress. Useless to deny, yes, but imperative to direct and to guide change. Life seems gray in these impersonal, uniform places of business. They symbolize efficiency and accessibility, entrance to the global modern. But they also represent the easy loss of what has endured and developed for centuries, whose local traits define why we may be part of the community we are born into. "Do you worry that this kind of development will make you less

Norwegian?" I asked. He laughed: "You Americans don't understand. You have no sense of rootedness to your place. But we do, and always will. However much our lifestyle changes, we will always know what it means to be Norwegian. And that you cannot understand."

Maybe I can't, but as an outsider, as a citizen of the most immigrant of nations, there is at least one thing I can tell him: that the identity borne by tradition is a most delicate thing. However strong and set it may appear, it may be fast tainted by the allure of the new. This is something the traveling philosopher can try out: learn to teach the message of cultural fragility. Ask those you meet to imagine a list of those values and practices most sacred and essential, and then pledge not to give them up no matter what new enticements arise. Then you might be able to work modernization into the beliefs that have endured through the past. Some beliefs will stand. Others will have to change. In the course of figuring this out the limits of a changing culture's identity will be established.

If there is a population problem, can the large families so desired by many of the world's cultures be maintained? Each culture needs to find its way to deal with the assimilation of new information. Previously it was not necessary to think about global population pressures, and now it is. What is important is that each society prepare its own appropriate response. Can endangered species still be hunted by those who have done so for centuries? Not without awareness of the worldwide extent of the problem. The law should not be simply imposed from the outside, but presented as an imperfect antidote to our unchecked mistakes. Different societies offer different perspectives. That is the reason for cultural diversity in the first place. The route to solution should not quash local identity but look to it for advice.

But we will all continue to be influenced by ideas that threaten to simplify the world. Brazilian statesman and anthropologist Darcy Ribeiro writes in his novel *Maira* of a native who converts to Catholicism, interpreting it as a way to save his people:

> This is the only command of God that completely moves me: that each people retain its identity, with the face that God gave them, whatever

the cost. Our duty, our destiny—what to call it?—is to resist, as the Jews resist, as the Gypsies, the Basques, and so many others. All are improbable but alive. Each of us improbable people is an aspect of God. With its own language that changes with time, but changing only within limits. With its customs and peculiar ways that also change, but changing only according to its spirit.[4]

To change in accordance with one's cultural spirit does demand resistance, but never isolation. It requires the ability to confront the exterior seductive threat with the strength of being able to recognize who you are and what pressures to conform will finally break you. Ribeiro's Maira learns from Christianity, but in the end he must reject it to return to his tribe as part of the clan of the jaguar, in the end a stronger pull than the rituals of an imperialist otherworldly God.

But most peoples do not have the luxury of isolated integrity, especially nations desperate to be part of the world community of modern, accessible countries. In February 1991 the national post office of Mongolia issued six rather unusual postage stamps. The theme appears to be "the Flintstones visit Mongolia." Each stamp features the modern stone-age family in a distinctly Mongolian scene, from Fred and Barney riding dinosaurs across the Gobi desert, to Wilma, Betty, and the kids meeting a Mongolian family at the door of a friendly yurt. These are actual stamps used to mail letters from Mongolia to the world; in addition, they are produced to sell to collectors across the globe.[5]

My first reaction was one of surprise: I wouldn't have thought many people in Mongolia had heard of the Flintstones, much less be inspired to commemorate them on official documents. But how could I be so naïve—it seems the whole world watches television, and the characters from a 1950s cartoon sitcom are fit to be honored in the world's farthest reaches as these places come closer than ever before. Comic-book reincarnations of these relics from ancient American TV history are today much more popular abroad than in the U.S.

It is both funny and disturbing to see Fred and Barney on Mongolian postage stamps. It suggests that someone in the newly noncommunist regime thought that this kind of gesture might demonstrate the nation's stated commitment to be "number one in privatization" in the former Soviet bloc. Meeting the images of the imperialists on their own ground—in the great vacuum-tube melting pot. Is there anything unethical about a cartoon camel racing against a dinosaur?

It's the easiest kind of cultural common ground, depicting a lesser-known culture according to rules set by a global TV presence. It was the Hanna-Barbera Corporation that told the Mongolians how they had to paint the stamps if they were to be allowed to use the Flintstones characters. So Mongolian culture ends up looking like a cartoon. And this is no way to respect and protect any nation's character as it seeks to join the world's market and community of free nations. We wouldn't put the Flintstones on our own stamps. Or probably anything from a country as apparently distant as Mongolia. But we Americans are happy to export our pop images as far and wide as we can.

But I guess it was their idea, was it not? That the friendly cartoon images would make Mongolia seem that much more familiar? The cultural caricature required is somehow disheartening. Lies passing back and forth on international mail in the night. This suggests an imperative for those who have the opportunity to travel, to represent, even inadvertently, a whole way of life as you visit a place different from your home: *Tell the truth about where you come from, and learn the truth about where you go.*

Silly for a philosopher to be going on so casually about truth, I know. Thousands of years of searching and none of it has been found for sure. Well, at least tell as much as you know. Do not patronize. Do not romanticize where you travel to or where you come from. Use experience to transform prejudice and expectation so contact between cultures can change both sides.

Still, I wonder how much we really can learn from a brief encounter with any distant way of life. Is my experience of any other way of life than my own any more than a romanticized cartoon version of rich and possible worlds I will forever be excluded from? I spent only a few months in Nepal, and I have only a very specialized kind of knowledge about their music and, from there, the culture at large. I spent two years in Norway, and I speak the language better, and there are always reasons to come back. My role remains that of a commenting outsider, whose views are considered somewhat informed, if always a bit foreign. What am I then allowed to say about each place I visit? As little as possible in the generalizing sense. As much as possible from the precise and particular experience. This is what should be easiest to share.

The momentary visitor only pretends to know much of any unfamiliar place they alight in. Some take notes, others take charge. If you are sensitive to the world of differences, you will want to listen as much as you talk, be changed even more than you change. The unknown and distant will solicit your own boundaries of self and identity, make you draw lines that define where you are and how stretched you will allow yourself to be. And there will certainly be limits. These come up any time we want to pick some aspect of the values of our own culture and imagine that they should apply to all. Just when should this be allowed?

Food. Water. Shelter. Community. Individuality. The world of human cultures offers many ways to realize these needs. Once you are ensconced in any one of these many ways it is easy to forget the existence of alternatives. If a culture works, it usually prevents some organic and evolved kind of consistency, always difficult to explain or give reason for. Each answer is just one of many coherent solutions to the same problem. But from inside one wall we cannot see through others. Afraid or just confused, we choose to fortify our borders further. Or we travel to try to understand.

Some human needs are universal, along with some aspirations. Whatever the universals turn out to be, their achievement may be reached in conflicting ways. The acceptance of these many ways should not imply blind relativism, but respect for a person means to respect what they have learned to believe in, even if the belief seems to inspire questions. The most understandable kind of challenge is when a way of life begins to brush against global problems that bind us together and require consensus. Global problems may necessitate the alteration of specific cultural values, but this should never be carried out in any oversimplified manner. There are philosophical and environmental absolutes that may temper relativism: finitude, biology, the sense to find the new and also to find a home among others, both alike and unlike us.

Who is the 'we'? Who is the 'you'? Who are 'they'? Ideally I would like to break down such barriers, but I am speaking to people who are both the same and different. We who represent nations that export and control the modern image are of course the first ones seduced by its false appeals. I have argued that individuals can make an effort to counteract the illusions, but perhaps the whole emphasis on the individual is a fault of the modern way. Still, that is where I am coming from. It is the group in which I feel most at home. Does that make these suggestions too personal to be of use to anyone else? I hope not; for whoever reaches from one group to make an impression to another has the opportunity to prove popular prejudices wrong.

That is why we should care about the foreign, that is why it is always accessible if we are open enough to the balance of similarities and differences that characterize the full reach of humanity. The solution is to break through the bright and shiny obvious images that we export so inexpensively around the world and to bring instead a composure and attitude that encourages welcome, saying, even tacitly, that we are ready to treat the rest of the world with respect: to only teach tentatively, to be open to learning what is "otherwise" with the widest kind of sensibility.

ELEVEN

Beyond the Selfish Landscape

Can too many people spoil the spectacular? We often want what the land cannot sustain. We would rather have our own identical and fenced-in backyards than cluster our homes together to leave more room for common open space. If one person is abusing their property, building too much or using too many resources, we want the right to make the same selfish blunders ourselves. It's a free country, goddamnit. Don't tread on me.

Yet at the same time we expect things to go just right for us. We don't want to see any smog, we don't want any traffic as we race to get to work on time, and we don't want anything built that ruins our view. Selfish desires such as these have their good side—perhaps they lead us in the other direction to want to protect what we have and rally together with other people who want the same thing. Look at these rows of identical houses being plastered across the landscapes nationwide! Someone out there believes everyone wants the same thing. We can all have that only to the extent that we want to live in a spread-out world of sameness. Perhaps all is well. If everyone can afford a big house with all amenities in a neighborhood full of people with similar privileges, what could be wrong with that?

I think deep down many of us feel there is something wrong with the spread of residential and commercial sprawl across the landscape. It's as if the compartmentalization of our lives is finding concrete form in the way we build our places. Why do we find old houses charming? What's so cute about old towns? Not just that they are different from the mainstream ways of today, but that they manifest a certain necessary essence that our freedom to construct efficient landscapes has removed.

Maybe it's only that things happen so fast today, that in the old days less damage could be done because everything happened so slowly. I don't think speed is everything here. We have become people who want things only personally, not for our communities. We have driven our desires inward and then built places that reflect these inward desires.

The late Alexander Wilson, a Canadian landscape architect, describes the practical ideology of suburbia quite well:

> The mass building techniques practiced in North America both require and promote uniformity. To build on land, property owners first have to clear and level it. Everything must go. Once they put up the structures they replant the land. Obviously, building contractors cannot restore the land to its former appearance—an impossible task, because they've had the topsoil removed and heavy machinery has compacted the remnant subsoils. But it is also ideologically impossible. A suburban housing development cannot pretend to look like the farm, or marsh, or forest it has replaced (and often been named after) [you know, "Fox Run Estates," "Marsh Haven"], for that would not correspond to popular ideas of progress and modernity, ideas based more on erasing a sense of locale than on working with it.[1]

There must be something *comforting* about living in a landscape where your house looks equal to everyone else's, with the promise of shared values so clearly visible. It's supposed to look fair to all, but I intend to show that this is a landscape quite *selfish:* it's not fair to the land, and it's not fair to people's need to depend on one another and live together to define a real place in the natural and social world.

If we really wanted to save the commons and not carve it up into everyone's little piece, then how come there aren't more clustered developments surrounded by open space? Sure, there are some, but often these are surrounded by gates and you still must drive miles from their perimeters to find anything to buy or eat. The greatest tragedy of that kind of isolation has to be the example of the Heaven's Gate cult, all of whose members committed mass suicide inside a prosperous, safe, gated community. Their leader's final words, captured on video, were, "We're getting ready to leave this place."

Of course it's not fair to use extreme examples, but we want to create places, not that we want to leave, but where we want to stay. Some of us can always run farther from the centers to quieter and wilder places, but that won't help solve the problems where the people are. Flight from so many cities led to the inner dilapidation of our sense of community, and we no longer buy or work near and among people we live with. Our settlement pattern has been thinned out into ambiguity.

Should we create new towns in the open ranges of the West instead of new residential enclaves? Zoning makes this difficult, and zoning is supposed to reflect people's preferences. One defender of the separation between workplace and homeplace said, "Who wants to live next to a 7-Eleven?" The local shop has evolved into the 7-Eleven and been stripped of its locality. We use the place all the time but we don't trust it. We only want it when we need it. The question shouldn't be "who wants to live next to a 7-Eleven" but "what kind of local shops and services should we build and how can we reconceive our dwelling needs so that they could be zoned to be together?" Why put it all together? To save the beauty that brought us all out to this beautiful state. To build out of wood and concrete a world that shows that people care about each other and are willing to cooperate. To show that a human place can be about the human good and not just a testament to private wealth.

Many people are suspicious of such clustered plans. They don't trust the community as much and would rather surround their private homes with buffer zones that they know won't get developed. People sometimes say they move out west to be in the free and open sky and to get away from planners who want to tell them what to do. But planning should come from the people, so we get what we all deserve, as a vast community. The important parts of the land belong to nobody: they are collectively shaped and defined as a mix of private homes and public lands.

This is where the regional planning process becomes an issue of values and philosophy. As much as we talk about new forms of public transport, new ways of building housing so that it is closer to where we buy and where we work, new ways of living where we might walk or bike from home to the places we need to be, we must realize that we live in a nation where only 2 percent of the trips made are made by public transportation. In Europe, in areas of similar or higher economic stature, up to 40 percent of travel is by train or bus. It's a whole different world, and different choices have been made along the way. You might say it is because those "old country" towns are so old, they came into being before grid-based planning and before the car made the grid an idea that could be easily realized without regard for the real texture of the terrain. But it's more complicated: people, and the state, made choices. People wanted to interact with others in their neighborhoods each day, on the way to work, shopping, and traveling. There are cities, there is the countryside, and there are villages. There is no sprawl without the car. There is no sprawl with the individual holding supreme rule over the community. There is no end to the potential of sprawl, save the desensitizing of people to their homes. When all is anonymous and accidental, not necessary, we will cease to have anything to care for in our towns and let them all go to seed. We will get whatever happens, not the beautiful and successful city we wanted.

Here are a few stories from the wars of people and place:

In 1988 planner Joel Russell was asked by the town of Chatham, New York (population 2,000), a well-preserved small village upstate, to consult on two proposals brought to the village board. One was a small strip mall at the edge of town—standard fare, a few small shops and one big supermarket a few miles from town. The second was a mixed-use scheme that would put a smaller supermarket and apartments on the derelict site of the old rail yard, right near the middle of town off Main St., together with an initiative for the town to repair the train station itself and turn it into something of public value. But residents complained, worried about downtown parking, and couldn't rally behind the downtown project. The strip mall was built with little opposition, and easily lured shoppers away from downtown with its promise of easy parking and big discounts. Do we get what we pay for? As James Howard Kunstler tells the story in *Home from Nowhere,* the mall had "an air of inevitability around it."[2]

What could the town have done with the old train station? Lots of things. A bigger town, Spartanburg, South Carolina, also had a derelict train station. Local writers got together, assembled a book of their work, borrowed the crumbling train station for a night, and had a huge party. The city government grumbled and said no one would come to their party in this dying downtown. But hundreds of people showed up, bought out copies of the book, came to believe in the local culture it stood for, and now there is committed interest in rebuilding that downtown.[3]

What can you do with a dead mall? All over America developers are trying to figure that one out. Renovate it? Problem is, it's so much *easier* to build a spanking new mall on a "vacant" wooded site a mile up the highway. Just as it's *easier* to shop miles from town next to that asphalt wasteland.

There are good stories out there. The town of Pittsford, New York (population 25,000), purchased the development rights to half of its remaining open space with a $10 million municipal bond, which voters approved, to acquire 1,200 acres of farmland, woods, and wetlands in the name of public interest. A city study found that because this land has been kept undeveloped, the average taxpayer in Pittsford would see a tax savings of $3,600 over the next twenty years, because the town has avoided the costs of having to provide additional public facilities to the developed land.[4]

There's hope in big towns as well. Denver, Colorado (population 500,000 in the city, 500,000 in the suburbs), has seen an influx of people into its formerly stark and empty downtown. Indeed, thousands of new apartments are under construction on the fifty acres behind the old Union train station. It's the new hip place to live in Colorado, called "LoDo."[5] People who describe the outer suburbs as sterile are flocking to a city center that has great bookstores, entertainment, facilities, and many available jobs. Now remember, people have moved to Colorado for the great outdoors and the economy, so why do they want to live in the middle of a city? It's a place with a history, real authenticity, and genuine "girth" that cannot be duplicated on empty, sprawling, outlying sagebrush.

Now I'm not saying that you are a better person if you move into an apartment building just to be closer to a lot of like-minded ex-suburbanites. Planning should be about choices, not constricting choices. But at the same time it will only work if we can step back from our own dreams and look at the quality of life of the community as a whole—basically an unpopular view.

A few years ago I spent some time searching for the most beautiful town to live in within reach of where I work, a university in New Jersey. I wanted a place that felt like a town, that had a history, that was also close to natural beauty and not immediately poised to engulf it. Such places are rare. There are enough quaint towns around, but most are in the midst of eroding that very quality through unmanaged expansion and no communal vision to stop anyone from doing with their property what they will.

I did find a town with most of what I was looking for. There's one Main Street heading straight away from the river. The town is surrounded by small mountains, mostly protected land, so it can't really fall victim to sprawl. Main Street has a bunch of small shops providing essential services. A pizzeria. A deli. A local newspaper, comes out once a week. A gun shop right next to a health-food store. (Yes, this is America.) A bookstore, several real-estate agents, and more than enough antique shops since the place is a popular tourist destination on holiday weekends.

What kind of businesses thrive in this town? Not many. Everyone has to drive or take the train to some bigger place except those of us inclined to find some kind of work to do at home. It looks like a real town, but this look is more veneer than solid community. The older houses are small, diverse, close together or attached to one another. Why is it that newer houses that go up look more alike, are as big as possible, and have walled buffers between one yard and the neighbors? We want personal space. We don't trust whoever's on the left or the right. We like the look of the small town, but we can't be bothered to deal with real encounters with people.

There's one grocery store in town but most people drive twenty minutes to the big-box superstores on the ravaged strip highways not far away. But lest you be too easily convinced that American shoppers are happiest in an all-in-one big-box superstore, consider the most popular tourist attraction in upstate New York, not far away from my town. What's that, you say? Niagara Falls. More people go to the Canadian side. It's Woodbury Commons, a place you can arrange to visit on a package tour from Tokyo. At first glance it looks like a newly built village, a new town for the millennium perhaps. There's even a gazebo with tastefully scaled buildings around it. Something that looks like a church tower is in fact an information booth. What is this place? It's the world's largest outlet mall. Every store is housed in a quaint old building offering discounted goods from all your favorite brands, usually just a few dollars cheaper than the usual price. Nevertheless, this is a cosmopolitan attraction. Just the rumor of a good deal will bring tourists from Tokyo and Berlin. The world's travelers will go thousands of miles for a glimpse of a real American town, with some good deals to boot.

This is Main Street as theme park where the price is right. Except nobody lives here. We retreat to a traditional townscape ideal to save money in a friendly spot. We started with a picture of the small town, and everything about it that makes it a nice place to live. But by the end of our journey we have seen that idea trivialized, caricatured into an aesthetic to slap on to a shopping mall. You can't buy community this way. It's little better than Disney World's Main Street, U.S.A., which, I'm told, is the most popular place in all of the Magic Kingdom.

We want beauty but don't live in beauty. We visit it, we travel through it, while making fun of it. Our nostalgia is not a longing for the past but for places that have real meaning to us. Sure, you may have grown up in a suburban subdivision and be full of fond memories of the place. I'm not here to deny you that memory. I just want you to have choices, and not be forced into a settlement pattern that offers private security but public sameness. We have a right to diversity, and should be able to prove that we don't need to be told to care about common resources. We ought to want something more than our own backyards. Front yards that look toward neighbors, not gated fences that announce the presence of the latest invisible electrified security systems. If we choose not to care about each other, then we will get the communities or lack of community that we deserve.

Am I saying that the prosperous spread of fine houses, blooming like mushrooms over the hillsides after a sudden rain, are in any sense a detriment to the prosperity of the town or the region? They cost the community much more than they give back. The developer gets rich, a few people get some nice houses, but they do not benefit the rest of us. Why not? Because our taxes rise to pay for all the new infrastructure. Bigger is not usually better, but mainly serves to exacerbate problems already here.

What can you do to truly invest in the community? Eben Fodor, in his fine book *Bigger, Not Better,* advises the following: Invest directly in local people, through better public schools and job training programs. Invest in the community with good, sound planning, public parks, public centers, and drawing points to gather people around a common place. Above all, protect the local environment because that is a clear asset, aesthetic and economic, that keeps a place with economic as well as intrinsic value. That's one reason we like some places so much more than others: they're beautiful. Finally, fill local municipal jobs with local applicants, demonstrating that the government is loyal to the community. And when outsiders do move in, welcome them, draw them into public matters, and do all that you can to insure that they will reflect good civic pride in their attitudes and actions. Don't stay a stranger . . .

By its own nature planning is always outstepping its bounds. Though it is usually described in number-crunching, policy-wonking terms, it only makes sense if one concentrates on its daring side. Planners throw out impossible questions and then take them on with utmost sincerity: What will we be doing fifty years from now? How will we inhabit this place? How will we curtail sprawl, while still encouraging growth? Planners rarely will argue against growth. They will only want to redefine it into something that still seems bigger than the present, if described in a different direction.

There is utopian planning and realistic planning. The first simply imagines the world as we might wish it to be, and the second tries to make sense of the present mess and chart a way out. It is much harder, because the world will always be messier and more uneven than our possible visions of it. The most basic risk a planner can take is to dare to dream, to put forth an image of how people might live differently while altering our part in the ecology. The step least likely to be taken is to consider the limitations of the power designers have to change the way people think and live. How will the message get across? The value of the new design must be carefully communicated and demonstrated, never assumed.

Ecological visions of how we should live usually involve utopian slogans and principles that suggest a design for settlements and activities deeply different from the present. The path that reaches from the present to these visions seems tarnished from the outset, because it involves so much compromise and the necessity of working with present systems, which are often anathema to environmentalists. The pure and future society is much more appealing as part of the near-religious appeal of environmentalism than the difficult road from present indifference or despair.

The most interesting ethical problems involved in redesigning our future involve discovering how to change people's minds about what they want and believe in. It has happened before, it will happen again; our priorities do not remain the same. When I have lectured architecture students on the evils of suburbia—why live one place, work somewhere else, and shop somewhere else, all far away from one another and dependent on the car to get between them—the inefficiencies of this seem obvious to me but they have retorted, "Hey, who are you to knock the way we live?" They want to discredit my speech as nostalgia for the imaginary small-town bucolic happiness of the way we were. "All right," I accept, "what are you nostalgic for?" "Easy," they respond, "the malls. The malls of childhood. All we have now are bigger malls, not the places we used to live."

Perhaps what has already gone by always looks safer than what is to come. We yearn for the meaningful previous landscapes, the comforts of the home we left and can't go back to. This is why the new may be able to learn from the old. There is no earlier way of life that our world will return to. We *should* be moving forward, even after all this duress.

But forward to what? What is progress if it is not going anywhere in particular? The rhetoric of planning shows that it's harder to convince people to stop changing and opt instead for some kind of steady-state vision. Any world in environmental balance still must appear dynamic, evolving, with the glimmering hope of improvement in this world and not the next.

Our landscape of cul-de-sacs, tract housing, malls, and highway-side office parks has developed, say its developers, in response to people's needs. Americans want these things, so business provides. That is the basic defense of the status quo. Sure it ignores the role of advertising and marketing in the creation of needs, but it does raise this important ethical point: how do people come to want the things they want? Most Americans seem to dream of a big-enough house on a small plot of land to call their own—this carves the countryside up rather than concentrating settlement and surrounding it with woods. We prefer a clear border between our family's place and anyone else's. What would it take to change this preference? Concerted educational effort? Visions? Economic realities? Even more complaints about traffic?

Today we have to find a way to reclaim optimism and at the same time admit past failures in projection, and not repeat the naiveté in extending present ways of doing things. When it comes to planning this country, we have to dare to deny the inevitability of suburbia, and create new kinds of communities that will resensitize people to consider the environment as part of their daily lives, not a separate question from it.

Is it always moralism to try to tell people what is right and wrong instead of offering evidence for them to figure it out for themselves? The accusatory approach of much environmentalism will not serve to convince those who disagree with your priorities. On the other hand, it is easy to get people to agree with principles—agreeing on practices is much harder, and materially giving personal wealth or opportunity up for the good of the society is even harder to push for in today's independent climate.

If you just say that America's mall-strewn highways are ugly, most people will agree. But it's a free country, they might add, people are supposed to be able to get what they pay for and build what they will. Better to present the evidence that there are better ways to build and to live than to announce the superiority of an aesthetic lifestyle police.

Let's present options. Let people evaluate them. There are ingenious pictures of alternative visions: build this way, and you may add the same amount of new construction without disturbing the picturesque look and feel of the landscape, whereas the conventional method would be to subdivide everything so everyone gets their identical piece, effectively ruining the view for all. Megastores like Wal-Mart could locate in ailing downtowns, or at least adjacent to them, thus attracting more people to centers of population rather than now-empty sites on the highway.

Conventional development suggests that people don't care about community anymore, as long as they can travel easily and conveniently from home to work to the store. There is no reason to attempt anything more, and a convenient shopping emporium means a huge store that has everything, with plenty of parking.

Is it only romantic traditionalists drunk with nostalgia who find anything wrong with this? Remember my students whose fondest memories were the malls of their childhood: we all love as much of our pasts as we can place ourselves into, so we both embrace and spurn change. But this is nothing sentimental—despite all our diverse cares of individual and community, we have ended up with by and large a *selfish landscape.*

Gaze down on it from the air, and you will gasp at its expanse. Wherever the land has been seen as raw, useless, and empty, we have spread out our identical single-lot dreams upon it. We all want our own square, and that's where we will focus our love of the land. The market makes it available, because that's what we tell them we want. It's safe, it's available, it requires the least cooperation and the most homogeneity. It's so much easier for the market to sell us just one thing, in exact, duplicable quantity.

Why is it that there are so many more options when one looks to neighborhoods and places of the past? There may have been more respect for diversity, or more likely a much slower pace, and less opportunity for single developers to exert their swaths of power over the land. You cannot buy or sell community, and that must be why it is so hard to find.

I wish I could conclude by saying that what we need is a reasonable, compromise solution to a battle too often waged in a rhetoric of extremes. Choose your side—no growth, or free growth. Forget the talking heads, but go instead for a carefully considered mean.

Unfortunately, suburbia has been touted as that mean for decades. It's not the city, it's not the country, but a tree-lined residential haven smack between the two. Yet compromise has easily eroded the best that nature and humanity have to offer each other. In towns, in cities, we have each other, and we can walk and move at a human scale to collaborate, meet, work, shop, and live. As we've detached these integrated parts of life our mind fills with the void of the road.

The road is still beautiful, long, empty, snaking across the desert. But that's an ideal road, a symbol road, that we quickly forget when lumbering up the freeway, just one of the herd. Even as we travel slowly together we can't commiserate because we're sealed in, alone.

Compromise is not the shortest distance between two extremes. It's no easy pick of the best of both worlds either. We must articulate the advantages of defining a community so that we can make best use of the land, as something both to use and to love. Not only nature should be preserved, but the qualities that make any place great and durable. Nature cannot just mean those parts of the world where people are not. Nor can it be a garden that we thin out of the wilderness with our evenly sporadic habitations. May we trust each other enough to share the beauty of the land and the wealth of the community. Any one person's slow success or sudden windfall ought to engender responsibility to the community that has sheltered you and welcomed you in.

It's easy to imagine that we succeed alone. But we only advance by the grace of nature and the support of the community. We need to live, work, and design places that reflect this grounded sense of being that can last for many centuries.

TWELVE

The Nine Points of Eco-Cultural Restoration

C an culture and nature be restored together?

Probably the most famous intrusion of philosophy into this question is my colleague Eric Katz's article "The Big Lie," which states that restorationists are not actually restoring the land to any real thing called nature but creating an artificial idea of what nature should be, and redesigning the land to approach this.[1] Kind of a glorified form of gardening. Although Katz's approach seems primarily negative and critical, his goal is in the end to stand up for the preservation of wilderness and the wild as something that we cannot remake but we can only hope to save.

Frederick Turner turns this argument around in a more positive light, announcing that gardening is exactly the metaphor we need to expand to make restoration both a more positive and a more understandable thing.[2] We till the soil to derive sustenance from the Earth, and we grow decorative plantings to enhance our surroundings. Humankind finishes nature, improves it like the *techne* of Aristotle.

But what is the picture used to guide us? Restorationists cry for native plants, an original ecosystem, a primeval goal of how nature should be. I can see why the philosopher would then cry out, "It's a concept! A human construct! Art, not nature." *No Nature* is the title of Gary Snyder's collected poems. A beautiful title. A Zen koan in two words. It's not what you think. It's not to be found out there in the wilderness. We went to looking for truth out there, but in the end *we made it all up*.

So what. Nature, wilderness, the garden. Each of these has meant many different things through history. Whereas French and Italian gardens were traditionally formal and exact, like those surrounding the palace of Versailles, the English garden evolved into something wild and unkempt, evoking the Arcadia that was already lost by eighteenth-century England. The tension between these notions of nature frames the action in Tom Stoppard's play *Arcadia*. In this scene Lady Croom protests the restorative plans of her fashionable, trendy gardener, Richard Noakes:

> Sidley Park is already a picture, and a most amiable picture too. The slopes are green and gentle. The trees are companionably grouped at intervals that show them to advantage. The rill is a serpentine ribbon unwound from the lake peaceably contained by meadows on which the right amount of sheep are tastefully arranged—in short, it is nature as God intended. . . . Here is the Park as it appears to us now, and there as it might when Mr. Noakes has done with it. Where here is the familiar pastoral refinement of an Englishman's garden, there is an eruption of gloomy forest and towering crag, of ruins where there was never a house. . . . My hyacinth dell is become a haunt for hobgoblins, my Chinese bridge . . . is to be usurped by a fallen obelisk overgrown with briars![3]

As another character puts it later in the play, this is "the Age of Enlightenment banished into the Romantic Wilderness."[4] Is this not simply a conflict between two aesthetic ideas of how we should shape nature into something we approve of? Gardeners like Noakes may have been the first restorationists, though they were not doing so for ecological reasons, but primarily aesthetic ones. They wanted the wild, and imagined a picture of it, then set out to create it. Today the aesthetic vision of restorationists includes criteria such as ecosystem health and viability, a positive value for native species, and a return of wild creatures who have vanished upon the encroachment of previous human design. But is it more than fashion?

We envision the past to generate ideals. Restoration, whether of landscapes or of human structures, has a cultural side. People are making decisions about land and changing that land. We are not deferring to the land or showing humble respect.

Look! As I write on this matte-gray computer screen, beyond through the window a ring-necked pheasant is crossing the lawn. What a beautiful bird! How strange to see him on this ordinary suburban tract. But he's a native, and I can see him almost every day. He likes the cut grass. He's more often here than in the woods. Actually, today I've seen a deer, a red-bellied woodpecker, two wild turkeys (they went for the headlights as I lingered at a stop sign), and the monster woodchuck who lives under the house. All these wild creatures seem to *prefer* the somewhat manicured landscape. In the wild, I would find fewer of them. There were fewer such animals when I grew up in this same house. Are we closer to the wild today? Or is the flowing, changing nature of nature just revealing itself with time? It's true as one grows older that the old days grow sunnier and greater in memory, but uncertainty increases as well.

I could scrap the mower and let the grass just grow, though. Become a meadow, after a few years a forest. Watch succession around me. Actually I would prefer it. I hate lawns. I would see fewer exotic animals. More dreaded deer ticks, the tsetse fly of exurbia. . . . Would I be restoring some ideal existence, or just being lazy?

At the corner of LaGuardia Place and Houston Street in Manhattan, there's another overgrown lot. Worth millions to the speculative developer, I'd imagine. But wait, there's a plaque on the side of the fence surrounding this condom-infested thicket. . . . This is an ecological art project, a fragment of wild Manhattan, as it would be if untouched by human hands. You have to laugh. It's an overgrown lot. But it does look like a fragment of new-growth woods. Over time, it will have something more to say.

That's the thing about ecological restoration. It takes time for its effect and success to be known. We can't pretend to be nature, but only aspire toward nature and set up the conditions for a natural order of change to proceed.

A Deeper, Solo Ecology

What has deep ecology to offer restoration? Put simply, deep ecology is the belief that we can only change our relationship with the environment if we make deep changes in the root ways we conceive of the connection between humanity and nature, reforming the values at the core of our civilization. So generally defined, deep ecology would then include all environmentalist approaches that believe changes in thinking can make a difference in how we act. In practice, deep ecology as articulated by Arne Naess represents an individualistic view of the human-environment connection. A person looking within considering the world that surrounds them, examining how the self is defined relationally, how we gain our identities only through links with our context. It has traditionally been built on intuitions of how nature helps build this identity, not masking it or becoming something to fear or subdue. Deep ecology has been picked up by people looking for a name for this kind of intuition and is sometimes offered with a kind of religious fervor, or at least religious sentiment, encouraging these intuitions and "subjective" responses, not asking that they be put aside in favor of supposedly objective science.

Not surprisingly, many supporters of deep ecology are people who find the most sublime experience of nature to be that experienced when one is alone in the wilderness, living in awe of a power always a bit beyond the human ability to conceive or destroy. It is an outline of a somber but solid feeling of respect, which recognizes that the world is more than any human conception of it, so we must accept mystery and know when to stop manipulating and adjusting, designing or refining. Deep ecology encourages humility, and would say that restoration also needs to be attempted in the spirit of humility.

Now this is not a definition that everyone would give for deep ecology. Others would embrace or spurn it as a more extreme position; some devotees of wildness would say that it is pure hubris to say that we can return damaged land to any kind of natural state. These staunch defenders would say that it is most important to save what little untouched land we still have, and keep it away from any kind of human hand.

This defiant view does have its value. It is true we cannot claim that a human-made landscape is the same as a wild landscape. But there is no reason we cannot aim to preserve and to improve at the same time, in different places, keeping the ideologies from getting in the way of each other. I think deep ecology is strongest when we consider it as a call to ask deeper questions about the mutually symbiotic definition of humanity and nature through each other, and not separate the needs of one from the other. This sense of deep ecology is much more friendly to restoration, and much more useful.

A More Social, Gregarious Ecology

Deep ecology frames environmental issues from the point of view of an individual looking out at the world, learning to ask deeper questions, while social ecology starts with the premise that human beings are creatures of a social world. This is not the same as a socialist ecology, which might argue that human individual interests are determined by social structures, and can only be solved by egalitarian social structures. Social ecology need not go that far—it only wants to emphasize that we individuals are not as free as we would like to imagine to think what we would like about nature. Our institutions encourage us in certain directions: as the city becomes more isolated from material production and agriculture, nature becomes more easily an ideal. We build out of it gardens to fit our various aesthetic criteria. We go into nature to get away from work, from urban life, from the noise of daily existence. Nature becomes escape, a place of recreation separate from real life, not just because we imagine it so, but because the structure of our lives encourages the gap. We do not base our experience of the wild and natural solely upon idea but upon the world we live within that we have built, constructed, and come to expect.

What would it mean to restore an environment like the South Bronx? Fresh tomatoes and hot peppers thriving in abandoned lots in this most beleaguered part of New York City. (Why can we imagine Chicago with native prairie vegetation, and the same act in New York seems absurd?) Nature in the city seems invariably mediated through society. We need nature there because our food comes from nature, and we need clean air to breathe, water to survive, but trees and green to feel accessible to the more than artificial parts of our environment, however it may be hard to find them. But their *meaning* is at least colored, if not created, by what they symbolize for us, by how anomalous they may seem to denizens of steel and concrete.

Community gardens in cities can be considered acts of restoration. But very often cultures are being restored as much as originary places. In the Berkeley Street Garden in Boston, you'll find Vietnamese women wearing traditional straw hats, farming vegetables, and even rice, on tiny plots searching for a glimpse of their old way of life. The next garden plot might be tended by a gay couple, with ornate floral arrangements and pink flamingoes. Don't know what's being restored here, but it is a happy place where different senses of aesthetics and ways of life can coexist. Still, I remember the place before it was cleared. It looked more forbidden, untended, perhaps natural, certainly wild. Has restoration taken away the wilderness and put a culture of nature in its stead?

Restoration is clearly not gardening with the models of beauty or subsistence as its goal. But it is a kind of stewardship, or tending of the Earth, with a new goal of returning ecosystems to basic states of *health,* directed by humans, where humans should in the end not be excluded as a rule, unless perhaps in certain cases. The recovery from sickness cannot just appear healthy, it must be genuinely alive. It is often announced that there is more forest in New England today than a hundred years ago. But Stephanie Mills points out that a thriving wildland must not only look beautiful: "One must also allow that without elk, moose, caribou, wolf, cougar, and lynx, or without the *Homo sapiens* part of the ecosystem—indigenous subsistence cultures—those woods are a little thin."[5]

The place for a human culture in the re-created land, whether subsistence or otherwise, should not be overlooked. Social ecology would emphasize that restoration is still the construction of a kind of artificial nature as desired by and made by certain social groups and forces—that is, we have become wealthy enough and smart enough to believe that we should have clean running water through our cities, with salmon leaping upstream through the future developments of Seattle, with a challenge to show that humanity can *build* the wild into our increasing taming of the world. Restoration seen as such is still management, not a deference to a natural context that is always more-than-human.

Restoration Situated Smack between the Social and the Deep

Restoration must be more deferent to an ideal of nature than gardening, but more proactive than the simple cordoning-off of wild-as-valuable places. As such it needs to be situated right between deep and social ecology, a kind of balanced practice, not a theoretical extreme. When seen in this way it will *not* always be most appropriate to try to redesign a place using only native species. Who exactly counts as a native species anymore? *We* are certainly not native species to the lands we are restoring, and a goal of 100 percent native species in a particular ecosystem will probably be an ecologically naïve way of improving a place. But an investigation of what exactly warrants the term "native" in an ever-changing natural world is worthwhile. Upon discovering that the red pines she is so fond of are not native to the Upper Michigan peninsula where she lives, Stephanie Mills muses:

> I'm an exotic here, too. It was an admission of being confused. Like the pines, I don't quite see myself as being optimally suited to land

citizenship around here, although the simile only goes so far. Scotch pines are a lot hardier and unquestioning about their immigration than I am.[6]

No principle borrowed from science should become a kind of extreme political rallying point. Solutions in the mutual tending of humanity and land demand careful compromise.

The traditional American wilderness-park model looks like this to me: busy, winding roads approaching the park entrance, lined with fast-food chains and ugly motels, lots of parking lots, supermarkets to stock up on supplies, the generic, unthinking, flavorless landscape with little connection to its actual place. Then there is the border of the park, and inside everything is protected, preserved. A living, breathing model of the separation of humanity from nature. Real life on one side, preserved life on the other. We admit defeat by accepting this difference. I find more promise in the landscape of Switzerland, where the trace of human settlement is everywhere, but it is integrated with a spectacular landscape such that the entire country seems like a park, where the lives of people are deeply entwined with the mountains. True, even the summit of Mont Blanc seems strangely civilized, and no bear has been sighted in Bern in over a hundred years, but a striving toward a culture within nature has at least been attempted. And you don't need a car to get around it all.

A nature that admits to culture is a much stronger, if more difficult, goal for restoration to approach. We restore our land for our own health as much as the condition of the country. Neither we nor nature are broken things that can be tinkered with and fixed. As Barry Lopez writes,

> Restoration work is not fixing beautiful machinery—replacing stolen parts, adding fresh lubricants, cobbling and welding and rewiring. It is accepting an abandoned responsibility. It is a humble and often joyful mending of biological ties, with a hope, clearly recognized, that working from this foundation we might, too, begin to mend human society.[7]

With this conciliatory, combining drift of thought in mind, against my better judgment, I have prepared a list of general points to consider in the framing of restoration efforts. Keeping with a tradition, why not call them the Nine Points of Eco-Cultural Restoration. This list is subject to debate, development, revision, or disposal, but here goes:

1. *Know your place.* What it is, what it should be, how large it is, how large it should be, how much of it we should take up, how much we should lead, how much we should defer to nature or to the more-than-human world.

2. *Know your scale.* What is the proper size of human intervention. What is too much, what is too little. What is the right amount of presence we should have such that we can prove that we have a place in the world, where we have an environmental identity, and we are not afraid to fit in to what surrounds.

3. *Know your culture.* Learn where your ideas of nature come from, how they are culturally determined, how they are essential, how much they can change, and how much they must remain unchanged so our identities don't falter.

4. *Know the natural part of your culture.* Know what part of your society and ideas is dependent on the land you come from, the location of where you live, and the ways you have been formed by and form this place.

5. *Know the cultural part of your ideas of nature.* Realize that nature is determined by culture. Be prepared to revise your ideas, recognize different peoples' needs and differences, and how to manage and defer to the natural world so that a plurality of ways of living with the land, the water, and the air can be encouraged.

6. *Know your power.* Know just how much you are able to do to this place, the extent of this power, the ability to alter the course of things in your immediate environment.

7. *Know your limits.* Know when this power will fail, know the point beyond which the world is still mysterious, awesome, uncontrollable, and beautiful.

8. *Construct an ideal.* Have a goal to aspire toward, but do not get caught up in the vision. Create a picture of how your place can be improved, relish and develop this picture, but do not get so caught up in this picture so as to forget immediate reality. As surrealist mountaineer René Daumal wrote: "The first step depends on the last. The last step depends on the first."[8]

9. *Accept the reality of change.* Admit that change is a part of nature. Find a way to go along with that change. Set up that change so you may change with it. Make sure your ideal vision is a flexible one.

Now this list is only a very general starting point, aimed at outlining the compromises necessary to understand and implement restoration, as well as widening the discourse from direct ecosystem reconstruction outward to an examination of how we need to (re)construct ideas of nature most carefully, as we create landscapes, and as we envision a place for humanity within them.

One Scenic Watershed Stands Out

The watershed has been called the basic unit of place on Earth, because it is the most primary natural resource we need to conserve and understand, so the range of its flow must be something we know well, to define where we are and help to clarify the limits of our place. Water has been revered by most cultures, as can be seen in some of the beautiful names for water found in many languages: *Agua Aqua Apa Uru Wasser Woda Waha Vattn Vann Vellam Vesi Shui Mizu Maji Moyam Ma.* That last word is suspiciously close to the word for "mother," understood just about wherever you go.[9]

I've recently moved from New York City, ecologically a rather perplexing locale to get a bioregional handle on, up the Hudson River, still in the same watershed but a bit closer to the source. True, I looked for a place still accessible to work but far more natural, closer to the more-than-human world. But a beautiful place was not enough. I also looked for a place with a history, a culture, a local sense of itself that could hold its own against the pressures of development for people like me, those who work far from where we live by economic necessity, still wanting to define and experience a relation to nature.

In the late sixties a huge dam was planned for the area, which luckily remains one of the most beautiful spots along the Hudson River, with mountains and ridges plummeting down on either side. Folksinger Pete Seeger cruised up and down in the same years campaigning for an end to pollution and a preservation of the area's historic qualities in his three-rigger ship, *Clearwater*. Each summer, the Hudson River Revival gathers thousands of people for music, food, and celebration on the banks to build a culture that respects the water, supports the watershed, and bonds itself together around the place.

Early American connoisseurs of landscape found the native ground lacking in specific history. Robert Frost even called our land "still unstoried, artless, unenhanced," obviously ignorant of the vast native traditions that have told the Earth into its speaking being. But today, we can look back at the Hudson River, in its proximity to the eastern centers of population, as a landscape rich in history and importance in the development of a new native American sense of place. The Hudson River School of painters daubed romanticism into being on these shores by glorifying the mountains that plummet down to the water's edge. They're larger than life on canvas, but the drama is in the mind as much as on the map.

For two decades an organization called Scenic Hudson fought Con Edison's plans to build a huge hydroelectric plant into the idea of Storm King Mountain, a rockface celebrated and illustrated by numerous painters and poets. Central to the kind of argument used by the organization was the notion of "scenic preservation"—saving still beautiful landscapes that are important not only because of their natural beauty but because of their historical importance as part of the romantic, hyperreal past. Though statistics on contamination of the river and upset to the local ecology became important, it was this cultural ideal that fueled the protest movement. In 1980 the power company surrendered its five hundred–acre site to Storm King State Park.[10] The river was granted a reprieve, and appreciation for the natural and historical importance of the lower Hudson Valley has only grown since then, as more and more people stream into the area, looking for a landscape to live and visit that has not been ruined by the greedy expansionism of suburbia.

A local quarry in Garrison has been turned into a nature sanctuary (called, rather strangely, a "unique area" by the state) named "Manitoga"—the place of the great spirit in Algonquin. Industrial designer Russell Wright fought to heal the "open wound" of this quarry for thirty-five years. Today the place is a nature center renowned for its connection to culture, offering performances of music, poetry, and theater in an amphitheater that has been created out of the ruins of the quarry itself.

Although the Storm King campaign happened mostly before my time in the environmental movement, I have noticed that the name elucidates a smile in the faces of those who remember the fight. Kirkpatrick Sale told me the other day that when Seeger's *Clearwater* first tried to land by the dock in Cold Spring in '69, the locals threw bricks and stones to keep those commies off their shores. But when they discovered a few years later that the battery factory in the center of the village was the worst cadmium pollution site in the entire country, flushing pure toxic waste daily into the Hudson, the populace began to turn around. People appreciate the uniqueness of the area today, and more than anything else a sense of local pride in the restored and protected local landscapes, so venerated by artists and writers of the last century, is acknowledged as a central part of our immediate identity here.

We do not exist without the connections to the place where we live. It is a privilege to be in a place, and belong. Those who experience such a feeling had best do all they can to preserve it.

THIRTEEN

A Plea for Quiet Preservation

Maybe you've seen the brochure. It looks just like a real National Park brochure except it isn't—it's a fantasy brochure for the Maine Woods National Park. Fabulous idea, to preserve those testy northern woods so marauded by forestry companies and now being sold left and right for development or other nefarious purposes. Of course it should be preserved for all to enjoy! One thing we all know for sure is that we need more national parks. Right?

Take a look at even the lesser-known trails of Acadia National Park. Every junction mapped and signed exactly. Overused paths that are eroding down to bare roots and rocks. No place to park! Mountain bikes zooming down carriage roads that are so well-restored that they are nearly like paved highways through the woods. Often a toxic haze of pollution on a summer afternoon. A famous destination, for sure, among the nation's most-visited national parks. A beautiful place, but a hard place to find even a bit of that wilderness experience we expect from our priceless, preserved lands.

True, it's on the Maine Coast, an island accessible by bridge, and not a vast forest tract hard to get to from here. But with national park status comes more access, more facilities, more official efforts to downgrade the very qualities that make a place worth preserving. Always?

Only when a park becomes successful and well-known. The old irony of loving a place to death.

Is there an alternative? I spent last summer on the coast of Maine, and indeed I discovered several places on the coast that have remained much wilder than the national park, are also preserved, but care has been taken so that they are not too well known. They sport a different kind of facility, a different way of interacting with the public. Without giving their names away, I plan to describe a bit about how they present their charms to the visitor, as a clue for how to protect the wild and still keep it wild. This is not to be an argument for inaccessibility, but an effort to remind us that it should always take a little work to find the things of greatest beauty.

The politics of preservation are so difficult and the work so incessant, sometimes we forget what to do with what we have preserved. It is of course a mixed blessing that national parks are overused—at least it shows the people of this country care enough to visit the wilderness and keep coming back. Recent conservation thinking has explored the idea of preserving places primarily for their own sake, not for human recreation, with specific plans not to improve facilities or at times even to take them out when they are there, in approximation or restoration of a wilderness aesthetic where little visible trace of human tampering should remain, save the boundary at the edge of the place saying something like "you are now entering official wilderness. Expect nothing more from us and remember, we will not be coming to get you if anything goes wrong. You're on your own. We've saved this place for the rest of nature, not necessarily for you."

It is a bit of a paradox. We want as many people as possible to care about wild places, and we want people out there in the thick of it, ready to experience nature, but we're all disappointed to find popular places teeming with too many people. But can we secure the future of beautiful, valuable places like the Maine woods without bringing too much attention to its value? I think there are ways—as long as the public doesn't expect that calling something a park means everything is prepared for the visitor on a silver platter. When you meet the wilds, you should be ready to change your life.

Let me describe three places I visited last summer, on or near the coast of Maine. Each represents a different kind of public land solution, and I describe them not from the point of view of how they are managed, but from the perspective of the naive visitor who arrives not knowing what to expect. I don't want to tell you exactly where they are because I don't want to call too much attention to these special places. You'll find them if you want to, with a few good maps and the real desire to get there. Just as the best travel guides give only hints for finding the best places, it's more interesting to get you to want to find a certain kind of place than these specific places. There are probably places like this close to where you sit, though for them to succeed, not everyone can know they exist.

First is a place I spotted on the map as an island far out into the sea but still reachable by a series of small bridges. It had to be an interesting destination. Then I heard much of the island is a Nature Conservancy preserve. A few hours on quiet roads, few signs or clues, got us to the dirt road that disappeared into the forest. A small parking lot, and one trail through the woods to the sea. A large poster with a checklist of all the birds one might possibly see. A list of rules: please don't park anywhere else but in this parking lot. If there is no room, *please come back another day.* Imagine the audacity of not building enough parking for everyone who wants to get to this place! Of course not: it is nature that is to be conserved here, and we are only to be visitors, if there is room for us.

The trail, rocky and unimproved, comes out onto a pristine coast after an hour's walk up and down through woods. And there it ends. To the south one could continue for several hours to the tip of the island, where the rock formations are supposed to be quite unusual. But no trail has been built to the tip. Not unusual perhaps in the West, with your grand spaces, but in the East, almost an affront to people's civilizing sensibilities. "What, you're not making it easy for us to get there!" Exactly the point. You can get there from here, but you've got to find the way yourself. This weeds out most people who want their hands to be held out there in the wilderness. That's what brings us closer to nature, and closer to changing our way of life so we care more clearly for it, right? No, to find a deeper wildness requires some effort, uncertainty, doubt, and work.

This deserted island shore retained a quality missing at Acadia, a wildness that placed a humility right away on we human visitors, so that we stepped back to listen to the rush of the water's swells, dipped quickly into the frozen sea, nearly surprised a baby eagle, brown all over, watching guard over his domain from a scraggly tree. What is there to report from the wilderness? As little as possible. It doesn't exist for our stories, but to accept us as a humble part of the environment, just another migrant on the move. Someday I'll have to come back and make the time to walk all the way down to the island's end. I'll try not to come on a summer weekend, when the lot is most likely to be full.

Weekends are of course never a good time for wilderness, because those are the days set aside for everyone to get away from urbanity and activity to *unwind* in the sky and the air far away. So that's when the woods get crowded. Why not abolish the weekend, have everyone working and resting on different days, spreading out the stress on our lives and the land a bit? Technology should make that easier than ever before. Indeed, just as people decry that they have no time and no chance to escape their work they could now choose their escapes much more freely, and find even the most crowded places empty and reverent as they are supposed to be.

Not that we should scowl when meeting others out for the same kind of respite from the world, but we don't want to feel the wilds are overrun. Sure, most national parks are pretty quiet once you get half a mile from the blacktop, but the more access that is put in the harder this becomes. Keep the roads dirt, keep few signs up, just don't destroy the *clues*.

Here's another place in Maine, just inland a league or so, a small mountain with spectacular views. You take a few dirt roads in, a left and a right, and come to a small parking lot at the gravel's end. Here are various blueprint-like maps, carefully delineating which land is public and which is private, pointing out several trails one can take. They are marked, but just barely. No distance information, just arrows suggesting which way to head. One trail goes first down into a small hollow, and then steeply up a rocky, bald mountain. Because of this peak's location, the view, though reachable after only an hour's climb, is one of the best in the state. There are no other people here. Ruins of a truly phantasmagoric telephone tower, shards of mirrors, old rotting plywood, frayed wires holding the metal poles, aloft, more like an art installation than anything of practical value. This is the only thing here to mark this summit as something other than a wilderness. My inclination is that the thing should come down, though an artifact of decaying humanity has its own instructive virtues.

Take a different route down, you walk through an open forest where a distressed pileated woodpecker sweeps up and down the slope, looking for something. Soon you come out on a huge lakefront beach, with crashing whitecaps. An astonishing, empty spot! The lake, at least a few miles long, regales in untouchedness at first, but with binoculars I see that in the distance, on every point, someone is sitting quietly. A few canoes are moored. The lake is getting use, but quiet use, just enough use, so it still sings of the wildness that it represents.

I strip down and dive into the cold whitecaps, swimming over some wet shallow sawgrass by the shore, then on into the depths with their swells and foam. I feel enough alone, and what's remarkable is that the beach is just a half mile from the parking lot I started on up an old wood road. When this area was improved, they decided *not* to extend the new road down to the water. To get there, you still have to walk. This choice was made to keep the spot just a bit more wild. It wouldn't have happened in a national park. This would have been turned into a roadside destination. A big parking lot, interpretive signs, instructions for everything.

Of course it would have. National parks are about accessibility for all people, bringing the wilds within reach. It was Edward Abbey who proposed in *Desert Solitaire* that if we really respected our parks, we'd keep the parking lots outside their borders and insist that those who wanted to enter leave their automobiles outside the sacred line. He wrote that in the 1960s; wilderness is still a powerful but fragile thing. True, one ought to be able to get a taste of it from behind the windows of a machine, but inside it we need to flee from the carapaces around the loose human soul. You have to walk, run, or swim into it and not feel all is human around you. To be human inside the more-than-human, that's the goal. We need to preserve this possibility, but not spend too much effort in advertising. Some work must be necessary to strip down and discover beauty, as Spinoza ended his *Ethics:* "All things excellent are as difficult as they are rare." We have had the tendency for centuries to muck things up, to take the road just that extra bit farther than it was ever meant to go, in the name of openness and progress and ease and the inevitable . . . well, just the inevitability of it all.

Wilderness is about restraint, discipline, and thinking beyond oneself. Hopefully not that endlessly Protestant kind of restraint that can become so regimented and dull. It is the restraining of one kind of human ingenuity in favor of a parallel human ability to care, to let go, to feel the buoying force of the wild world around. No amount of information will take you there, and no amount of safety brought by trail markers and signs telling you what to do at every turn. There must be some doubt allowing you to look beyond what the instructions tell you, like everything you take the time to discover for yourself.

Then, to a third place, down a long dirt road in the middle of a peninsula extending out to the sea. It's a wildlife refuge, so from the designation it's not just for humans alone. Several short trails, this time with interpretive display signs, many about how to photograph wildlife, as the project has been set up to honor a famous photographer who recently passed away. These amenities, though, are just on one small section of the reserve. The rest is accessible without trail, the coast to be explored when the tide is low, the inland to be bushwhacked through.

It was a hazy day of low hanging clouds that seemed to occlude the horizon. Sea and land blurred together into the distance. The tide was way out, and I made a shortcut through mudflats from one point to another while my feet sank deeper into the muck. Plenty of birds, from gulls to herons to tiny sandpipers running on the ground not sinking in a bit.

I had brought along a small sound recorder and a fine microphone to expand my sense of *listening* to the wilds. Try it sometime. When you're wearing headphones and have the mike turned up, the sonic presence of the surroundings are intensified, like looking at the coastline through binoculars or a telephoto lens. There is so much more to hear than with the naked ear, not always specific things, like birdsongs or crashing waves, but an aural sense of the whole place. We use our ears differently than our eyes. We listen to place ourselves in the world, to feel where we stand, not so much to pick out objects as to know exactly where you are.

Start to play around with this technology and you'll soon realize how hard it is to escape the din of human sounds. There are airplanes flying overhead everywhere, even if in the distance. The faraway chuggachugga of a lobster boat, or a distant car on a wet road. You can hear them all. It can take a several-hour walk into the wilds to begin to be free of human motorized sounds. Then you can begin to appreciate the subtleties of a sonic refuge. It's not a place of silence, but of delicate juxtapositions.

I stopped for awhile to consider the harmony of a seaside bog, beach on three sides, with winds rustling through small jack pines. Against the gravel the sea beat slowly, in the grasses, a special duet among grasshoppers or cicadas. Above, a soft whistle in the pine needles. In the distance, the regular call of a foghorn on a barrier island, barely audible. Still human out there somewhere.

This was not Thoreau in his cabin making sense of the pure array of sounds. I was wired in through a technology, intensifying the reach of the human ear. We have all become far more enmeshed in technology than Henry D. could imagine, requiring it for news, information, entertainment, imagery. This sound enhancer I was wearing made what was out there all the more intense. I could *hear* the subtleties of the wilderness in greater detail, like what a microscope or telescope does to what starts out beyond our reach. What interested me was the special blend of seaborne wind and the invisible grasshoppers communicating with songs jumping out from the tiny blades of grass, all above the built-up whoosh of pine needles chafing against one another. And then so far out to sea, that one human sound.

It is no shame it is out there. That is reality, life. But I was happy not a single automobile could be heard. It can be hard to escape the sound of cars, even far into the forest. One reason to keep walking, walking on, far down the coast and off the trail, is not to find silence but to discover a whole world of sound, that admits human presence but only in deep moderation, where our footsteps on the pebbles are just one part of the swaying, blowing world, for a moment nothing with the whole power we know we have to destroy and gloss over and to utterly miss the beauty of what is going on.

Wilderness does not require no human presence, just a sense of respectful presence where we do as little damage to what we love as we can. This place I have visited is a wildlife refuge, a kind of preserve begun by hunters so they would always have something to kill. Killers can have plenty of respect for what they take, and in the midst of the chase, easily know that they yearn for a piece of the world where humans are secondary. Theirs is a concern for the possibility of sport, for individual creatures who strike a bargain they never even hear about, where they're preserved and live happily only if once in a while a few of their numbers are taken. Well—such places have evolved. This one allows no hunting, ever. But the birds fly on to places where they are once again fair game. It's one kind of preserve. Not first for us, but for the others.

That's a wildlife refuge. The first place I went was a Nature Conservancy preserve, where nature as a whole is set aside. The second is state-owned multi-use land, where all the uses must be carefully balanced against one another. In all of them the individual traveler can feel she is deep in the wilds, in a way that is much more difficult in the state's lone national park.

Remember, I'm not concerned with management strategies, or the complicated legal wrangles that led to each of these kinds of preserves. This is about the experience—what it feels like to be in places quietly preserved, without large public celebration.

America's national parks are some of our greatest assets. They are known the world over and the destination of countless pilgrims from distant countries, who often care little for our cities but know that the wild parks offer something they don't have closer to home. But with public recognition comes the demand to make places available to all who so much as hear about a new wild place to go.

A Maine Woods National Park? Careful of what our preservation is for—when I think national park I see National Park Luxury Lodge, National Park Scenic Drive, National Parking Lot and Traffic Management Plan. Who will this park be for? How will it be advertised? You could easily say that it is only small parts of national parks that are routinely destroyed by overuse, but often it is the most beautiful parts, from Ocean Drive to Yosemite Valley. If the north woods does become a national park it must be a different kind of national park from any we have yet seen in the East. We want it to be protected, available to all, accessible to most, but not to the detriment of what it is. You should still work to get there. Information should be available, but not the kind of information that packages and homogenizes the kind of experiences you are meant to have there. No one should have to hold your hand as a stepping stone between the self and the wildness that we all need to discover in our own way.

This is a plea for preservation, for quiet preservation. Not secret places known only to the initiates, but a sense of planning wild places from the beginning that keeps them saved for themselves and not mainly for us. We are welcome to visit anytime—if we can find the way in.

FOURTEEN

Why Wild Philosophy?

Environmental activists, wildland and wildlife managers, environmental policymakers, and politicians have every right to ask what place philosophy has in discussions of ecology. Every philosopher ought to ask herself the same question, so as to avoid being caught in the conceptual spirals that can be the hallmark of the discipline. D. T. Suzuki once said, "This is what I love about philosophy—No one wins." It is Hermann Hesse's glass bead game of concepts, the free flow of the test of ideas. Fun, frustrating, endless, beautiful at best, nit-picking and cold at worst. We are not satisfied with belief. We claim to want to explain things, but we remain best at asking questions.

But environmental philosophy is *applied* philosophy, which means it uses this questioning approach ostensibly to help solve real-world problems, in this case, the clarification of how humanity should relate to the natural world. We want to help to decide how humanity should relate to the *wildness* in the natural world, to examine the fate of wilderness as an idea, to help define the wild place as something that can be understood and cared for in all parts of the world, as a concept that may change fluidly as it is reinterpreted inside many cultures and many political systems, to hopefully emerge as something, not that all people can agree upon, but that can be thought about and saved in so many ways.

I will quickly admit my biases: I believe in the value of wilderness. The wild has a place in the hearts of all living beings, somewhere, and that includes all humans. The idea of the wild includes a sense of danger as well as purity, of ultimate naturalness as well as fragility. There are people who can live inside of it, but to love it is to acknowledge a value more than the human, something wider, something larger, that we must work hard to participate in while it is so much easier for the rest of nature to inhabit it. That is the fate of humanity—to have to struggle to fit into nature after our own nature has thrust us out.

The love of wilderness and the desire to maintain it is part of humanity's rise toward a less selfish state. It is a sign of our growing ability to look beyond ourselves, to expand our care to aspects of nature that are important not because they are useful to us but because we respect them beyond the limitations of use. The love of wilderness as something precious and worthy is part of the march of civilization, and should never be opposed to culture.

Though I do not doubt its value, I also don't think it's the only part of nature worth respecting and explaining. It is probably not the most important way humanity should look at nature, though it is one of many important ways we can relate to the world around us. It is important to say this because as much as wilderness itself has been under siege by those forces in our culture that want to see all of nature as something we can use, the *idea* of wilderness has come at the same time under conceptual siege, sometimes from very surprising places, namely the pulpits of historians and philosophers who say they are *for* the environment but against wilderness, because they see the wild as a narrow and very exclusionary way of looking at the natural world, not representative of the real and diverse ways human beings work with and re-understand the land, changing and developing in different ways through the machinations of history.

In environmental history we have seen William Cronon decry in the pages of the *New York Times Magazine* and in his big anthology, *Uncommon Ground,* the idea of wilderness as something naïve and unrealistic to those people who actually work with the land.[1] Its greatest fault is that it separates humanity from nature, perpetuating the illusion that has diverted our species from the support of life for thousands of years. He asks instead for an environmental ethic and aesthetic based on respect not for the wild reserves thousand of miles from our homes, but for the trees in our backyard, for the health of the family farm, for the understanding of exactly where our food comes from. For him, wilderness exists only as an idea, an idea developed for those who live in cities isolated from nature, where they can imagine the mountains however they will.

Environmental philosopher J. Baird Callicott has been pushing for several years now the argument that believing in wilderness is a kind of old-time religion, based on backward and originally colonial American ideas of separating humanity from nature. As such, it is an extremely limited notion about which to found the discipline of environmental philosophy, and because of this, it is a damn shame that it has got so much attention from environmental philosophers in the first century of our discipline. It's time to move beyond this naïve separation between ourselves and our surroundings, and replace it by sustainable development and biodiversity.

Callicott believes that "implicit in the most passionate pleas for wilderness preservation is a complacency about what passes for civilization."[2] This is an interesting notion, though I don't believe it for a second. It is only a somewhat enlightened civilization that could believe that saving some wild country out there for its own sake has value. This desire is a civilized notion, and something from our era, not any past idyll. The fact that some of us care to save such lands is a step in the right direction. True, it should not be the only kind of environmental sentiment that receives philosophical attention, but it should be brought into the wider debate of what kind of relationship humanity should have with nature, not set aside as a deviant direction.

When it comes to saving wild country, Callicott believes that we should stop talking about something as woolly as wilderness and instead set up "biodiversity reserves," saving endangered species and whole ecosystems in the name of science. That is all fine and good, but I would not call the notion of biodiversity any less culturally constructed than the idea of wilderness. And wilderness still is, to me, a much richer and valuable concept, one that might need some renovation, but something that should be developed rather than set aside in favor of more positivist approaches. I still suspect the notion of the *wild* is more inspiring and compelling than the idea of biological diversity, but I might be just the kind of hopeless puritan romantic that Callicott wants to dismiss.

Yet the suggestion that sustainable development might somehow replace concern for wilderness is even more perplexing. The Brundtland Commission said sustainable development is "meeting the needs of the present without compromising the ability of the future to meet its own needs," and that is as wishy-washy an avoidance of our moral responsibility to future generations as anything I could imagine. If we believe in the future, we have to decide things for that future, and not let the future take its own path. If we decide to preserve wilderness in perpetuity, as our forebears in conservation had the insight to do, we take the risk of claiming to know what's best for the future. Modern UN and World Bank schemers are too slippery for such real moral commitment.

Sure, sustainable development is a useful concept to try to elucidate to plan change around the world in the coming decades, but it is no replacement for real respect for nature. I don't see why as esteemed a philosopher as Callicott thinks that it somehow supersedes real concern for nature. It's really a suggested approach to a whole different problem.

For why should sustainability be *opposed* to the identification of, concern for, and preservation of wilderness? I have never been able to understand this fallacy myself. I think it's because we all like to extrapolate or inflate the primacy and completeness of whatever point of view we are championing as the true, blue, new right way. Callicott wants sustainability, and for him it supersedes all that came before. Many environmental philosophers, not so interested in people and their problems, put forth wilderness as what matters most. Even William Cronon, when pressed to stop all the nay-saying and announce just what it is that he does believe in, couldn't have agreed with the old naïve view more when he said in the pages of *Environmental History* that "wilderness is my religion."[3]

It is easy to see why the wilderness can be a source of spiritual experience and challenge for so many through history. From Moses to Muir, many have needed to be out there away from the civilization that created them to catch a glimpse of the God who so often slinks from the details of the constructed human world. No one can deny that the possibility for such experiences is out there. Yet it has never been the *only* place to see God, and no one should put the wild forth as the only part of nature that matters so. It is one of many places to touch the greatness that is inherent in the fabric of this world.

But wilderness philosophy is not wilderness religion, and the philosopher who wants to support wilderness should not turn away from critiques of the idea of wilderness in disgust, crying blasphemy. Wilderness is much more interesting as philosophical possibility than as religious icon, because there is so much more to say and wonder about. The responsible philosopher of the wild won't just love it in silence, but will be able to combine his own support with the relentlessness of questioning. I support the intention behind the critical efforts of Cronon and Callicott, to caution against the totalizing tendencies of some all-or-nothing wilderness demagogues, but I protest the negativity of their tones. It is so much easier for intellectuals to say no than to say yes to anything, for that is the way we are trained to think. It is harder to turn skepticism into support, so that we may refine possibilities and honestly change the world. Yet this is so much more important. So I believe that it is imperative to question the idea of wilderness, in order to defend it more forcefully rather than hasten its conceptual destruction.

Here are three basic critiques of the idea of wilderness that deserve thoughtful consideration by all supporters of the wild:

1. *Wilderness comes from civilization, and it is not an idea that makes much sense to the history of human cultures.* I agree. There was never any need to worry about preserving the wilderness when it was some-

thing formidable and dangerous, against which humanity defended itself feebly in order to subsist. Times have changed. We have proliferated across the planet. We no longer fear the wild, by and large, but we lament its passing.

This is no mere romanticism. It is an achievement. We are now able to care about what it is not primarily of use to us. We may love it for its difference. Sure, this makes nature something separate from the mainstream of human slash-and-burn mentality and activity. But it is a nature still part of nature, a place we come from after a long and hard cultural evolution. It is nowhere we can return to easily, but it is a pure part of the environment that we now may be able to integrate somehow into our complicated lives.

The need to love the wilderness is a result of a history that has pushed a separation between humanity and nature. This is an unfortunate path, but it is one that we have ended up taking. The wild will surely win in the end, long after humanity has been rendered irrelevant, so we need not worry about its ultimate survival. Our challenge is to see if we are compatible with its present health and flourishing, and I sincerely hope we are up to the task.

That being said, we must be careful not to make the model of humans separated from nature that identifies wilderness to be the *only* way or even the most important way we as a species relate to the environment. This brings me to the next critique.

2. *Wilderness is not everything.* Its preservation has *never* been the only goal of the environmental movement, or ever the most important goal. True, it may seem to be the most dramatic, the most obvious, or the most photogenic goal, but it should always be seen as one extreme of a diverse movement that exists to encourage our species to reflect carefully on our dependence on and attitude toward the vast world around us.

It is essential that we never use concern for wilderness to distract us from concern for the more immediate ways human beings depend on the environment: using it for food, resources, and designing our habitations so they do not cumulatively pollute and degrade the surroundings. I would even admit that these other areas are far more important for most of us in day to day life than the saving of wilderness. More directly important, that is. Knowing the wilderness is safe and out there may be more symbolically important. Many Americans are happy to know that national parks are out there, established to protect in perpetuity the most spectacular aspects of our natural heritage. We like to believe our country holds such places to be self-evidently sacred, even though much money might be made mining them, logging them, or selling them into commercial tourist slavery. But there are plenty of other places being treated more capitalistically. Saving a few places does not mean calling for an end to all commerce.

I would hope that more and more countries in the world will see the realism inherent in singling some areas out to be set aside as wilderness. It does not mean a declaration of the rights of nature before the rights of people. It only means the people as a whole decide that sometimes nature must be given its own chance. But the problems the many diverse countries of the world will face when describing wilderness may be quite different from what America has had to face.

3. *Wilderness does imply conflicts between nature and people.* For as many examples of indigenous peoples that can be brought up to show that humanity might live in a simpler form of harmony with nature, there are as many instances where it is only the fact of a small population that prevents a people from over-harvesting its land. There is much we can learn from the world's traditional subsistence peoples on how to live closely with our surroundings, but in one sense we avoid the real issue by talking too much about indigenous rights when we are pitting humanity against nature in search of the wild.

More often people are agrarian or traders, and they work closely with the land, and they buy and sell what they find there. Setting a place aside as wilderness does take it out of the marketplace, and whether we like it or not, this often sets it *against* the interests of people who live nearby and have had to earn their living from the land. They should be compensated, and they should be brought into discussions of why wilderness can matter to all of us. They should not be punished for having used the land. Sometimes they may be put in charge of the newly demarcated places. Sometimes they are not the ones who know how to manage best.

Indigenous, primal people are changing. Hunters and harvesters are changing. It is not in our interest to halt this change. Their histories may include original and clear ideas about respecting nature. But they may not have needed a word for wilderness. If they need it now, it is our job to teach them. To discuss it, not to preach or inflict. Cultural identity is a fragile thing. Every group wants to maintain it, but they rarely realize how easy it is to lose. Setting cultures aside as museum pieces will not work, nor will easy media promises of an instantaneous world available on the Internet right now for all. Each tribe, each region, each culture, and each country must outline its own way to deal with most-certain change. Inspiring a care for the wild may bring humanity together once in a while around a common goal, but it should allow each people to find its own route through the problem.

In some places wilderness will admit the presence and activities of people who have tended the land responsibly for generations. In other places the fragility of the situation might mean that the old ways must go. Each case deserves separate consideration. If we are smart, we will hope for many creative approaches from the world's disparate situations for all of us to make sense of the wild.

No proclamations will make easier the difficult choices minority cultures must face amidst pressures of development and preservation of their inherited lands. There is no easy way to save the wild as well.

Science is not going to save the wilderness. Biodiversity may be very important, and its value may be clearly established by conservation biologists. But it remains a specialized concept. In contrast, the wild is an idea that will be compelling to far more of us: it is pure, sensual, dangerous, and alluring. We cannot resist it. Science can only support our love. It will not replace it because its language is more exact.

Economics will not save the wilderness. The wild may need a place in the nations' budgets and expenditures, but it cannot be quantified, and above all it cannot be reduced to dollars and cents. You cannot make enough money on wild places to justify their existence in cost-benefit analyses, unless you sincerely bend the rules to put a pricetag on the priceless, and attempt to buy what is not for sale: beauty, purity, survival of the beyond-human right in our midst, reminding us to turn off the running total of calculation in order to truly perceive where we are and what kind of world it is that we live in.

Management is not going to save the wilderness. It may be practical and possible to draw a line on the map and say: look, this side is wild and is governed by rules and that side is tame and there you can do what you want. Something is backwards there—legislation cannot set boundaries in which wildness is supposed to be confined. True, we have to set up such laws because people seem to need codes to keep us in check. But this is a sad fact of human irreconcilability with nature: we don't on our own fit in. Yet if we find the wild in these planned-out wildernesses, its presence will be in spite of the rules.

So take us out there, to breathe in the alternative. Even so, experience is not going to save the wilderness. You can go there and love there, or even refuse to come home and instead live there, but its safety will still be in danger. There is so much back home and across the world to do.

Philosophy is certainly not going to save the wilderness. Especially if it only pokes thorns in the sides of everyone else's faiths and arguments. Ideas have through history changed the world, but I doubt that they have saved the world. Will humility save it—if we just dare to step back and tread lightly but seriously across this planet that is all that we honestly have? Will education save the wild, if we simply teach more and more people to consider to care? Will poetry save the wild, if we learn to bend language as far as it can go so that it will be its most beautiful? As Swedish poet Tomas Tranströmer writes, "The wild does not have words." We don't have much time. We have to do everything, and nothing, acting always with both passion and care.

Go out there. See what you know. Come back with more. But don't forget to come back. We need all of you somehow, in the midst of this fight. None of these approaches *alone* will do enough to save the wild, but if they all respect their own limitations and the contributions of other, quite different ways of seeing the wild, then something, let's hope, can be done. Their will be disagreements and incompleteness, but all we can hope is to work together, and although the wild will surely win in the end, perhaps it can include us in the victory as well.

FIFTEEN

Knowledge versus Information

A recent *New Yorker* cartoon sets the stage. A couple is speaking at a party. The woman says to the man, "This is supposed to be the age of information, so how come nobody knows anything?" This is a serious matter. We are shocked into complacency by the ease of looking anything up. There is no need to hold onto knowledge when you know exactly where to find the facts and bring them to your fingertips. Let your fingers do the walking, said the phone company about those fabulous Yellow Pages. Now the computer promises a world of information at the fingertips.

What does it take for information to become knowledge? In ordinary language these terms are confused, and why not, since these are such confusing times. It won't help to try to constrain the terms, to make them mean less than they already do in the wide usage of reality. Of course I would like you to welcome my own definitions: Information is what can be counted, measured, stored up, turned into a material object and handled from one person or one file cabinet to another. *Knowledge,* however, is more nebulous. It's learning what to do with information, how to pick and choose from among the details, how to make an informed decision when you absolutely need to decide. How to figure out when you need to pay attention, when you have enough data to go on. How to play the game once you have learned the simple rules.

It's harder to take account of but we devise tests to measure it all the time. We want to know how people *perform* when left to their own devices. Sooner or later we need to turn off the flow into the in basket and leave space and time in which to *think*.

Information is what we have promoted so successfully in our technological society. In the spread of more and more of the stuff, we've forgotten how to guide people to turn data into knowledge. That step is glossed over, as if it were second nature. But it's harder than ever to promote when it's easier than ever to turn the page. This isn't what the experts say. They tend to trump up information as a sacred principle that our age has finally owned up to recognizing the importance of.

Information as Entropy

The concept of information as we know and love it today is generally traced back to Claude Shannon, a scientist working at Bell Labs in the 1940s. How much could be carried in a telephone conversation before the content of a message would get lost? We hear the message, we expect some words and sounds, we are surprised by others. The amount of *surprise* is the amount of information that enters the call. The average information contained in a long series of symbols is a measure of the statistical rarity or "surprise value" of a series of signs.[1]

The information content of a telephone call is a measure of all that could have been said, not what actually was said, just as entropy at a given temperature is a measure of how many different ways the molecules could have been arranged without making any difference in the substance, information is a measure of how much one phone cable can communicate without requiring another cable, or a thicker cable, or a wider cable with more bandwidth. Persuaded by von Neumann, Shannon named his quantity "information entropy," and it thus became a measure of disorder, not order. Because entropy is the measure of the information that we have no interest in knowing, not of what we need to know.

Although Shannon's views have made possible the entire proliferation of the global telecommunications industry, most experts today think he was dead wrong. But there is a real difference in the way they disagree. Proponents of information as a fundamental property of the universe think Shannon didn't make information important enough, while critics of the whole value of the information revolution believe he made it into something too important.

Information as Noise

In his book *The User Illusion,* Tor Nørretranders tells us that consciousness is not all it's cracked up to be. In fact, we don't really need it to live, to think, to be human. It encourages self-centeredness, it denies the development of identity and purpose through communication. Information theory should make the individual (or the user, using his own mind, say, as a computer) less important than the message, what he or she can get across, can put forth into the world so that others can reach it.

Nørretranders is an example of the kind of information critic who thinks information has been taken too seriously, as opposed to Stonier's view that it is not taken seriously enough. We have been bewitched by information, we think we want it so much, but we have turned it into something that obfuscates rather than reveals meaning. Well, perhaps that is what it has been since it was first defined.

Shannon's information theory defines information as something that doesn't matter very much. It is a kind of entropy, a form of noise, a confusing distraction that is basically incidental to purpose. It is a concept that helps the phone company but confuses the rest of us. Not just conceptually. The concept of information becomes the building block of a society that pushes facts and data endlessly back and forth, ignoring the questions of use and meaning. It is only incidentally concerned with what we may do or not do with all the information wildly available.

Shannon wanted to know how to transmit messages error-free,

how to save money in doing so. Sufficient bandwidth ensures the situation, but tells nothing about what we know or don't know. Still, for most of our ears, information has been a "plus" word, something we associate with the good. "For decades, information was identified with order and entropy with disorder."[2] This is Norbert Weiner's view, nearly the opposite of Shannon's. For Shannon, information is entropy, a full surge of possible confusion. Can this be true? "Entropy is a measure of an amount of information we have no interest in knowing."[3] This only means the information is *there,* something we could possess if we could be bothered to go get it. That's the way it is!

"Shannon's notion of information is a measure of surprise, unpredictability, unexpectedness."[4] *So why do I want to make it into something good or something bad?* I want to keep it inert, quantifiable, measurable, but still confusing. Thus it can be fun, inspiring, potential, but ultimately something outside us. Its connection to knowledge will always be tenuous, pointing, not supplying.

"Information is not very interesting. The interesting thing about a message is what happens before it is formulated and after it has been received."[5] What matters is what inspiration *does* to us, what it inspires in us and where it encourages us to go. This is the route toward knowledge, the prelude to action. *Learning* is something that can be set off, not codified. But there is something seductive about information. It points to more information. It wants to envelop all concepts with its generic potential. Like the ideas of evolution, relativity, logic, and even identity, it is always threatening to bite off more than it can chew. "*Meaning* is information that has been discarded. . . . It is only when you have got enough of the stuff that you realize it has no value in itself."[6]

A man enters a library, scans the bookshelves. All those musty pages, all those long words, all those recombined letters, all those ink marks etched for centuries onto thin pages of compressed trees, bound inside leather, cloth, card all with thread and glue. The meaninglessness of the process, the brilliance of the technology. And yet, and yet . . . What will it do for him? Why should he take time to take any or all of it in?

A magazine has been redesigned, a popular monthly on technology. "Our new articles are brief, snappy, to the point," writes the smiling editor on the new mission pages. For who has time to read *anymore? The pace of life is quick, we need bolts of data, surges of information. Information is good, it is good to be informed. Why?*

So why does information seem inherently free to me? Because the copy is as good as the original, as regards to its information content. As regards to the object as fetish (a book, a CD, an original masterwork of art) it cannot be. But these aspects of the thing are outside its sense as data. The fact that information is free is a big problem for software companies, as they have to come up with new ways to charge for something people already have and that will work fine forever. Information is free, and knowledge cannot be bought and sold.

> The modern information society is really good only at moving information about. . . . Gigantic quantities of bits can be transmitted via satellites in orbit around the earth and in cables deep down on the ocean floor. A myriad of information is constantly on the move worldwide. But all these channels fail to answer the vital question: *what are we to say to each other?*[7]

What we need to say can often be gotten across by saying nothing at all. The student who calls his parents only when something is wrong. As long as he is not calling, they assume he is doing fine. Nørretranders wants to call this quality *exformation,* but I think that's a bad word, too much like *extropian* or *exfoliate.* Perhaps the ever popular word *content* is what he is after, the substance that media must deal with, transmit and broadcast and receive, the quality and meat of the message that is so easy to overlook when swept up in the gleam of the technology.

So is information entropy or organization, disorder or order? Is it the sudden phone call we can't ignore, upsetting our quietude, an unwelcome buzz from outside a calm inward balance? Or is it the news we constantly craze, that we need to move on, to feel deep in the flux, part of the flow, up to the minute, never bored or caught in cycles that simply repeat?

Nørretranders has a bit of an either-or, analytic philosophy approach, showing how a message is transmitted even when nothing is said, to show that much important knowledge is *tacit knowledge*. I think he is on the right track here, but he doesn't really distinguish the difference between what it means to know and what it means to communicate. Knowledge is a synthetic process, but at the same time it is more than recognizing the importance of links.

I think of information as the raw material that is there to push forward our own serious and original thoughts. It's there as a resource to set us in motion. Whether it is fundamentally part of the human way of codifying the world or beyond us, out there in nature all the way before evolution, is beside the point. What has changed most with its great availability is that we are seduced by its magnitude, and are encouraged to jump from one place to another with smaller and smaller details at each place and no goal for the game but to keep on the move. It's fun, it's amusing, it takes up time, it is full of surprise and delight that only a love of disorder can permit. Indeed, when I hear of Shannon's information being described as "a measure of unpredictability and unexpectedness" then I like it more, it sounds more spontaneous and all in the realm of the improvised with sudden insight. But that's not what he means, what he wants is hiss and fuzz.

To know is to *see* an unexpected connection and know where to run with it. To grasp an unexpected parallel, to make links where none are visible and to fashion a previously unheard argument between them. Then, to impart knowledge is to know who wants to hear this new story, when, in communication, to know which stories are right for whom.

And of course a good story transcends the plot, or the events being told. It is not reducible to information in the common sense. Knowledge must be necessary to human development, and it must be a fundamental part of the human story since the beginning.

So might it not be more accurate to look at knowledge, not information, as the very part of nature that we partake in that makes us human?

180   *Knowledge versus Information*

Knowledge as Adaptation

Why do we need to know at all? An evolutionist might answer: in order to survive. The quest for knowledge is the human fate to be part of the living, changing world.

Henry Plotkin believes that knowledge is adaptive behavior. We need to know to adapt to our surroundings. Likewise the adaptive traits of animals are knowledge, like wing markings on a moth. Here he does have a point, but it's not to make humans seem more animal and evolved—it should make animals seem smarter and more amazing. Think about that moth and you'll see why most information is not knowledge. We don't own it, it doesn't do anything, it's nowhere near as impressive as what the moth can do.

Adaptation is for something, reacting to a situation. Knowledge ought to be for something so we know when it is important. Now, is information for anything at all, or is it against meaning or message? "How can the wing-markings of a moth be knowledge? How can a lymphocyte be said to know something about a virus?"[8] Human knowledge too has goals, and it has evolved. It does not come out of nowhere. It is a special kind of adaptation. Here's how Plotkin wants to defend this position. Not only is knowledge a form of adaptation, but all adaptations are for him forms of knowledge, because they are directed toward a goal:

> Adaptations are 'in-formed' by features of the world; they are highly directed kinds of organization and not random, transient structures that may or may not work. Adaptations *do* work, and they work precisely because of this 'in-forming' relationship between organismic organization and some aspect of the order of the world. This 'in-forming' relationship is knowledge.[9]

Or is it merely rote response to information? Tom Stonier finds a way to talk about this same aspect of the living world to make information look more prevalent and axiomatic. Never mind knowing, because first the world is a plethora of messages just waiting to be decoded:

The poison glands of ants serve as a method of defense and for subduing prey. Some have evolved to serve as recruitment or alarm substances. Some lead to ritualized attack behavior. The message comes before the meaning. Many primitive animals, including protozoa, have "eye spots" which guide them to the light. For a paramecium light constitutes a message which when decoded means, "food over here."[10]

Does it make sense to say that knowing happens automatically, without active work or decision-making, assembling, parsing? In a way both these theorists agree, though Plotkin uses the adaptive example to show that the fact of knowledge links us to the rest of life instead of separating us. For Stonier, the prevalence of readable messages makes information more obvious as a fundamental principle of the universe.

And I still want to know the difference between what I *know* and what I know where to look up.

People Think That They Know!

A few years ago I attended a very religious, Hasidic wedding in the city of Brooklyn, my father's hometown. You know, one of those traditional affairs where the men are separated from the women by a long, opaque curtain. Austere in a way, but still an occasion for wild, ecstatic dancing on either side. A strange event—people, family, relatives from a whole other world.

I remember one conversation in particular. I was standing talking with my cousin, from Germany, another philosopher, griping no doubt about the tough times of the profession, the lack of clarity in its direction, the impossibility of finding work. A tall, quite old man came up to us, a rabbi I had remembered from previous family occasions, mostly funerals. He was often presiding. This venerable rabbi cocked an ear to our conversation. "Ah, knowledge, ehh? Sure," he began to ruminate. "People think that they know. But what is it that they know? Nothing. They know . . . absolutely nothing. For what is it to be known? What is there to know? How would we know if we know?" And he questioned and he questioned, moving on, wondering, shaking his head in a confident kind of hopelessness. My cousin laughed to me afterward, saying, "You know, we are probably the only two people at this whole shindig interested in what that guy has to say."

So you think you know something, eh? You think you're so smart? Well, what do you know? How do you know that you know it? What is the gauge of knowledge in a world flooded by facts? How does information, the promulgation of data and details all around us, become ideas that fill us with understanding and inspire us to act and change the world?

Is that the way it works?

Knowledge seems relentlessly difficult to talk about or to learn. Is it what is measured on tests, what originality can be spontaneously written down by the student? Even that seems an artificial way to discover what we know or don't know. How much do you remember a year or even a month after the test? Not much. Knowledge must be more than some answers that are too easy to forget.

So is memorization knowledge, the vast internal potential needed to remember in an oral culture? I remember being most impressed to meet an old man at a barbecue stand in Georgia who had committed all of Milton's *Paradise Lost* to memory. That's many, many lines. How could he do it? Had he internalized knowledge, or information? Presumably if all he could do was recite the words without knowing much about them, he would be a guy who had stored up a lot of information. If he could talk about what he was reciting, be deeply aware of it, have a considered point of view of it, then he could be said to possess knowledge.

Yet must knowledge be so analytical? Might it instead be a sense of "feel" for the material, an immediate phenomenological sense that of knowing what something is for, how it *connects* to everything else? Connection is easy with information, it's in fact the basis of how one navigates through the Web, from one idea or place to the next. Understanding might, in that medium, just mean knowing how to get from where you are to somewhere else, inhabiting the connections, moving on.

I have said too many times to you how I doubt that this medium contains enough *depth* to really be called a repository of knowledge, even of information of any level of substance. The Web *advertises* for information, and I don't mean commercially, I mean conceptually. It gives you a taste of the facts, like an encyclopedia. Remember when your teachers told you not to use an encyclopedia as a student in junior high school? What was the reason? It was too easy, the subject matter already predigested, the answers already available as if there were no doubt as to what is correct and what is not. True, the Web offers an anarchic array of opinions, a free-for-all not polluted by the authority of editors and publishers, unless you choose to let them sift through your information for you. This has both good and bad sides. *You* must then do the assessing, while the medium just encourages you to move on to another place, to peer, to uncover, to explore a few more details. It's quick and seductive, fun to play, like a game of discovery.

It may be that deeper knowledge takes an amount of time that few people want to commit to the project of finding things out. A book of several hundred pages takes many hours to read. If you're writing about it you may still write just a few lines about it, but if you have read it seriously and the book is any good, it should convey a certain specific kind of feel that cannot be summarized. It could be a consistent argument, it could be a tone, it could be a coherent story with a beginning, middle, and an end, or it could be a solid attempt to *deny* all those traditional aspects of organizing knowledge in favor of some radical alternative to the assembling of knowledge.

Knowledge, then. Can it be assembled at all? Perhaps we are presented with information in various forms, various levels of depth, so that we may *internalize* it and transform it into knowledge inside us, something that we retain. I don't think that's it. Information is what's easy to retain: details, details, details. The big picture, especially an open, incomplete picture, is much harder to fathom. Progress, improvement, direction, is always toward somewhere we can't quite see.

In technology change may move toward the solving of a problem, or toward some strange opportunity that existing machines make possible even though they were not designed to do so. In art the whole notion of progress is under fire, although in our self-obsessed times we value originality more than ever, and here information sometimes seems at cross purposes because the facts clearly don't belong to anybody, they are up for grabs, and the same whoever has got them, until you start to bend them for your own purposes.

Self-knowledge is something we're all taught to want, from that first day at the psychologist when she asks you, "So, do you really want to understand yourself?" at which point I would always answer "no" because I'm afraid of the kind of knowledge that would be about myself alone, with some goal of "figuring myself out" rather than learning how to make sense out of the world and make some work that makes a difference out there. But many people seek a deepening of the personal as an antidote to the general availability of information, an alternative to the sameness that the vast availability of superficial bits of data threatens us with. What to do with all the details? How to decide which special bits of information are what you need?

It is important to know in an active sense, not simply to possess information that can get you far. Good decision-making in all fields comes from an ability to know what to do with all the information presented before you. To figure out the puzzle, to shape an answer when you never have all the pieces before you. This is somewhat generic and banal advice, but it's still true.

Buzzwords such as "information society" and "knowledge economy" suggest that these nebulous qualities are being valued and traded somewhere out in the mainstream, but I suspect they're hunting, too. We're all grasping for some ineffable result from all the details available in our world today. I keep coming back to that word 'details' because it seems both pejorative and familiar, instead of the impersonal 'data', which suggests a machine processing it all rather than a human mind. Because we don't go through thoughts the way a machine does, despite the assertions of generations of cognitive scientists. I don't believe them. Call me a romantic, but I want human thought to be mysterious and nuanced, in the way information can never be. I'm happy to let computers store data for me, but I don't want them deciding things for me, such as what mail is important, what musical decision to make at this or that moment.

Is information the quantifiable, knowledge the qualitative? Perhaps not. Information certainly can be stored and stacked up and counted, but it is still difficult to measure *how much* of it we have. Knowledge is supposed to be testable, that's how we decide who gets the good grades and who gets the bad. To some extent it is easier to measure than information, because it isn't hard to read a few pages of someone's writing to determine whether or not they are repeating material by rote or striving to connect ideas in spontaneous and original ways and really *working through* the material. Knowledge may mark a lack of fear of deviating from the script, of collecting the information and being unafraid to turn it into something new. Even when you talk to someone you can quickly tell whether they are listening, whether they are spouting a few interesting facts by rote, whether they can link what you say with what they know in interesting ways.

Of course some people can know a lot but still have nothing to say about this knowledge. Anything specialized can be self-involving if not self-revealing. Who has time to talk about the obscure or even the deep? Human interaction has been devalued as much as the quick fix in ideas has been celebrated. Well, perhaps it has always been this way, with any depth hard to sift out of the appeals of the immediate world. I do think something is different now. We take it for granted that there is so much out there, way too much to ever get ahold on. Information is overwhelming! It promises instant access and connection to the whole world, but picking and choosing is harder than ever as we can go everywhere and nowhere, and not feel bounded or necessary. There is a sad detachment in complete freedom from place, disembodied work, cyberspatial drift.

The Uses and Misuses of the Internet in Education

It's easy to spot a student paper that is based primarily on information collected from the Web. First, the bibliography cites no books, just articles or pointers to places in that virtual land somewhere off any map: http://www.etc. Then a strange preponderance of material in the bibliography is curiously out of date. A lot of stuff on the Web that is advertised as timely is actually at least a few years old. (One student submitted a research paper last semester in which all of his sources were articles published between September and December 1995; that was probably the time span of the Web page on which he found them.)

Another clue is the beautiful pictures and graphs that are inserted neatly into the body of the student's text. They look impressive, as though they were the result of careful work and analysis, but actually they often bear little relation to the precise subject of the paper. Cut and pasted from the vast realm of what's out there for the taking, they masquerade as original work.

Accompanying them are unattributed quotes (in which one can't tell who made the statement or in what context) and curiously detailed references to the kinds of things that are easy to find on the Web (pages and pages of federal documents, corporate propaganda, or snippets of commentary by people whose credibility is difficult to assess). Sadly, one finds few references to careful, in-depth commentaries on the subject of the paper, the kind of analysis that requires a book, rather than an article, for its full development.

Don't get me wrong, I'm no neo-Luddite. I am as enchanted as anyone else by the potential of this new technology to provide instant information. But too much of what passes for information these days is simply advertising for information. Screen after screen shows you where you can find out more, how you can connect to this place or that. The acts of linking and networking and randomly jumping from here to there become as exciting or rewarding as actually finding anything of intellectual value.

Search engines, with their half-baked algorithms, are closer to slot machines than to library catalogs. You throw your query to the wind, and who knows what will come back to you? You may get 234,468 supposed references to whatever you want to know. Perhaps one in a thousand might actually help you. But it's easy to be sidetracked or frustrated as you try to go through those Web pages one by one. Unfortunately, they're not arranged in order of importance.

What I'm describing is the hunt-and-peck method of writing a paper. We all know that word processing makes many first drafts look far more polished than they are. If the paper doesn't reach the assigned five pages, readjust the margin, change the font size, and . . . voilà! Of course, those machinations take up time that the student could have spent revising the paper. With programs to check one's spelling and grammar now standard features on most computers, one wonders why students make any mistakes at all. But errors are as prevalent as ever, no matter how crisp the typeface. Instead of becoming perfectionists, too many students have become slackers, preferring to let the machine do their work for them.

What the Web adds to the shortcuts made possible by word processing is to make research look too easy. You toss a query to the machine, wait a few minutes, and suddenly a lot of possible sources of information appear on your screen. Instead of books that you have to check out of the library, read carefully, understand, synthesize, and then tactfully excerpt, these sources are quips, blips, pictures, and short summaries that may be downloaded magically to the dorm-room computer screen. Fabulous! How simple! The only problem is that a paper consisting of summaries of summaries is bound to be fragmented and superficial, and to demonstrate more of a random montage than an ability to sustain an argument through ten to fifteen double-spaced pages.

Of course, you can't blame the students for ignoring books. When college libraries are diverting funds from books to computer technology that will be obsolete in two years at most, they send a clear message to students: don't read, just connect. Surf. Download. Cut and paste. Originality becomes hard to separate from plagiarism if no author is cited on a Web page. Clearly, the words are up for grabs, and students much prefer the fabulous jumble to the hard work of stopping to think and make sense of what they've read.

Libraries used to be repositories of words and ideas. Now they are seen as centers for the retrieval of information. Some of this information comes from other, bigger libraries, in the form of books that can take time to obtain through interlibrary loan. What happens to the many students (some things never change) who scramble to write a paper the night before it's due? The computer screen, the gateway to the world sitting right on their desks, promises instant access—but actually offers only a pale, two-dimensional version of a real library.

But it's also my fault. I take much of the blame for the decline in the quality of student research in my classes. I need to teach students how to read, to take time with language and ideas, to work through arguments, to synthesize disparate sources to come up with original thought. I need to help my students understand how to assess sources to determine their credibility, as well as to trust their own ideas more than snippets of thought that materialize on a screen. The placelessness of the Web leads to an ethereal randomness of thought. Gone are the pathways of logic and passion, the sense of the progress of an argument. Chance holds sway, and it more often misses than hits. Judgment must be taught, as well as the methods of exploration.

I'm seeing my students' attention spans wane and their ability to reason for themselves decline. I wish that the university's computer system would crash for a day, so that I could encourage them to go outside, sit under a tree, and read a really good book—from start to finish. I'd like them to sit for awhile and ponder what it means to live in a world where some things get easier and easier so rapidly that we can hardly keep track of how easy they're getting, while other tasks remain as hard as ever—such as doing research and writing a good paper that teaches the writer something in the process. Knowledge does not emerge in a vacuum, but we do need silence and space for sustained thought. Next semester, I'm going to urge my students to turn off their glowing boxes and think, if only once in a while.

When I wrote those paragraphs above in an editorial for *The Chronicle of Higher Education*,[11] I was surprised how quickly my words were reprinted all over the world. This has proven to be the most popular of all my writings. I found myself cast as a voice of dissent, which I didn't mind, but also, in particular, as an enemy of technology, which troubled me more. This is when I learned that the right few words written at the right time in the right place can have more influence than those big books that I labored over for many years for the edification of the few and the dedicated.

Ours is an age of instant data and sudden polarity, and any opinion is more likely to be listened to if it is easy to categorize. We are all supposed to be for or against things, and if we waver, protest, or point out the complexities, we are dismissed as academic wafflers who have forgotten the value of clarity.

I resented being called an anti-technologist! Whenever something is examined seriously, its value is probably a mixture of the good and the bad. So it is with the Internet. A technology improving dramatically with each season, it offers instant access to the kind of information that would have taken days or weeks to amass previously. This is truly remarkable. Facts are genuinely at our fingertips, something promised but never delivered for years.

We can get information faster, but are we any better trained to sift through this information, to apply it, to know how one detail connects to any other, and to combine all to make a creative, balanced, and informed point of view?

We take knowledge all the more for granted if we blur it with information. They are by no means the same thing. Information is the details, all that data so easy now to access. Knowledge is being able to put it all together and draw a clear conclusion. This is what students are not being trained to do, or if they are being trained, they do not get personally involved. They trust all that data they download a lot more than their own ideas.

But I don't want to complain any more about this. I teach engineers philosophy, literature, about the meaning of communication. I love technology and use it all the time, from clarinets and cars to word processors to digital audio systems to hiking boots and backpacks. These tools are my life, and most of your lives as well.

A teacher's duty is to inspire, and you can't inspire by becoming known as an oracle of complaint. I don't want to be remembered as that cranky professor who pointed out that the Internet makes students forget how to think for themselves. The Web can have that effect, but it can do much that is positive. I've changed my approach to it. I'm *insisting* that my students use it as much as possible. But I don't want them to download information, and I especially don't want them to print out all those Web pages and hand them in to me with a satisfied grin: "See, I've been working hard on research." Not at all—I want them to use the Internet for what it was first designed for, *to connect with people,* real people, with fluid, forming, developing and living ideas.

Books and writing are still the best place for well-formed and articulated ideas. But on the Web you can engage in ideas in motion, and find the people who wrote the books and immediately engage with them far more easily than was possible before the advent of the online universe. Whereas in college I heard (possibly apocryphal) tales of spirited students who picked up the phone and called up Bertrand Russell ("Would the gentleman please try again at a more appropriate hour . . .") or Mme. Claude Lévi-Strauss ("Don't worry, *mon cher,* no one else understands my husband's work either"), today an enterprising student can track down the e-mail addresses of the writers and thinkers we have been studying and contact them with astonishing ease. If the student writes a well-worded, careful, and important question, then the mind at the other end might very well answer. And not just direct the inquirer to some published reference, but take the time to answer. Some of us are besieged by scads of unwanted junk e-mail, but most of us still sift through the chaff and consider the genuine inquiries with gravity.

A few years ago, I had my environmental ethics class read John McPhee's classic book *Encounters with the Archdruid* about the late, great arch-conservationist David Brower, who was then still going strong (at eighty-seven) in his drive to place at least 2 percent of this country's land under protection as wilderness. (He was fond of pointing out that 2 percent is already under pavement.) A recent book by philosopher and mountain guide Jack Turner, *The Abstract Wild,* argues that the whole notion of managing wilderness kills the wildness that we love in it at the outset. One of my students, Christian Schmidt, e-mailed Dave Brower and asked him what he thought about this critique. Brower replied that he hadn't read the book, but it sounded "like more word games being played with 'wilderness,' something too precious to deconstruct, with our time too limited to waste on such pursuits."

That's what I thought Brower might say. But I'm impressed that a student managed to get ahold of the great activist so easily. Who knows? Brower might very well take a look at Turner's ideas, and environmentalism might be pushed along just a tiny bit. Not every student got through—the quality of the question makes all the difference. That's what I'm now trying to teach them: how to use the Internet to reach real, living people, not just pre-digested, flickering ideas.

This is such an obvious thing to do with the Web, and students are certainly doing it all the time, from making dates, buying stocks, auctioning cars, all on the Internet. But when it comes to school, they still more often think of downloading data to pad their own thinking with juicy-sounding facts and soundbites. Sure, the Web offers plenty of information, for the sifting, for the taking, for the search for biases and figuring out exactly who is behind the information.

It is always people who are behind information, sometimes hiding out, but most often accessible. If today's technology is the harbinger of a global culture linked by the increasing proliferation of computers worldwide, then it will be not an information society but a *connection society*. Use these machines to connect, to dialogue with the people behind the ideas. The Internet will only thrive as a medium toward community when it can bring people together. Books will live on, and we still need to teach the value of sustained argument, careful thinking, and how hard it is to get it all down on paper.

But we can teach our students how to use the Web to make books and ideas have a life of their own. They are produced by people, and we can teach them to find those people, contact them, engage with the authors and the subjects about their ideas and their situation, and learning will not take place in a vacuum. The big difference between the computer and the TV should not just be how close we're allowed to sit to the screen, but how much we are able to engage and change what is out there behind the glow that glazes our eyes over while promising us the world.

Still, "people think that they know." What are we so sure about? Knowledge may have little to do with information. It may build more on experience, and deepen itself automatically with time. Just over the last few years I have come to appreciate things that seemed to just drift by before. Friendships, memories, repetitive tasks that seem so simple but so necessary. All those anecdotes I have collected, little stories that I have been berated for repeating. Yes, I have been criticized for just knowing stories, nothing else, as if these tales blind my ability to think. Sometimes they do. But I want nothing more than to repeat them, incessantly, if they are good enough, and find others that are worth repeating as well. Not because I am a particularly good storyteller. Only because it is hard to find a good story. A good story must be spread around.

Story might be a better model for knowledge than a scientific experiment. It lasts, it is remembered, it can be passed from one human to another with a modicum of depth even as it transforms its details in ways that cannot be predicted. Lessons can be offered from such stories, but if they are good, there is also art, something more than a lesson, something with beauty before reason.

Knowledge must have nuance, encompass confusion, make amends with chaos without calculating every variable of it. The known must accept the unknown. That's the best thing about knowledge. Now information, information cannot do anything with its opposite. There's either a one or a zero, one cannot comment on the other.

Heidegger wanted poetry to solve the problem of abstracted knowledge, and I'll second that and combine it with the demand for story. But it won't be easy to define what poetry is, never was, never will be. The poetic life is not the carefree life of hunting down experience and living with it in lushness and grace, no way will it be that easy. It's the associative life, the search for links not between facts or places where the facts live, but between relentlessly disparate experiences. This happens here, and that happens there, and they have nothing to do with one another until you discover not the reason but the sense of bonding between one happening and another, along the search for newly meaningful ways of walking between and among experiences.

This isn't about making art out of life, but living life in a proverbially open manner, with time to take things in, to blend them, and to learn what the facts have to do with anything that matters. No world was ever assembled out of just the facts. You must continue to ask where everything comes from, and where it must go. Only then will you be able to take an idea and run with it.

SIXTEEN

That's a Damn Talented Elephant!

I'm not much interested in the past. There's too much to worry about right now. And the answers to all the best questions are definitely still to come. I want the culture of nature to be far-reaching, looking forward over the arc of the millennium with dream-like daring, striving for thousand-year plans based on conviction, not just data. Wouldn't it be nice to believe that our species has a long way to go, so much more to learn, and even more time in which to learn it?

Yet who can forget the loss of innocence? What kind of death wish keeps us obsessed with dinosaurs and ancient dead trees, volcanoes set to blow right next to the world's largest city? You've all seen the Far Side cartoon: "Things look bleak. The earth's getting warmer. Our population is skyrocketing. And we've got brains the size of peanuts." We've all been there, or if not, we'll be there soon.

Still, there is solace in imagining we can communicate to the remaining creatures of this world, either those still alive or even those long dead. Remember those famous Netsilik words of the old shamaness Nalungiaq, about the time when people and animals spoke the same language: "Nobody could explain it, that's the way it was." Perhaps that's the way it still is. Consider the following story of art and its appreciation crossing the bounds of human and animal.

There is art everywhere in our world, so much that we usually take it for granted. Music blaring softly indoors and out, spectacular advertisements plastered on every free wall. There may be no current shortage of art, but we have forgotten how to assess it, how to make it mean as much as it can. Art is the free play of consciousness, or human creativity beyond consciousness, as we can often make things we cannot explain. This is the strength of sudden insight, creative awakening, spontaneity, or call it what you will.

Artists of all media make things that they do not plan, that succeed just when they surprise. And yet, we often approach these works with questions about what the artist was thinking. We want her to be there, and ask, "What did you intend by this? What does it mean?" or, given the proclivity to analysis that marks our time, "What can we *infer* about the artist from the work?"

For art has become a synonym for self-expression, based upon some axiom that every self has something worthy to express. This is true. Every self has a value that cannot be denied. But some art is better than other art, even though all selves have equal worth. We must not be afraid of our likes and dislikes, but return to the quest for them beyond personal taste. Art must have a conscience—it should not fear the absolute. There ought to be a good at the apex of it, more certain than mere opinion.

The search for absolute art used to be much more popular, much easier to accept. Artists labored to illustrate or sing the divine, and the standard of correctness was seen as omniscient, larger than the human, anything *but* depiction of the artist's own self and its turmoils. Still, the best works brought a unique spin on the eternal, making the gods a bit more tangible, ever more real. The absolute was held up as a standard, though then as much as now, no one knew what it looked like.

G. I. Gurdjieff conducted experiments in search of absolute music, sounds that would have a specific, predictable effect on the listener. He felt close to success just once, as he reports in *Meetings with Remarkable Men,* when he found music that led nearly all in the audience to quickly fall asleep.

Paul Klee, a musician as well as a visual artist, thought the great age of music had passed long ago with the purity of the baroque, but that the twentieth century would bring the great age of painting and drawing, because the canvas was finally freed from the illusory need to depict reality. Now point, line, and color could be explored in and of themselves, dancing with rhythms and patterns, approaching the abstractness of music in the sense of being about nothing else except itself, severed from the stigma of having to replicate the visible world.

The loosening toward abstraction that characterizes much of the mainstream of twentieth-century arts is one of the great achievements of our era. Before modernity art seemed ever pushing forward, always claiming to encompass and supersede all that came before, standing on the shoulders of giants just to do them one better. With this century's explosiveness this no longer seems possible. Rules have been cast aside, through layers and layers of further letting go.

The freeing may leave us with little guidance, but if it has liberated us, we have learned how to see so much more. Nature now looks like art, instead of the other way around. The drip patterns made by water on a desert cliff can resemble a painting. The songs of larks over the rustle of a meadow can at last be accepted as music. The darting of herons after fish in the river can be seen as a dance. Abstraction has drawn us closer to the art that has always been out there in nature. The result of this is that we all should feel more alive. Art that raises the right questions may have great importance for a culture in dire need of self-questioning, like our own at this precise moment in time.

So we may not know how to tell what is good or accomplished, but we find art everywhere around. Even in the zoo. In the early 1980s, trainer David Gucwa noticed that one of his charges, an elephant named Siri, was playing with a stick, doodling in the dirt in her cage at the Syracuse Zoo. Over the next two years, he engaged in a remarkable experiment that tests the boundaries of trans-species communication, as he supplied Siri with pencil and paper, later paint, and the elephant commenced to produce works that many humans have marveled at and can easily be called art.

The drawings are minimal, but intriguing. This elephant knew just when to stop. The works look at first glance like an Asian calligraphy—

not dashed off, but the sudden release of a spirit that has been pent up for a long time, an animal in a cage.

We have no choice but to take them seriously as artworks. That's what minimalism and abstraction have opened up for us—the chance to see art all around us where previously we would find nothing. We praise simple forms, colors, and shapes and find so much more immediately to see.

The book David Gucwa put together with journalist James Ehmann, *To Whom it May Concern,*[1] is so successful because it does not presume any conclusions about the validity of elephant art, but just presents the works for us to consider, juxtaposed with written reflections on elephants throughout history. Gucwa and Ehmann then mailed Siri's drawings to all kinds of "experts" to get their reactions. Onondaga Chief Oren Lyons said, "You can't speak for the animal. All you can do is appreciate what she has done—if you dare." Animal psychologist Donald Griffin wrote back, "They are complicated pictures, but I don't know what they tell us about what the animal was thinking. Of course, I have the same feeling about all modern art." They sent the drawings to the late Willem de Kooning, who responded, "That's a damn talented elephant."

A Native American has us reaching out to take the more-than-human world seriously. One expert on animal cognition gets uncomfortable when that cognition appears creative! But I think it takes the greatest courage for a recognized artist to want to trust the elephant, to want to appreciate her work, not to imagine she is trying to tell us something that can be easily explained. De Kooning knew that art is more than psychology, and that abstraction must lead to an openness to seeing artistry where previously it was invisible. He had the guts to realize that to appreciate the creativity of an elephant implied an advancement of the human character, not a belittling.

Just a few years later he was to face the same scrutiny as Siri. Later in the 1980s de Kooning was diagnosed with Alzheimer's disease, but he kept painting until 1990, seven years before his death, in a more delicate, outlining manner than his earlier bold and full works, but with a visible sense of purpose still. His work through 1987 has been deemed by some worthy of exhibition (beyond that his paintings have been kept private thus far). Critics are divided: Did he know what he was doing? Should these works be kept under wraps? Or are they the natural culmination of the fabulous career of one of the most enduring great abstract expressionists? Can we consider these works as art, without recourse to an obsession with disintegrating pathology?

Perhaps it would be nice to be able to apprehend art without knowing anything of its history or context, to gauge the effect of works on our consciousness, without information that will goad our conscience. But that's not the way it is. If we don't know more about the artist or his time, we want to know. If we can't, we imagine, we extrapolate, we *hunt* for significance.

Whereas de Kooning's earlier works are often bustling with energy and activity, too much to fathom or explain, these late paintings are sketchy, hints at compositions, promising possibilities rather than completing them. In some ways they are easier to take, but woefully incomplete. We search for direction behind them, traces of fading genius, tendencies perhaps of mastery that outsiders and novices can more quickly grasp. This is the attraction of pathology—we are impressed that anything at all can be produced by one suffering, one reduced or incomplete. See how many parents post the art of their children on the walls of home, and are genuinely impressed. (And often they smile that they swiped the paper away from the kid at just the right time.) See how surprised we are that the old and infirm can do anything at all!

De Kooning's cryptic canvases filled several halls in New York's Museum of Modern Art in the spring of 1997. Were they the final gasps of brilliance or the record of a talent fading? I watched visitors to the gallery, checking out the fading marks of de Kooning's genius. And I carried to the show the book of elephant art, showing it to friends, remarking on the way both exhibits of work do not encompass their significance in themselves, but lead us immediately to important questions. There seems to be a polarity. People seem to squirm on one challenge or another. "You mean de Kooning liked these?" said one artist of the elephant drawings. "Perhaps he was already senile." Or another gallery-goer: "These paintings don't do anything for me, but I sure would like to meet that elephant."

My original intention in bringing these two artists on trial together was to stand up for both of them, to reiterate that any artist, human or animal, expert or novice, always has an advantage over the critic: they have created something, they have made the work, and no kind of attack, judgment, or explanation can ever take that away. But wandering through the maze of de Koonings, all from his final painting years, so simplified and declining, arranged chronologically like a clock winding down, tentative marks upon an increasingly white space, fading away into silence, I felt not only a sadness but a certain injustice inside: this is not fair to this man's work, these pieces mean nothing without the paintings that came before them, it is not honest to show all these together without presenting his earlier, stronger work.

At the same time I had a nagging suspicion that we might prefer our artists to be suffering, disadvantaged, waning, out of control, and smile at how illness and infirmity makes them calm down. Why does sickness make us that much more sympathetic to art? This is a culture where we are taught to increasingly envision our own stories as narratives of recovery. We are not sure what art means or what it is for, but we assume there is some good in it if it makes us feel better.

The elephant reaching out beyond her ken to make marks on a page, the final canvases of the ailing Dutch master. These tales show that self-expression can and will prevail. Awareness matters less than drive, action stymies explication. But self-expression is its own tyranny as well. It may be important for all of us to strive to make art to ground our selves, as a kind of therapy, to hunt for a firm ground in this fluid place. Yet that is not the primary purpose of creative work. Art still aims to make itself necessary by aspiring toward destiny, and it ought to enhance, not stifle, the ability to tell the good from the bad.

It is time to stand up for the achievements of this past century in the arts, not to shoot them down. Art's modern battle to free itself from all constraints mirrored blind leaps to liberation in our recent past: music that is four minutes of silence, paintings that are completely red, performances deliberately unfocused or untrained. We had to go through these steps to cleanse our culture of excess, drive, and even the will to progress, to imagine that the great march of our Western way was going any one fantastic place in particular. It is not. We are en route to many places, many ways to indicate good from bad, many ways to be aware of our creative responsibility.

Arthur Danto has argued that by taking such risks, art has become philosophy, trying to approach the absolute not with beauty, but by asking the right questions, and refusing to let us stop asking. This will only work if philosophy at the same time moves closer to art. The vast frontier of questions must be spoken beautifully, framed elegantly, and not allowed to drift into arbitrary abstraction away from the rest of us who ought to care most about it.

Hard to find artists who will call their work abstract. Too easy to find philosophers who admit that their thinking is too abstract. Each endeavor must illuminate these concrete experiences, the living causes of wonder.

We of the culture who do not know just what to believe in have been blessed by the openness brought by our recent history. It is no accident that we are finally able to look at the art of elephants with some seriousness, or to be forced to admit that art teaches us not so much about the artist, but more about ourselves and how much explanation we demand before we can really see.

A shadow, a light, a melody that triggers off a memory. The cry of a crow, the moving warble of a group of flying cranes. All contain possibilities of song, chances for communication, someone trying to speak. Never forget the elephant. Or the dinosaur, the vulture, the plunging waterfall, or the oldest living tree on Earth. They all contain infinite stories and must never leave our memories empty.

Art does not belong to us. It abounds everywhere. When it works, it goes somewhere we were not aware of when we began. We are responsible for how little we know; it's no one's fault but our own. And yet the more one learns, the less sure anything seems to be. That's the danger of education. That's the fault of the information society. Too many images, too much trust in our ability to classify what we see. Throw as much of what you know away as you can, and you might at last be able to see.

SEVENTEEN

The Firefest

Our old spectator attitude to nature is now unthinkable, because we now know that everything "hangs together" and we experience it as such. I am for a fresh intensity in our conception of nature, because nature itself is threatened.

—Finn Alnæs, preface to *Ildfesten* (1978)

Astromia is more than all, and greater than the greatest. For it has no beginning and no end. Astromia was, is, and will be the uncountable universes. But stars arise and perish in the unending.

—First lines of *Dynamis,* second novel in *Ildfesten* (1982)

One day in 1985, when living in Oslo, I received a letter from Norwegian author Finn Alnæs, known as a writer of long, turbulent novels, the most artistic spokesman of the country's *økobevegelse* (eco-movement). I had written him several days earlier asking if he wished to be included in my book on the Movement in Norway. This was his response:

Yes I have written much on a concept of ecology that embraces arts and culture as well as natural and social resources, but I do not yet want to publish anything, nor even talk about it. There are many parts of my novels with ecosophic relevancy, as you term it. Yes, you (we) may select such a part. For the time being, I appreciate the opportunity to work undisturbed by public reaction, responses. Sorry I'm not translated into English or American. The problem is to a large extent my vocabulary. The translator would need all Norwegian dictionaries, so many dialects and historical variants are used.

But there is a marked difference between me and the ecophilosophers you are considering for your book. As an artist I have an opportunity which they lack, namely to put persons in situations that urge them to act with their entire minds, even bodies. It's outbreaks from the human heart, expressed with, I hope, some intelligence and knowledge of our century.

Alltid Jorden. Alltid Kosmos. Velkommen to Vangen, my home. You will be fetched from your office in Oslo by a car driven by an old friend, and brought straight to my door.

So. Here I am. Riding darknorth in the car.

"Is Finn a well-known author in Norway?" I ask the old friend.

She sighs as it is a boring question. "Do you mean is he popular? To read the works of a real artist takes time, and commitment. And many people have neither— Don't you agree? He is certainly one of the best we have, and so few people appreciate him."

"Isn't he becoming more and more recognized?"

"No. Less so with time. His novels get more and more difficult."

There: Day One

The house is large, quiet, at the end of a narrow track. Used to be a farm, clearly. Inside are shelves full of books, and, on the wall, giant photographs of swirling water, wind, and rock, sometimes with the faces and bodies of one of two women superimposed or underimposed within them. It is often difficult to tell which is meant to be the 'figure' and which the 'ground'. Alnæs is a photographer of some reputation. Don't know what reputation exactly. A rifle lies propped up in a corner by the bed. Many notebooks, some on the shelves, others hidden in tight iron cabinets with the legend "notebooks." Nearly a complete collection of the classics of Norwegian literature. Philosophy as well: Nietzsche. Kierkegaard. Zapffe. Naess.

"So, Mr. Rothenberg, what exactly do you want from me? Come

now, be systematic, be clear. I have my ideas. I see in your collection that I shall be the artist, not the philosopher. You do not need my explanations or solutions, no, but, heh heh, I do have them, certainly. I can give you outbreaks from the human heart, passages which live in a way that those of your other authors do not.

"What's that . . . you've heard enough beautiful descriptions of pessimism, depravity, hopelessness. You do want answers? Well, so do I, but solutions are not the same as art. But I will get to them . . . they are to be found in my future works! You are asking for unpublished unfinished material! The answers are coming! Don't you see?

"Oh yes, there has certainly been enough negativity in our world, in our time. We have had enough philosophy of lack . . . look at our own Peter Wessel Zapffe. [Zapffe is the Norwegian philosopher and humorist whose works such as *Om det Tragiske* put forth a view that as man comes to realize the full extent of his humanity, he will realize that he must abdicate his position at the pinnacle of evolution and voluntarily die out. Z called this *biosofi,* the first of many words created in Norwegian to express a newly paradoxical setting of man within nature.]

"Oh you could in some ways call him the Nietzsche of Norway, but oh, there are *mangler* within him. . . . Hmmm, what's that in English?

I think: "Hole, loophole, missings, *nei,* pitfalls, that's the best."

"ZAPFFE! Why the rascal should have hung himself years ago! It's a sin that he's still alive. The swine will live to be over a hundred, and he still goes on about how mankind should simply choose to wither away. . . . Well, are you putting him in your book? Dangerous . . . we cannot let such seductively pessimistic ideas spread too far.

"No . . . I've never met him, but, oh I know him well. Yes . . . I know Peter Zapffe well. I have read every line he has written, again and again, and I have taken notes. You want to see? . . ."

He takes a book from the vast collection: "Here, I have marked in the margins in code. 'S+' means a particularly good use of style. Yes, here he puts forth an argument on why we should not have children. 'S–' points to a particular deficiency in style. There are many of those."

I notice somewhere a "Z." "What does 'Z' mean?" I ask.

"Ah . . . well, that is where he reveals something quite special about his own character, something he may not want to reveal. Oh yes, I know him well. There are *mangler, mange mangler* . . . what did you say?"

"Pitfalls."

"Ah yes . . . words are so important. We always need new words. The establishment has taken, stolen away our words and institutionalized them. We had *miljøvern,* now we have *miljøverndepartmentet.* We had *naturvern,* now we have *naturvernforbundet.* You see. THEY have them now.

"That is why I always suggested new words. The protection of man's part in nature must be widened to include all! Why not *økovern,* or, even more general, *samvern*? But nobody took to using my words. I don't know why.

"The problem is so simple, really. Each of us must realize at once that we are Cosmic, part of the Cosmos itself! If that is fully understood that will be enough.

"So . . . you want to try to translate something. Well, why not start with this. Yes, why not start at the beginning:

A Universe Comes into Being

. . . a ray of the lifefield streams
from a previous lightland through darkness,
pauses at the first point, and turns to fire;
now compacted energy
spews matter forth
with a resounding peal
fire-substance emerges.

A time has begun,
a space has been shaped,
a universe, one, among unknown many,
has come to;
unfolding itself in dynamic balance,
billowing round in a dance of oneness,

between that choice to shape
             choice to lay waste
exchanging, co-swirling,
brilliant, eclipsing,
eternally moving,
free force
             to imagine . . .

from *Korona*, unpublished

"Now you see, it is important to realize that ours is but one of many possible universes. We cannot know. But this doesn't mean it is worth our time to wonder what these other universes are actually like, or what other intelligent beings might look like. That turns it all into a game. . . . You know that Carl Sagan, he really is ridiculous, eh? No . . . reality as it stands is the most fantastic thing possible! If we can only understand and know real love, nature, and art, then the world's difficulties shall be surmounted."

"So, I don't think much of science fiction. No, never, in fact. But the stars, yes, the stars.

"There are comets in the air these days, you know. Perhaps tomorrow we should go down to Lillehammer and buy a telescope. We must see them. But no . . . the moon is full. . . . We will see nothing. . . . But, maybe it is simply enough to know that they are there."

"My first critique of pessimism or blind imagination was directed, in my second novel, toward the whole of modern literature—you know, Beckett, Ionesco, Joyce—all so preoccupied with emptiness, meaninglessness, and alienation. In my book *Gemini* there are two brothers, both writers. At the outset of the work one has just died in a climbing accident, yes, the one who adhered closely to the credo of modern, negativist literature, which he stated as below:

The Law of the Virtuous Negative

Show no joy in life.
Have no respect for anything.
Be not affected by anything.

You shall not believe in beauty, or explain it with inflated words.

You shall not believe in love, or explain it with inflated words.

You shall not believe in God, or explain Him with inflated words.

You shall not believe in humanity, and we are not worthy of inflated words.

You shall not solve the world's riddles, for they cannot even be clarified.

You shall use small words, the smallest possible, about a being who is without a fast identity, without place, without time, without standing, who runs without beginning and end—and scarcely runs at all.

You shall consider nothing except irony, sarcasm, contempt, indifference, dread, and disgust . . .

You shall laugh, but your laughter shall be bitter, biting, ice-cold . . .

Yes, you shall laugh. But do not make yourself laugh by looking at the sky above you. That is only for naïve dreamers, earthbound astronauts, astronomers, and those who wonder about space.

Fall not into some anachronistic notion of "God's nature." That may have meaning for men and women of the past, but here there exists for us only a new urban nature made, of things, by the international "citizen of the world."

You shall show rust-beaten images of this rust-beaten humanity.

You shall believe in what remains of Man, in Man's remains.

You shall be sick, because the world is sick. You shall be modern, because the world, in every era—ha ha—is thus.

You shall be the virtuous negative.

from *Gemini* (1968)

I inhale deeply. "Well, quite a mouthful. It's based on *janteloven*, no?" (a similar credo setting down the principles of the humility of Norwegian peasants, written by Danish author Axel Sandemose in the 1950s).

"What, oh no, what do you mean? It is based on the Ten Commandments. *Janteloven* is also based on the Commandments."

"Oh. Of course. And surely neither can be seen as the answer? They are exactly what needs to be answered, yes?"

"Exactly. The answers are coming. They shall be the substance of my future works. As you know I am in the midst of writing a cycle of eight novels called *Ildfesten* (The firefest), which in time will answer such important questions, and show where and how the grounds for optimism can be shaped. But I have so little time! So much to say! I work simultaneously on all the six remaining novels. I shall decide myself when they are to be published."

"So much to say, yes, diversity is the key. There are so many ways to say it. I am a mangfoldist, yes, of course. Art is the perfect place for diversity, where it must be considered as paramount.

"But diversity can be dangerous as an all-powerful slogan. That is why the eco-movement failed. Everyone crying out in their own way in their own worlds. Lots of stars, but no real leaders, no unity, no agreement. Yes, a lot of strong individual personalities in this Movement, but what to hang it together?

"We could never unify. And the authorities took our words. And no one would accept the new ones."

"Well, in this book I am writing, I will introduce a new word to the American public—*ecophilosophy*. And I have the chance to choose and shape its meaning."

"Yes . . . then it is most important. We must be clear, and embracing, but not to shut out any of the many meanings of the term. Unity with diversity . . . that is the basic problem. . . . And I will provide the answer, yes, in time."

"But, oh, there are conditions, consequences. When a man climbs up toward a summit alone, by a new route on a difficult wall, a hairline crack, one never knows exactly what he is doing. So it is with art.

"Now some climbers make a point of documenting all their climbs and letting everyone know it is they and not any other who has made the first ascent . . . but is that so important? Climbers must trust each other if they are to climb together. They must collectively see their goal. So it is with eco-activists. But artists . . . with us we must encourage diversity above all:

> Literature needs a diversity of means and methods of expression because life itself is diverse. Yes, I know I repeat myself, but is it not so

necessary to drum this in again and again? When shall we all realize
this simple fact: that we are not served by, and shall never be served by,
that which requires all to be the same? The power source of this idea
has always been stupidity and intolerance. The slogan, "first destruction, then build anew" springs forth only from such narrowness. There
has never been the need to destroy anything before building anew in
literature, because anything unable to live dies of itself. ("The Art of the
Novel and Norway," 1965)

"You see . . . even back then I was talking of culture in ecological
terms, speaking of life and death. And this idea that we must scrap
our present society and systems before affronting the future is equally
unsound. We must envision change itself in an ecological way. This
leads to what the philosopher/astrosopher/ecologist Fartein Glitra in
my book *Dynamis* calls 'desperate optimism':

> "Friends," began Glitra. "Life is diversity, and for each of us this has
> many connotations. But Alex here, as we experience him, is among
> those who would show us that certain forms of blackness always
> end in contempt for humanity, and that contempt, if we do not let
> it pass, can slide into fascism or follow fascistoid currents. But this
> depends on to what extent one presents at the same time a citizenry
> which dies out. Yet Alex has shown in his books a fascistic contempt
> for man which does not attack in particular civilized man, but the
> very phenomenon of Man. It is here the conflict between brothers
> is greatest, and if you shall go in with them, you must, as Alex has
> himself, pose the following question: 'How high can poetry lift itself
> over its lowly subjects?'" (*Dynamis*, 1982)

"Good, interesting. Yes, I am beginning to get interested in this
project of yours. You see of course that the philosopher Glitra is here
speaking of Alexander Steina, the optimistic author in *Gemini*, and his
deceased brother the 'virtuous negative.' But, in describing the 'conflict
between brothers' I mean at the same time these two brothers, and
brothers in general. And Man in general."

"Yes, I see that."

"Good."

I see now that there exist at least two people that are called Finn Alnæs. One is the brilliant, relentless struggler toward optimism and vitality in a world that seems incapable of listening, and the other is a lonely man lost in a swirling cycle of novels, dreams, and his own chance at answers that stand to him as far more important than anything else on Earth.

That night I dreamed of traveling to a reunion, a place where many old friends were, and many new people to meet. It was a cavernous dormitory, many people, many rooms, everywhere, yes, just the type of people one would expect to meet in such populated caves. Some I knew, some I did not, but all were expected, and I thrived upon the busyness though I knew it was false.

Day Two

"Yes, interesting dream, that. Sounds like a distinct reversal of the situation here."

"Yes, we two alone in the forest. Quiet. Such peace to work."

"Hmm . . . alone enough to think about words. For example the word 'world'. Soon it will mean everything, all. We have to decide, set its limitations, discover it anew. Sure, the optimism is strong, it is to come. The pessimism is of our time. Yes, it is not hard to write about that:

> But see for yourself how a single lighted match can obscure the whole Milky Way!

And this is said to humanity:
You have found the means to destroy all that is here, and you have also accepted the possibility that you may use these abilities. The Earth has stood and still stands at your disposal. But do not take the right to prevail over all. Declare your respect for that which is greater than yourself.

But respect is not that which appears! You, who were once fresh cells in the organism have become a malignant tumor whose stifling tendrils have spread so thoroughly through all that they cannot be severed without the death of the organism itself.

And when the cancer is complete you will have reshaped the entire Earth in your own dreadful image. (*Naturkathedral,* 1978)

"See . . . the sanctity of religion can be reversed."

"But once I wrote primarily of concrete plans. In a concrete way. Yes, when I was twenty-seven I wrote the following for a speech:

I wanted for a time to be a playwright. For a while I discussed with myself the possibility of making my debut in English. It is awfully difficult to become a playwright in the country of Henrik Ibsen. Either you write like him, and that's wrong, or you write unlike him, and that's wrong too. But it's the same psychic mechanism hampering us from making a new world: If we advocate a new world, its is wrong (utopia). And if we plan the future based on "present facts"—everybody argues that something better might be done, at least here and there. Whatever we do, wrong we are! (Speech to World Federalist Youth Congress, 1957)

"But of course I wouldn't write that now."

"Yes, it sounds like something *I* might write. You know, that sort of forced clarity and argument that we arrogant youth use in trying to show the world that we are one up on them."

"Yes . . . But tell me: Do you think it's a tragedy that I am writing in a language of only four million people, for a little provincial nation, a mere spot on the edge of the world?

"Think that I could be writing for millions, I could reach many more people, so many who could understand. I see it as a tragedy."

"Oh . . . of course there are worse tragedies, I know. But I had plans for the world! I still have them, locked in that safe. Yes, they're still secret, so don't ask to see them.

"I had to leave the World Federalist Congress and that milieu. . . . I longed for Norwegian nature, and I knew that I had to write novels. And that requires peace and silence, not the realities of our confused world. It's sort of sad, don't you think?

"Well . . . I know I have to leave *this* place if I want to reach the people. And the people need us! We veterans of the Movement have lost the public. We cannot make any more mistakes. And we are tired of saying things the same way! . . . We need new words, sparkling words, to fight this pessimism.

"But what shall we do? Knock on the door of the network and shout, 'I want to speak to the people!' And then face the TV camera with rehearsed lines? No; just ten years ago one could write an article in any one of the major newspapers and it would be read by thousands. But no more. Our brains are numb. No wonder the real artists are going into the catacombs.

"No . . . the media has focused on our nonviolent actions, the protest against the damming of waterfalls. But the most important part of an action is the dialogue with the people through public debate. Yet that is not sensational. The media tried to create stars—and this is not hard in a movement with such strong personalities—Naess, Kvaløy, Faarlund—yes, this certainly will be a book of strong personalities you are putting together!

"What about all those who have been forgotten! Those who really did the work. Even in my mind now they sink into oblivion. . . . Yes, this has been a Movement with a lack of human warmth . . . all this protest-camp romanticism, sad; . . . still, there is something essentially human about this lack.

"There is much to write about here."

A cold silence in the room—yes, silence can be disdain.

"No. I do not want to connect my name with a defeat. I am no longer in this Movement. Perhaps I should not even be included in your book!"

We take a break and Finn asks me to study the photos of women and waterfalls on the walls.

"Is she not beautiful? Either watching the water or in the water. Her body was like water."

Silence. What can one say?

"Yes, she is the mother of my six-month-old daughter. They left only three months ago. She was forever incessantly jealous.

"Of what?"

"I don't know . . . couldn't she see how much I loved her? She's in all these pictures! Couldn't she see? . . .

"Oh yes . . . I have experienced the limitations of the picture. Do you notice how people would rather watch an image of an elephant on TV than to see one walking by outside the window? Yes. Words are the basis of all truth, all our ideas. Yes, we need them. Good ones. New ones."

Silence.

One photo especially struck me. One placed side by side with a reflection of itself about its edge. Mirrored. Like a Rorschach print. The nude body of a woman stretching forth, double exposed with a waterfall. The exact same shape. I knew not which was imposed on which.

Then next to it its opposite. The placing of the photos side by side bothered me a bit, as it created all sorts of unnatural symmetries—tampering with the symmetries of nature. Maybe that's what these women felt. Their symmetries had been tampered with.

When I Am Far (I)

When I am far
so am I far
all ways,
Know this.
Then can nothing be done.
Then can you hang pictures of me
on the walls,
set to the music,
we played together.

Mark me, perhaps, as a wall-spirit,
for my hands' and my mind's work
are everywhere still.

Dynamis

my thoughts detach as I drift to sleep:

killing you with silence
keeping dominance by saying nothing

janteloven

power.

Is she not beautiful?

He lives alone in the forest, slowly going crazy.
Your visit may be just what he has been waiting for.

But how can I write about him? He's shown me too much of his life. I know he is only talking because I assured him I am not interviewing him in any way. How else can there be openness? Any media is dangerous.

He comes hurriedly determined with a notepad up the stairs, right as I am falling asleep. He reads directecdly:

"What I am trying to tell you is . . . we have all been false leaders. In my art, in my work, in my life, people come into focus and then fade. Something can happen now, something might happen, something must happen, but we need LEADERS!

"How shall we explain it this next time, how shall we make it clear? We must help them, not try to tell them. . . . From among THEM shall the leaders sprout! We need more time! It is the only possibility. Good night."

That night I dreamed of what it would be like to see again one woman who has been writing me many letters since I have been away. Someone has been trying to convince her that I am perfect for her and she has begun to believe it. She has sent me many of these words and we are both beginning to believe them. In the dream the actuality of the meeting was questioned. And I wondered what of the whole business was to be believed.

Day Three

The woman or the water—which is figure and which is ground? I think I would like to have that picture on my wall (like a Rorschach test). But what would any women think of it?

"I answer in novels!

"In *Dynamis*, the philosopher Glitra meets conflict within himself between being a true friend and between treating all his acquaintances as if he were a chess-player, manipulating and using them solely for his own directed purposes. When he realizes how he is only able to treat people as tools to be used, he learns the tragedy of his limitations.

"That is what is so wrong with so many in the Movement. . . . They do not know how to live and act as human beings! They write, research, search for examples of the ideal, and try to find people who can tell them how to feel."

"Yes, that is what is lacking."

"But come . . . look at this photo on the cover of my novel *Musica*. It is an old photograph. She should have become my wife, years ago. For some years we lived together in a tiny, tiny room. See . . . here is a photo of it. . . . That stack of papers is my office, the whole contents of my first novel.

"She gave more to me than any single person. I can't believe she is dead."

I didn't ask whether she had died then or more recently, but I sensed that there were other reasons for their separation.

> Freedom of the spirit can exist only when the expression reaches those who hold other points of view. Where the expression holds only for those who are like-minded, freedom of the spirit is kept in, like the mere skin of reality. The expression is locked in quarantine.
> (*På frihetens pinebenk*, 1972)

"Yes, I have always been concerned with reaching many different kinds of people. That's why I assembled this book of essays, *På frihetens pinebenk* (On the torture-rack of freedom). The first half was on politics, the second on culture. But people weren't ready for such unity in diversity. Nobody listened. The book did not sell. I won't do a book like that again.

"But to reach diverse publics, yes, I remain a mangfoldist!

"What did you say? . . . When have I reached the most people?

"I would have to say when improvising speeches before large gatherings. Yes, that's when inspiration can come. People will feel that and then listen.

"But I see what you need now . . . it is from the future! I can give you nothing now. For me to answer your questions you must go away, so I can continue working!"

"Well, let's not make the world wait too long."

"Yes, quite right. We must translate something else. We have begun with one universe; let us continue with the origin of our own species:

> Humanity!
> Of course you are magnificent.

("see . . . that comes from Nietzsche")

> And so much is possible for you.
> But have you yourself made your own brain,
> this immense bundle of nerve cells
> arranged in mysterious perfection
> which can tell how sperm and egg
> unite to become a person?

("and that, you see, is from Zapffe. Continue!")

> And where were *you* when your sun came to,
> in a mass of gas and dust?
> Where were you when the first whirl was shaped
> in the cloud of creation?
> the first eddy in the

primal mist,
by chance . . .

("yes, good, this is getting interesting . . .")

Or was it God's finger that set the
system in motion?
Then where did the gas and dust
come from?

Gemini (1968)

Yes, the stars. That night we went outside searching for the comets. But it was hopeless. The moon was too bright.

"You know what I am afraid of most?

"Flying."

"But surely you must fly sometimes?"

"Yes, and when I do, then I am the most courageous person on Earth."

Later, leafing through *Dynamis,* I come across the following passage:

When I fly, I am the world's bravest man. Every single second I struggle with the fear of death, calculate the probable time and distance of the fall from the plane to the ground. And if one day the plane should really tumble, I will be the least panic stricken, because I will already be exhausted with fear and tremblings. We mountain climbers know how to deal with danger. But we would never surrender our equipment and protection.

Who is speaking here, I wondered. I said nothing. Our conversation, though, continued:

"Well, since you are always asking me, how do you think we can save the world?"

"Ha ha. You will have to read my novels! And I have not even begun one yet."

"You know something: if you want to become my enemy, don't be honest, and make me work in vain.

"You do not want art, you want answers! I had planned to give you outbreaks from the human heart, but you want my opinions, my plans, well these are secret for the time being. They are for future books, not your book, or for any book at the present moment."

"Well, can an outbreak answer anything?"

Silence.

Smiles.

"Tell me. Do you think the author can be a character in his own work?"

"Always is."

"But then it isn't fiction!"

After much deliberation, we decided to watch an American film on television that night. It was about a time when the media controls all, when a TV newscaster goes through a metamorphosis, first to a madman, then to a comedian, then to a prophet of the uplifting spirit of humanity. His show becomes the most popular on the air, thanks to a cold, determined program director played by Faye Dunaway. But after a while his message is no longer profitable. It turns against the giant corporations. Then the arch corporation director takes our newsman into his office and preaches to him that he must become the prophet of the almighty dollar. He is convinced: "I have seen the face of God!" our hero blurts. "Well, perhaps you are right," says the arch-capitalist. A ridiculous film, really. In the end they have to kill him. Finn asked three questions during its course:

"Why is there always so much shouting in all American films?"

"Not all."

"Do people live in these skyscrapers, or just work in them?"

"Both, actually."

"Is she sexy?" speaking of Faye.

"She is supposed to be. But there is a brooding kind of evil to her in this film that tempers it."

"I really shouldn't see such films. I'll turn into a troll in the morning."

That night I dreamed about all the women I knew who are like the one in the film. Cold, determined, bossy, but with a determination that is attractive. I know only a few of this type. Each time I approached them in the dream I remember being overshadowed by a certain elderly philosopher . . . Glitra or Naess. He had been there before. Hmm . . . yes, it's all been done and said already, never mind about the words.

Day Four

I knew something was wrong when I came down to my desk and saw that my notebook and the translations were gone.

"Yes, they are not there. I have locked them all in the safe. You don't realize how vulnerable I am. You could do anything with this material, I really have no control. I suggest that you go back to Oslo, decide exactly what you want from me, and then come back. Then you can have back whatever you need, if I know exactly how you will use it. See, I told you I would turn into a troll if we watched that film. It made me suspicious. I can trust no one anymore. . . . I have made mistakes in the past. I cannot make them again."

"Now wait a minute. You have no right to confiscate my notes like that." I realized I was in a tenuous position here. I needed that notebook back. Much of it was on other things than Finn Alnæs. On the other hand, I am not so sure he would have liked me to write down all the things I have down about him, on those last few pages.

"Besides . . . only a few pages concern you. And they're just fragments of translations . . ."

"No. You are some kind of journalist. I am afraid that you are writing down everything that I say."

This was true. I was writing down everything he said. It somehow seemed worthy of being written down. But I must not let him discover this.

"That book was empty when you arrived!"

"No it was not." This was true. "See, it is dated October 1985. I started it over a month ago." It contained all my notes on the whole ecophilosophy project.

"See, now this first page is about a book on gestalt psychology. . . . Here, the figure-ground distinction is introduced. . . ."

"Wait . . . that is just what we talked about. It is about me!"

"No. It is about a book called *Gestalt Therapy* by Frederick Perls. Look, here is an excerpt:

> The primitive says "The Earth is starving, therefore we are starving." And we say, "We are starving, therefore let us wrest something more from the Earth": symbiotically both attitudes are bad dreams.

"But that is so relevant to what we have been talking about!"

"Well . . . of course it is relevant. That is why I have come here to see you. This was my preparation. Here, another excerpt, from the same book:

> To the extent that there is a discrepancy from the verbal concept of the self and the felt awareness of the self—*this is neurosis*—so notice the difference as you slip from one to the other.
>
> Healthy verbalizing takes off from what is non-verbal. . . . But when one fears contact with actuality, with flesh-and-blood people and with one's own sensations and feelings—words are interposed as a screen between the verbalizer and his environment and between the verbalizer *and himself.* The person attempts to live on words—and then wonders vaguely why something is amiss!

"Well, we talked about this, too."

"No, we didn't. But perhaps we should have."

"What?"

"Now look at the next page. It's about Wittgenstein. Have you read Wittgenstein? No, I didn't think so. Of course I haven't really read him either, but here are some notes:

> 219. When I obey a rule, I do not choose. I obey the rule *blindly.*

> 333. Only someone who is *convinced* can say that.

"Did you ever think of that? Both the words 'convicted' and 'convinced' lead to *conviction*. Ah, perhaps it doesn't work in Norwegian, *kanskje?*"

"No . . . I don't know."

456. When one means something, it is oneself meaning.

"Well, it is a good thing there isn't anything too personal in this book of mine, isn't it? Now would you let me do this with your notebooks? I know you keep them under lock and key, as you would like to keep this one. I know they are in there, yes, drafts and sketches for *Gemini, Musica, Dynamis,* and future novels: *Korona,* and who knows what else . . ."

"Yes, yes, I know. You know how I am. Forgive me this one indiscretion."

"OK . . . now next are some characterizations of the poles of intrinsic value by Archie Baum, an obscure southwestern philosopher. Have you heard of him? I didn't think so. Yes: 'Hedonism exists between pleasure and pain. Romanticism between desire and lack of desire, voluntarism between satisfaction and frustration, atmanism between . . .'"

"Enough, enough! I don't need to hear any more. I'm sorry. It is wrong of me to keep this. Nothing there is about me." He flips quickly through the pages that are about him without reading. Luck.

All is returned intact. Maybe this is not so good.

"All right. You can have it all back." But we have not understood each other. "You came here looking for optimism, pure constructivism. I have wanted to give you art. These two are not the same. In the future they may become the same. You are asking me in the present for the future."

"Well, I hope we get there before it is too late."

"That is a very Zapffian answer!"

"Yes, I suppose it is."

"The novel can be the only truly ecological art form. That is what I interpret Zapffe as saying in his best moments." Alnæs is returning to himself.

"Yes, in other forms much must be left out. In nature nothing can be left out. We must accept all as it stands!

"In a novel, nothing need be left out. I am an epic writer . . . the Earth, the Cosmos, Astromia."

I am ready to cheer.

An artist who works alone: should one work so alone? He in his own world interests me. In his way, he is the most integric ecosopher of them all. We know well the paradoxes:

The more understanding you have, the fewer are those who will understand you.

When art calls one can no longer be a responsible and political citizen. And can one only be optimistic as an artist who creates his own epic worlds? Is this act of creation what it means to be ecological? To create one's own universe, yes, one, among unknown many?

Who will be changed by it? Who will glean hope from it? Whoever can take the time I suppose. Whoever can be induced to dream a similar dream.

Where in all this are the world's problems touched? Does the muse drive one away from them to the stars, the comets, upon ski tracks over viddas?

Yes, Finn, you can show us the joy of being part of the Cosmos, Astromia, and all. But maybe to really take this choice you must leave us behind.

Oh, I can't breathe or continue, the tragedy and condition are so clear. And I can tell you no more, for I have learned what shall be the substance of my future works.

And I don't know if I can let these words stray from me too far.

I remember now two pictures above one another above the stairs, both of a cabin in the rain, with a slow exposure to show the tracks of the falling water. The upper one was gray, the lower slightly golden. He had said:

"See, in the opposite direction from this first photo was a full rainbow. The second was taken right from within the rainbow. So now you know what it looks like inside a rainbow."

I didn't question that.

I never saw Finn Alnæs again. He spent several more years writing feverishly, being misunderstood, and feeling very much alone. In 1992 he was found dead at his writing table, after a tough period of suicidal tendencies, alcoholism, and neglect.

He left at least four novels partially written. The *Ildfesten* cycle will never be completed.

When I Am Far (II)

But likewise, my friend,
will I be far
all ways.
Live then all the days we had together.
Think never I and you. Think we.
Live this.
And never forget that we are here now.
Now!
Your friend greets you
this way
to sunrise.

Dynamis

EIGHTEEN

The Innocent Climb

I remember first a long walk up through mist. I am a child, stepping through the trees, those green disappearing shapes against the gray. It's disturbingly dark and strange. Endless up, marching up the wet and rocky trail. Higher the trees give way, get smaller. Then a vast world of stone looms up. I am so small that the rock seems so much bigger than it could ever seem to me today. It is too much rock, too much to comprehend or want to walk on. I want to run, back down into the safe cool woods. But another part of me is happier in this rock world than anywhere else.

The clouds sink down, the world is invisible. We are marching up the huge stone ridge over lumps and bounds to a summit that will look just like any other place. There will be no view. We will all feel cold and wet and out of place. Except me. I am the smallest and will soon feel the most at home. From the time of this climb onward I will dream for years of mountains and their hard, open tops, the promise of vistas and the impossibility of really living for long up in the cold silence and way above the trees.

Think of the gait of a child climbing the mountain and how it instantly seems about three times higher than to those of us full-grown. The huge effort and mystery of it all! This, the highest mountain I had ever had the chance to go up at the age of nine. And to have to walk into a cloud to get there, so that anything around could be easily imagined to be true!

For so many years I sought to recover that sense of wonder, that joy at walking into a cloud for the very first time. There have been much bigger mountains, certainly. But I have also thought I knew so much more before I went up them. Their names, their altitude, their stories, and the confidence that I could make it. Yet it doesn't take long to lose the innocent climb. And the smaller we feel next to the greatness of the mountain the closer we are to inhabiting its greatness, the single idea I learned from Arne Naess that I most take to heart. I suppose now that's the meaning of the aesthetic goal of the *sublime*. Hard to wish for if we believe our humanity can rule all, solve all, encompass all, as all that talking now seems to point to. But one mountain, once climbed by a little boy who felt most strangely at home through wet pelting rain and invisible wind running faster and faster up the gray stones to the wet slick top of the second most-climbed mountain in the world, yes, one mountain can be enough to remind us that there will always be so much more than what any human being can do.

The world will live on. The mountain will live on, long beyond any uses for it we can think up.

The fewer facts you know about a mountain the better. To prepare to encounter it your mind should be empty, expecting nothing, or if you have to expect, to expect the worst: boredom, the too familiar, too many people, even the same people you would see at home. Even as a precocious mountain-mad child I had heard what a *monadnock* was—a huge lump of rock rising above rolling forests, a big hunk scraped bare but still left after the icecap had gone back. I also knew that Mount Monadnock, in southern New Hampshire, was the second most-climbed mountain in the world. Even then it seemed a rather astonishing statistic, realizing that number one is Mount Fuji, a national icon, a postcard Mona Lisa of mountains that is almost an indelible image inside human consciousness—fulfilling an international ideal of what 'mountain' is supposed to mean. That pure snow-tipped cone peaking through clouds. A Platonic form of mountain, inside all of us. Five billion views of Mt. Fuji. That's the global brain looking up and wanting to go there.

Mount Monadnock number two? Who in Japan has even heard of it? Who in Europe has heard of it? Who can draw it accurately from memory or picture it inside? How could such a relatively obscure peak be number two?

The standard answer: It's close to some of the biggest American metropolitan areas. It's easy even for a kid to get up there. In its own bounded way it's fabulously spectacular.

My own selfish answer: I've been up it so many times. Each time has a resonance, a significance as it marks my own life passage against the time of the mountain. The time of the mountain is geological, and it doesn't care at all for people or animals or trees or biodiversity or life in the least. It's a rock place, a world of eons and eras and millions of years conflated to timelessness. The mountain will be around long past any being that chooses to care about it.

These little stories of mine are so, so small. But I want to join up with that mountain, so I'll have to make them even smaller.

What kind of child so loved the mists in the morning, the gray occluded places where you can't tell where you are? He was happiest inside the clouds. Did that make the clouds inside him any less visible, any more soft and less hard? No one understood him. He wanted most to be taken seriously, to be listened to and not called "kid" or "cute." He would have to wait a long time for that to stop.

The mountain of course would accept him as he was. He could run all the way up to the rocky parts long before anyone older could catch him. He could enjoy the rain and was never worried about catching a cold when wet. Let the cold catch him. Let the wind envelop him, let the rain strike through.

He wanted to rise up, to peek through like that monadnock. But the glacier kept him down, that ice weight of adulthood and experience that is only amused by children, not really interested in them. He took notes, planned for the future, got ready for the inevitable. Note 1: be sure to remember to take my children *seriously*. Treat their ideas with respect, not surprise. Note 2: be sure to live high in the mountains, somewhere full of wind and snow. The air is clear up there. Nobody will bother me.

So few of us can be monadnocks. We are best kept down, shoved into the pen with all the others and encouraged to lie flat and only rarely speak up. Those that rise will find their heads scoured, scratched, and maimed. But if you survive you might in the end have something to say, though it will never be easy. You will still carry scars.

That's not to exaggerate his difficulties. They were internal, quiet wounds, but often he burst into tears for no reason. Not in the mountain, no, never in the mountains. The wind and ice are so clear and so safe.

It is many years later, and I am only that child in the reconstruction of memories. I am only a climber in a fabrication of the past. Who's to say which is closer to the reality of the present or to the geological reality of the mountain scraped bare, with a life span so far removed from human time?

Petrarch was worried that climbing a mountain took him too far from the proper contemplation of God. And these days all we seem to consider is ourselves. Every story takes us back into the self, and all we will end up knowing is how each of us, each lonely life, takes a walk upon the land and tries to remember something of how the place affected us.

If the monadnock is bathed in light you can find your way up above the forests. But how is it to understand the rocks in darkness? Climb a mountain at night in the wake of a lunar eclipse and you will see.

It was in the summer after my first year of college, I was nineteen years old. A lunar eclipse was expected, a rare but not unheard of event. We would climb from the forest into the open sky and observe. At night, guided by the bright and full moon.

There were a group of us: my first girlfriend, Bridget, my good friend Andy, other friends Somi and Paul. We drove up after dusk from the city and parked by the head of the old Halfway House trail.

An easy walk it was on the moonlit trail, the rocks like cobblestones on an ancient weathered street. Every beautiful way seems like it looks back to another time when more people put their feet to its earth: Monadnock, I had heard, was once a popular resort destination. There were scores of exact, tiny trails marked upon its flanks, attractions, tea houses, resting places, and a gracious lodge on its top. It was a grand destination, a title now reserved for Caribbean hideaways and faraway ski resorts. Without the airplane, Monadnock seemed a much more wild and distant adventure for the train and stagecoach riders from Boston and Manhattan. It was a long way off, a fine place to escape to.

Now it was another New England path much more wild than it was. Did this mean that we were slowly returning to nature? No, only turning our tendency to conquer elsewhere.

But on this night these facts did little to cloud the clear skies above our climb. The moon casts an unfamiliar shadow, especially to those of us too long in the city. Streetlights, it is said, tell lies. This was the real changing light of the night. It guided our rocky way up.

I thought of the legends of lunacy brought on by leaving children too long out in the light of the moon. It's not where we are supposed to be. But when we go there the forest does become a strange and privileged place. Everything's now like a fading black and white photograph, only the wind moves the shadows as you see them. You can look at your feet to make sure you don't slip but there isn't always that much to see.

Stepping slowly up beneath the moon. Careful on the rocks, always some are wet. Watch the faint shadows that are trees shrink as you get higher. In the distance views peek through, shimmers of the distant lights of tiny towns, or single candles burning in shacks deep in the woods, where someone sits and could not know they are being watched from far away on the mountain.

When you reach the long rock finger ridges you know you will make it. The way ahead is open, quiet, unvisited by any other animals on this night. The light is strange enough to keep them all away. And now even something is happening to the moon. A piece is being clipped away. A strange round shadow makes its appearance on the source of light. That's the Earth. That's where we stand right now, so far away. How can the line of this planet possibly make a difference to that faraway bright light? That's what has astonished people about eclipses for centuries.

I see now the cool rock dome in night shadows, seventeen years later. The shape and color are still clear. Or are they? Have they not become blurred with other mountains I have climbed at night, other moments when the deep silence of the world has been felt? Many times I've been on the rocks at night, and seen how lonely the world is. For as much as humanity reshapes this planet in our image, its mountains still seem unmovable and unfazed by it all. Nothing is expected of us by the night.

I'm trying to be specific, I want to be clear. The one thing about this climb that separates it from all others in my mountain memories is that the bright moon did not give way to sunrise. By the time all of us sauntered up to the summit, most quietly in awe, some talking to avoid taking in the emptiness, the shadow was swallowing the moon. Suddenly its motion sped up, and in an instant the light was swallowed up. The sky was instantly dark, and we had no flashlights. We had forgotten about this part of the eclipse—the light goes away. So we sat at the top of Monadnock with all the wonder of moonlight gone and the wonder of the eclipse darkening the sky. What to do?

"We wait, of course," I announced. "If we wait, the light will come back."

"But it's cold," said Bridget, holding my hand, though with that single sentence the temporary nature of our relationship seemed to come out. It would not last.

"Just enjoy the cold. Feel the intensity of the cold and the darkness. It won't hurt you." She looked at me skeptically. Some others had already started down, even though they could not see where they were going. It looked possible. "Well, we can also feel our way down. Sight as a sense is a bit overrated."

Stepping down you let gravity do the work for you. It's less effort but so much easier to fall, as the weight of the Earth just pulls you down, right there beneath the shadow of the Earth in a lean darkness. You rely on recent memory to know that the trail is safe, where it turns wet and dry, where it goes right and left, slippery or firm. Holding hands does not help as this is a single-file trek. Some are more confident than others. The group spreads out in time along the walk. Soon each of us is alone, going at our own pace not being easily able to see but soon easily able to feel. It becomes a pure and individual descent for all of us.

One by one we return to the clearing where we left the cars. Some people are taking too long. We're worried what happened to them. Andy and I rush back up, confident, wanting to rescue. We find Somi and Paul about halfway up. They were just taking their time. Not wanting any kind of push or rescue. We were the impatient ones. They said they were fine.

Not quite dark, not quite light when we are that the bottom. It was a special adventure about which little needs to be said. I've probably said too much already. Where are they today? Andy runs a successful computer concern. Paul tells nonprofit organizations how to run things. Somi is one of the country's cutting-edge graphic designers. Bridget has given up on men. We will never all climb together again. The mountain is still in the same place, not even wondering about the next eclipse. I probably think more about this ascent than the rest of them, and it still seems like one of the most important things I've done.

Why? Because I set myself away from the normal days. Because I took some risk to get tainted by the darkness after the light. Because I didn't know exactly what would happen, and because I brought my friends there with me.

But where are they today? That's the question I keep asking about which the mountain has nothing to say. Where are they today? These people, these memories, these reasons for the climb.

Four years later I took a woman up there whom I hardly knew. There's no point even telling you her name. I spoke alluringly of the mountain and of the need to camp by its base at night, so as to get a fresh and early start and be the first ones up. Never mind the darkness, we wanted to begin with the dawn and follow the tracks of the morning sun. Driving a few hours in the dark in a borrowed car, we were both conscious of the strangeness of the escapade. Other guys' idea of a good time was taking me out to dinner, she thought, while this one started with a mountain climb that would begin with us crawling into a tent in some illicit woods. I had this idea that we had to camp just by a particular pond at the base of the mountain, private property of course, but a good place to watch the sun come up. No one else would notice, or mind.

This time I did have a flashlight. We unloaded the tent and the sleeping bags, simply carried them off into the woods. The fiberglass tent poles sprang into place and the shelter was up. Both of us climbed in and took off our clothes and then we were naked underneath the down quilting. Maybe only fools rush in but those were different times. It was romantic enough and we were both somewhat interested. I remember she was very thin and nervous and cried out in a tiny voice. I remember the joy of being held so close but I do not remember her name. Thus the story and the acts last more than one's sense of the person, these persons that come and go, who go back and forth to the mountains.

Dawn as the sun shoots against the tent and makes sudden moving shadows through leaves in the wind, and I'm instantly ready to head for the summit before anything else happens in the world, to get up there before anyone else has even thought of having breakfast and jumping into their cars to drive toward the mountain from the city far away. Words are cascading through my head, phrase after phrase, as they often do early in the morning before the weight of reality makes them stop. "Let's go! The sun is out, the summit beckons . . ." "Uhhh . . ." she of the forgotten name says. "I'm ready to climb. We can be up and down before breakfast." "Coffeee . . ." she mumbles, not sure of where she is I reckon. "Water?" I offer. "Bubbling straight from the forest spring."

It wouldn't do. All I could think of was the incipient mountain and all she could envision was a huge mug of steaming black java. It hadn't even occurred to me. Back then I never drank anything with caffeine, and when I saw a mountain, all thoughts of food and libation desisted. But no, we had to pack up, get in the car, roll down the road into Jaffrey, amble into a main-street diner, and fuel up. After that she was ready for the mountain, but I saw she could as easily have gone home.

We went up, though; don't think I'm not used to dragging the uninitiated up across the rocks. She with the wrong shallow shoes and the mistrust of the mud and the awkward jumping around the wet spots and wondering why there weren't any sheltering trees up here. "Lightning?" she asked. "What if it strikes?" The clouds were building. "Don't worry. Not likely, and we'll be down before anything serious builds."

The clouds only pass by, no damage done. The autumn colors are full but the day is unseasonably warm. We are sticky and confused on the return. Who is she? Who am I? Why did we climb this mountain together at all? Years later it seems most important that I convinced a girl I hardly knew to ascend the most climbed of mountains with me. Only to have someone to go with? Never so self-centered, but instead the point is to have taken someone, anyone with a glimmer of interest, another searching soul, up into the world of this beautiful not so faraway landscape.

I saw her again many years later, and was too embarrassed to ask for her name. She's thinner, wiser, now a psychologist working at a hospital. She looked at me at the party with an interesting smiling gaze, as if to say, "you, you are a person worth investigating, figuring out. You showed me a different kind of place. I remember it well, differently than you remember it, and I have never climbed a mountain again."

And the last time in winter I am struggling through deep snow up the Pumpelly Ridge from the Dublin side. It's a crisp but frigid day, and my boots are soaking wet as I keep sinking in the fresh white cover. No leaves on the trees, the countryside always so much clearer in winter, and views of the land begin early on the hike. Winding, ascending, rough travel in the tough season. Hours to head up, smiling hours squinting in the sun. Today I'll never make it all the way, simply too far, too slow, and no human or animal has broken the trail. It doesn't matter. I've been all the way. The summit, a place that I know, that I hold secure among memories, alone and with others. Better to know it is there than to make it and be not satisfied.

I do not really want to describe these trips to you. I want to describe what they do to me, many years later. They hold me close to the monadnock, even though I have never lived in its shadow, even though I have always been a visitor even at those times when I understood some essential fact about myself or the world while up there.

I hear you can now take a tram to the top of Mount Fuji. That might make Monadnock the world's most climbed and still untainted mountain. Of course there once was a road up to its top, too, and a lot more people than go there today. If it's not tainted, it is at least full, weighted down, plastered or painted with all those human memories of walks up and across the land.

We wander to collect experiences, and as we amass them we find they are nothing but experiences. We may tell whatever stories we want about the mountains we have climbed, but in the most honest stories hardly anything happens. That may be why we turn to the land instead of to each other.

NINETEEN

The Zone

S pread the blame as far as it goes.
   Find whose fault it is, then take them to task.

Ten years ago the machines failed us as no one was in charge.
These are the facts:
250 times the radiation of Hiroshima and Nagasaki combined
135,000 people had to be evacuated.
1,000 immediate injuries,
10,000 square miles contaminated, the size of Maryland.
Dangerous levels of radiation were deposited in 20 countries.
By September 31 people had died from exposure to something
no one could see.

On that April 26th, 1986 I was in the Norwegian mountains;
drying out from the warm wet snow
tuned to a tiny radio, we heard the news.
"Radioactive clouds are coming your way."
We looked up at the sky, no one knew how to tell,
To know what was safe, and what was not.

———

Every country had to do something rather than nothing.
In England people were told not to drink the milk.
In Germany they said don't drink the water for a week.
In Lapland they killed thousands of reindeer the following Fall.
The reactions seemed random,
just to show that the powers had reacted,
But no one really knew what to do.

Today it's called the "Zone"
The reactor is sealed inside a concrete block called "the Sarcophagus"
It's the most radioactive building on the planet

Tarkovski put it in a film long ago, before it even happened:
the empty future, walking through nature
so tentatively, as if all were a time bomb,
already set off:
The 'peaceful atom' wipes towns off the face of the Earth.

Thousands of animals, plants, whole villages, buried
Hundreds of contaminated vehicles lie on the blacktop.
There's a huge fence around, no one is allowed in.
I have seen the faded pictures of empty helicopters and tanks,
so I am inclined to believe the worst.

Yet people have come back, making homes in the dead land.
Some are holding onto family plots,
Others sneak in to be left alone.
Everything they grow is contaminated—
except for the apples.
No one knows why the apples test okay.

When all else dies,
there still must be safe apples:
knowledge still there to be tasted once more

Are there lizard-headed pigs, eight-legged calves?
No one outside is sure who to believe.
Women give birth not to monsters but to disabled children.
Men suffer strokes in their thirties.
Death hits at random.

The old Soviet myth never promised that no one would be left alone.
Now some have found space and time here—
They say the Zone is kinder than the rest of the world.

Spread the blame as far as it goes
Whose fault, whose fault?
Some go home again, some forget
Some live as if none of this ever happened.

The looming subsumes us from war to peace.
To contain our rage in tiny bombs:
gleams of protest, wishes of death.

Rabbits, rabbits, I'm hunting rabbits.
If I catch them I'll make it through the winter.
Times are tough up here, I'm almost out of cash.
I write to you, my only friend, a man I have never met.

It's rage I'm hiding, I'll speak to no one.
By the firelight I'll assemble my devices that kill.

The world gets evil, I will fight back.
No one will know who I am.

Is this the way? Is this the way?
This is the way it will go:
you're all so fascinated by anyone who can
destroy with so little remorse

and who's not afraid to write
what's wrong with this world.

I want to come visit you, one day I will.
Perhaps the money will come.
I want to see another way to live.
You have friends, you have family.
That will save you from the darkness, from taking it all in,
from demanding that something be done.

Secret rage, private deaths, lashing out at the villains I choose.
It's wrong, and evil, but people will listen.

Why do they flock to the strange and the sinister?
The annihilation has already begun.
This culture will end itself, we all know that.
Rage will wake up the sleepers.
Shock of the new, shock of the old, the same old complaint.

No one knows who I am.
No one knows who anyone is, really.
Our secrets live with us, and we are as closed as
we pretend to be open.

I am the voice of repulsion.
I am the voice of the other side.
I am the voice of the danger of this world,
I am your worst fear, in your safest hour
it could all be gone, it might all blow away.

The package arrives, you imagine explosions,
could it be for me? you say to me:
Now you know which side you're on.

———

You remember the story (it's not yet over)
of the two brothers who both rebel against the world,
they each hide at the verge of civilization,
one in a shack miles from nowhere,
the other living content in a hole in the ground:
that one, you know, after he comes back
marries his high school sweetheart,
(a philosopher no less)
becomes a saint in the public eye, until
at last he turns his darker brother in.

The lonely northern one in the business of mailing death.

There's an argument somewhere, the story unravels.
There's a cat who mewls themes from Beethoven.

The dreams every morning in strange languages,
the perusal of deep books no one has written,

There is something about your voice I cannot hear,
I cannot hear your words.

The voice of the wind,
the whoosh down the hills
the arcadia of birds before dawn.
These birds, say the composer, are ideas.
They are not *like* ideas, that is
literature, not life.

And if ideas are birds, do they sing for a reason,
or, is all
explained by evolutionary desire,
to move on, to go forward,
to new forms random and unplanned.

This change goes nowhere, so the theory goes.
There cannot be a goal, progress cannot
be toward anywhere at all.

Destruction lies out there, intended or not,
someone wants to hasten the end,
to explode a point as if proof of the imperfect surge.

More disaster always lies ahead,
Dying *is* an idea, not like an idea,
it is the one that controls the many.

The wind buffs the building, outlines
its place in the air. So
feel the rush of the world,
hurtling on around us.

The leaves which have just come out blow down—
spring has come too soon, or too late, or too fast,
at least somehow not right, for they can't handle
the strain, are torn into the river, and flow down
to the sea in the storm.

Here the lightning's always waiting
even in the sun it may come down;
this place holds the rough tension that knows
all is not right with the world.

There is that hollow uneasiness.
like when you drive down the night highway
over a dried red stain of blood,

no impact this time, just a smooth sail
over the scene of the crime.

The fields over the Zone are burning,
they were set to take a stand.
Every inch of the ground is poison
Each whiff of smoke brings death to the lungs.
What did you expect?
Did you think discovery ever meant more than error?

The hum in the trees like an alien evening
The seventeen-year cicadas are back
Ten years since the accident
Eighteen since the bombs first went off
Time counts in cycles, we expect more.
Probability tells us: there will only be more accidents
That is the norm, the risk inherent
in experimentation.

There's an old swing set rusting in the woods.
The kids have grown up
The house has burned down.
The thicket has returned.

It's not really dangerous here,
It's just
that everyone has left.

They had no place to go,
but they left anyway,

eager to escape the recurring seasons
that haunt us each year again and again.

Clouds of flies in just one part of the woods.
So we can't pass through.

———

On the other side the tiny streams are crowded with fish
pushing their way upstream, relentless, gazing,
at least they know where to go.

Every journey begins with uncertain hopes,
when you give up on the destination you know
you're at last on you way.

There is a tunnel from the mountain to the city.
It's on the map but no one can go through.
It runs for hundreds of miles.
No one will let you in.
No one will let you out.
It's the only way to get there from here.

Someone blew up the mountain
a hundred years ago.
There's a scar, now a cliff,
a hole where there once was rock.

There's a line through the picture,
a schism in the mind
between wildness and order,
city and country, now—
we walk that line.

That's how meaning finds us in the woods,
as a deer leaps, warblers flit, either so much
going on all around or nothing, grayness or life,
depending on when and where you look.

The sun sets in the north, or the compass is askew
or we don't really know where we are anymore.
Change one detail and this world is a fiction
close one eye and you'll see what you want to see.

Will you? One of my eyes sees more red, the other more blue,
I have no idea which is closer to what is actually out there.

Each week the ascent is impossible to remember,
the tone of the trail totally new.
What else do you expect, really
as the earth unfolds, the petals scatter, the wind whips up,
there is no telling what will happen next.

Remember, then, remember it now
The world will never be the same again.

The old order is turned asunder
on that rainy island a thousand miles from here.

The rebel makes amends with the businessmen.
The roadbuilder says he won't build any more roads
unless they can be the right kind, those that hurt no one
and get everyone just where they want to go.

Every one persuades every other to follow one course or another,
facts get softer, values get harder;
the truth will never be the same.

I'm looking for a percentage, I want a number,
to hold my fate in a queue.
I want to be one of the numbers,
but I find I never fit in
to the rules, the criteria, the quanta that list us
in one type or another, one choice,
one way to make sense of the world.

So, what do you *believe,* they all want to know,
as I am charged with reporting the events,
and what happened on the journey,

and what to expect,
and when, and why
I resist doing what needs to be done
to answer these persistent queries.

Some may have given up,
others do hide,
behind images of beauty or despair.

You will wonder at the rest
brought by the rainfall,
and how the expectation is still greater
than the final sight of the sun.

The millionaire calls:
he hasn't much time
but he too has been racing the world
seeking an end for his money
and a beginning for peace,
to wish his path has crossed less evil than good.

I have come to cash in my trajectory.
How much will this map of my troubles be worth?
How many routes can be climbed still on Earth?

A bomb left a hole gaping at the street corner
Still at the edge of the river, ruined emptiness after fifty years.
Now Gehry's building something to take up the slack,
we've waited long enough, and the wars are over,
at last it's okay to risk it.

So strange to walk the streets of this city,
whose identity sings so much to us of the *oppressed.*
When the tanks rolled through the streets, and those days

when people were routinely disappeared,
from few, from hope, from imagination,
that's how I learned to long for this city
as home for the pathos of fear.

Now everyone comes here,
more tourists than France, overrunning the bridges,
crowding the alleys,
where else can you hope, where else seems new?
Above looms the castle,
famous inaccessibility,
now home of a hope that already tarnishes,
five or ten years down the line.

You need the darkness to want a way out,
the threat of repression tells that you have something to say.
Without all that is the false hope of money,
and how excited, you tell me, can one get worked up about that.

That building stretches and dances, to atone for the bombing.
So many years later that no one can remember why it all happened.
The windows are irregular, the walls all pulled asunder.
On the roof is a metal sphere with bars peeling off into the air,
like frozen feathers, soldered of lead.

Only scrub down the façades that you want to remember,
to celebrate their times or why they were built.
Let the others stay gloomy, sooted in coal, dark memories
of the city that's easier to take, more what you expect, so far
clearer than any abode
of possibility.

It's years after the fall, and I still can't describe it.
I never ran from the blast, I did not pull the trigger.

The avenues only float into consciousness as I learn enough
of the language so the map comes to life.

Was it true that once no one could get into the Castle?
Or is it only our whole inaccessible world that needed to be so
    metaphored?
We all pass through the frustrations when it seems there's no way in,
not long after there seems no way out
of the lines no one else has drawn.

The philosopher has returned to his homeland
he works from five to nine
he has a mission, but no hope to accomplish it.
He can mythologize the place no more now that he's here.
In his original language his audience is smaller than ever
but this is where he *must* be, his world is clear.

Why is there something rather than nothing
when nothing's good enough for me?

It is the morning after
the fog lifts
the empty city retains even more beauty
if you imagine that no one is there.
It is gray to the core, as it always has been.

The sculptor who labored for years on the dictator's statue
killed himself a week after his job was done.
The nation tore down the likeness soon enough,
that's how it is with politics:
no one can trust a face for too long.
The country can purge itself and still live.
The artist was not so lucky.

———

To call someone a philosopher is to pin him down
to demand not answers but an endless stream
of just the right questions—
some discipline, fervor is never enough.

He meets an ancient friend in his old neighborhood:
a woman, back then, who must have been just a girl,
it was so long ago and they both were there.
There were tears in her eyes, for they both had survived.
Afterwards, *I have no idea,* he then confides,
No idea who she was at all.

Footsteps on the faux marble floor
the stone blocks in the sidewalk survived for years
under Russian asphalt
lift concrete away, let rock face the sun.
The poet has no reason to be civil anymore.

You enter the room and the day is still sunny
then you hear about that girl beaten senseless in the park
You are the guest of a friend who knew her well.

Then you notice the *djembe's* head is suddenly cracked,
split down the middle
and you wonder if there is any connection.

One of those days
that's why we live in the city
that's why we live in this world
any day you could lose someone close like this
or someone far some other way
it all depends who you know.

———

Is it right to remark so glib
on possible disasters?

It's all far away,
right, it's no one *you know;*
tune out, choose your channel
we readers are insulated enough
from our own words.

If asked whether to save the hillside
or your own people, which would you choose?
(I mean if it were possible to save the tribe
and eliminate the world—
so the legacy would go on without a home.
Who matters most,
the place or the people,
the map or the map-readers,
the territory or its lines?)

It's all so quiet now right here
but so much is happening:
never mind what,
I can give you the numbers,
births, deaths, attacks, delusion,
think how many people the world over have nothing to do!
And if those who are gone had so much . . .

Seventeen years
to those that note the passing of time:
They're back!
The crunching of footsteps over carapaces underfoot
The slow swelling, the rhythms of the one-time forest
Crzzzzzzzzzzzhh Chrzzzzzaahhh . . .
What are these insects for?

They sit, bewildered, on fence posts, with glaring red eyes.
They can barely fly, like puffins falling from rocks,
Sparrows try to catch them but can't get their beaks around 'em.

Seventeen-year cicadas
strange animals in our midst once again
seventeen years ago I collected information
wondered if I'd remember anything when they came back
Still I don't know:
what do these things *do* in life?
what is the purpose of those who ask the question?

Do the cicadas have their own sense of time
a calendar, a number system, based on seventeen?

I read the news, I found some things out:
seventeen years the eggs underground,
germinating longer than any other insect.
Now that they're out all they do is sing and mate!
They don't even need to eat.
No wonder the Indians thought them a delicacy,
so much as the bugs celebrate the best in life.
You can pluck them from the air and gobble them right up then and
    there
A good source of protein.

Seventeen years, and back for just a few weeks.
Those lost red eyes—
why are we here?
what does this world mean after sixteen years underground?

Every seventeen years I'll check in on what happens.
I'll trace the memories of their return.
Seventeen years from now it may all make sense.

Certain situations will be resolved.
There will be other, outward problems to face.
I will not be able to solve them alone.

There will be low soft whooms in the trees.
Fluttering wings struggling to lift us between the trees.
We will stare up again and wonder:
who else has had to wait so long to face the air?
No reason to go on except the only reason that matters:
there is nothing else to do
this is the plan
this is our place in the plan
this is the sound.

What changes is the will to change

The birds have it all in them, they know all the songs.
If I am in a world of machines,
I hear them channel-surf the world of sounds:
towhee, falcon, peewee, caralarm, digiclock,
one switch and then another.
And if I'm a part of nature, then this is a composition or cadenza.
A virtuoso oneupsmanship of any song that can be sung:
hum a few bars and I'll turn it into something new.

All to get the babes or is it for fun?
Will the sun come up without the song?
Who is mocked but those who wish for a reason?
Perhaps each quip is a question of shorts,
asking the audience of the world if anyone does know the tune.

Early rising, improbable listening.
Hear the sense of the world and you might know your place in it.

To riff on what's there, to compose out of thin air,
these are the tools of the trade.

The bird on the wire hears the rain pelt the asphalt,
and the sound, yes, *the sound* of wet tires screeching to a halt:
there is as much reason to end up here as anywhere.
The slam of a car door, the demand of a sparrow on the sill:
I live in this of all worlds, and someone is home.

To pinpoint a location you will have to listen:
the babies have flown from the nest in the rafters,
either that, or they have fallen out, and they won't be let back in.
And the whistle of warblers, the shock of the goldfinch.
In the dark I the bird can pretend, in light I am overdoing it,
pretending to be what I'm not, like art, like imagination.

Will the changes ever change? Mock on.

One song after another, not to impress,
but to comb the soundscape for art.
We will listen to make sense of it,
and remember what we've heard.

Hear that gust of wind?
Hear the humidity lift?
Let the senses blend into the sense of this place, and no other.

The words are black, the screen is blue.
Leonard Cohen reminds us that the Torah
was written in black fire upon white fire,
so, why not write it all down on the machine.
Easy enough if you think you might be God.
And who doesn't, once in a while.

The home team is victorious once again,
and people do feel impervious, all powerful.
That's why the police await in riot gear at every street corner.
They've closed all the bars at eleven.
What's this, an outsider wonders, can't you guys take it *if you win?*
That's just the problem, we expect too much of it.
We want to take control, and wreak havoc on the city,
screaming, burning all night,
smashing the windows and having it all.

The roads are sealed off, it feels as if the war has just begun,
not simply ended.
After all, it was just a game, right?
Perhaps people are holding back the urge to fight for real.

There is this upheaval all over the world.
It is calm right here but all around burn the flames of unrest.
Or else here the greatest melee is among the calls of birds so
far away all in the hills might be silence.

We hide in the woods, we choose our battles.
Is the world at bay or all alive right here?
There are too many questions here, I know,
but I do not feel right in denying them.

Each way of writing jumps to another,
like the fleeing songs of the mockingbird,
like the swoops of the pair of pileated woodpeckers,
courting among the trees.

But there are reasons to expect more:
each day here starts with the loom of gray,
fog drifting in through the windows and then inside our minds.
And the sun usually comes out, the day becomes both lazy and awake,

and the sky behind all occlusion does remain blue.
Is this enough, or is it an escape?

I am held in by that song, I want to know what it means.
But I'll try to know enough not to imagine I will ever know—
let the amazement come first, let it drown out
the shock of the world.

puppupchoowee puppupchoowee
chhk chhk chhk
bip bip bip bip
whhy whhy whhy whhy
tk tk tk tk
peppeep pepeeep
whhhhhhrrrrrrhhhhrrr
chewewewe
piyup piyup piyup
pip pip pip pip pip
heerup heerup
fzzp fzzp fzzp
heeyo heeyo heeyo
hk hk hk hk
kreeeey kreeeey
gimme dat gimme dat
take it all in, take it all in
hhhhhhhhhhhhhh, tell me, tell me.
Unhh! Unhh! Unhhh!
No NO No No
Pleeeeeeeease, if not if, if not if
don't cry my baby, don't cry my baby
you you you you
up up up up up
and no more, and no more, and no more

take your time, take your time, take your time,
here and here, up and away, up and away, up and away.
Higher, higher, higher, higher,
heh, heh heh heh
cheep cheep cheep
sleep sleep sleep.
If you can, if you can, if you can
take more, take more, take more
write it all down, write it all down,
if you dare, if you dare,
if if if if if if if
trip trip trip trip trip if not if,
try, try, try, try, wooden, wooden, would you?

All we have are words
all we hear are sounds.
It is possible they have nothing to do with each other at all.

If you're driving long enough
the highways move like water
Connecticut acts as if Maine
New York and Boston are exchanged . . .
Only the forests seem familiar,
hold onto the trees, the trees
what exit takes you to them?
Every one and none.

I drove from the city to the end of the world,
a hook in the land, a spit in the water,
all to hear her story, and to change the bulbs.
Since the cancer she can't move her right hand.
Tough for a writer, worse for a painter.
Not resignation but hope:
"I'll have to learn to see different things."

Her family missed the point but the water is still blue.
"My mother saw me bleeding but was too drunk to care.
I was hemorrhaging but she wouldn't take me back to the city,
Just left me on a train, where there was no room to sit."
Blood dripping to the floor, only strength keeps you going.
Blood on your trail, nothing mama can do now.
Mama doesn't understand, she just put you on the train,
cruel, cruel, cruel world, left you all alone

and the blood drips and no one lets you sit down,
and you just know you'll be okay,
but you wish someone would care
or at least understand

This trial seems so much more than the weight of the world
bearing down
The zone of deadness, the slim chance to live,
the soaring past the odds, the lifelong habit,
no sudden way out.

I who am given no real pain choose the pain of the world,
so, who's it up to who gets to choose
what sufferings inhabit us, if you know, sure, if it's real,
you don't have the chance to doubt, the time to dream,

ah, but we all wonder aimlessly searching for our problems
until they grab us by the neck,

like the time when I was young that I felt so imprisoned
until at last I found myself in jail:
then, truly, my time was not my own.

When they let me go I felt the future descend, and myself
rise to blow in its wind:

I'll face my demons on my own time thank you.
We're all as lucky as we're willing to be.

This age of ours always hangs on
to the possibility that we will soon hear
the worst news at all:
no one, not anyone has
a good idea of how bad things might be.
Like that one country in the world with two official languages,
so many foreign films, and they're all foreign films,
have two languages worth of subtitles clouding the screen.

First in the language of appearances,
which needs so little explanation.
Then comes the language of memory,
which tries to tie every future to at least one single past.

Only if you can read both at once will they cancel each other out.
Only then is the screen of possibility clear.

See the one dead tree exploded by lightning
in the heart of a dry green forest.
Every day the needles crackle, clouds mount up
Any time it could happen again.

Poised for an idea you become that tree,
waiting for an answer to strike.

The Zone is the place where everything is permitted
but nothing is alive.
Red changes to blue; green but a passing hue.

To know what it's like just start in the city
and walk toward the edge of town.

When you enter the brand new empty developments
filling the white spaces at the brink—of the desert, the forest, the water
—you'll be right in a landscape ready for the siege
though it easily looked as if abandoned through fear.

Careful, it could strike you down too.
You are the only thing walking alive now for miles.
These shells of our homes like the empty bodies of
cicadas clinging by only inertia to the trees,
waiting for the wind to blow them down,
except we are working ourselves down and into the ground,
farther into the future
beyond the thought of seventeen years.

Might as well stop walking here:
I have enough trouble as it is
keeping fiction out of fact.

Did the accident of ineptitude end with The Zone,
or was it an act of imagination many years back?[1]

Memory moves the images out.
You must find a story out of what happens!
Just be sure to form it from thin air.

From the Summits to the Sea

I live up the slope from a river. This river has been around longer than anyone cares to remember. Humans have imagined it to be many things through history. To Hudson it looked like the dreamed-of Northwest Passage across the only hazily understood continent. A few hundred years later it was the paragon of scenic beauty for the new nation, overpainted, overrhapsodized as the ideal of the picturesque. Later, after they dug a northwest passage and called it the Erie Canal, the water was just a quick way to haul stuff from the sea to some Great Lakes still not really so far northwest. Then my river was a polluted brown sewer with poison muck on its bottom. Then the electric company wanted to deface it with a huge underground hydropower plant. Then we fought to clean it up and it looks better than it has looked for a century. You can dive into its waters from a sand beach at sunset and surface to see the soft sublime haze of the Hudson River School of painting. The illumination has survived.

And do the mountains care? Does the current notice? Does the tide mark the years or only follow the moon? I want to believe that they do, but I think they do not. Faith and reason here disagree. We are the species of worry, concern, and the idiotic power to lay waste to it all. We need to save this nature from one errant part of itself, or else change our mission into something that is worthy of the place that has made us possible.

It's a tough spiral of survival, the hunt for an excuse to make necessary the human race. The race for transformation, improvement, development, and renovation of the world. The need to believe we have moved forward from yesterday to today when all natural signs point to recurrence and return.

There is human time, and earthly time. It could even be said that the earth has no time, because it does not record its own movements from one eon to the next. Nature happens. We pull away from it and notice. At that moment we are outside. Reflection, as I reflected above, is not natural. It is dangerously unnatural, as it pulls a part of nature apart from nature. Centuries apart, millennia apart. We who want to get back to the wild garden fight our own destiny. Every species is all set to lose. They have their time at the top, and then recede to give the next one a chance as the climate changes and proliferation gets out of control.

But humanity rises to every challenge. Reflection comes not from idleness but struggle. I want what matters to be hard, not easy. We want to be tough, we want to show we can do it. Sure, change the world, make it matter, but don't sing the praises only of what now is no more. We must celebrate the real world, the rough world, the natural human and human nature red in tooth and claw. There is no calm and easy escape from civilization into the eternal woods once you know what is going on. There is no easy way into the turtle clan if you want to pick your totems well. Have you asked the turtles if they want you? What did they *really* say? You can only dream your place in a nature indifferent to your concern and consequence.

There are not right and wrong ways of living with regard to the Earth. But these are human matters, no choices that will be settled out there in the state of nature beyond our rules and projections. Only if we take it upon ourselves to protect the Earth and transform the human into something worthy of fitting into the natural will we improve today's situation. We will have to believe this is a path worth taking, and not look for justifications out there to make nature necessary or essential to some human sense of progress, changing, moving, heading forward with no goal ever set forth of what we'll do when we win.

Let's decide that what we want is to fit in. To a world beautiful and complete, one that doesn't need us unless we change our indifferent ways. Wait? I thought nature was indifferent, we the worriers? It only gets more confusing. All species are opportunistic, and think just for themselves. So are we no different, just another selfish part of the mix? We're too reflective, too powerful, have extended our reach like the starling, loosestrife, or kudzu. Weeds all, successful in the new environment without having to work too hard at it. But we should be smarter than a weed, we should know how to hold back.

Paradoxically, that might be less natural. More human. Unprecedented. Timely, not timeless.

Inhabit the ambiguity, don't try to resist it. Keep spiraling in and away from the center at once, doing all you can to make it hold. Move on without despair. Sing it all into significance.

I'm starting at a photograph I took of the Estonian Sea. There are four large stones sticking up out of the water in a shallow bay that extends many miles out. The water is gray-green, the sky is blue-gray, the clouds press down like a heavy weight from above on a light and flat Earth. The stones are perfectly arranged in a design clearly natural, what Zen gardens aspire to but cannot ever reach, how stylized they remain with the gravel of human touch. The moment was snapped, static, captured out of the unending flux. The scene has become an image, an arrangement of darkness, through color, to light. That piece of the world is only a fragment to me now, a work of art. It sings without voice, is silent music, an image pure and detached from its distance from me right now. Maybe this is all Heidegger wanted, the old Nazi, to apprehend the world as purely aesthetic far from the dark workings of people and their senseless cruel fights. Aesthetics do not take over politics. He knew it was wise and good to stay put in the forest only imagining the ocean waves, but he couldn't stay there. None of us can.

We who want answers or even questions in nature lose interest in history. There is only the now, the world is at it is and only humans want time. We will never know how it all began, because we can't have been there. We will not know when it will end, because that time will be long beyond our time, far past the end of the keeping of time itself, stuck in the cycles, nature once more all and one, ever more than our attempt to confine it inside image or idea.

NOTES

1. Ways toward Mountains

1. The letter is officially cataloged under the following heading: "To Dionigi da Bergo San Sepolcro, Concerning Some Personal Problems," in *Rerum Familiarum Libri (I–VIII)*, trans. Aldo S. Bernardo (Albany: SUNY Press, 1975), book IV, i, 172–80. Numerous other translations also exist, and this particular letter is reprinted in most editions of Petrarch's selected correspondence.

2. Dōgen, "Treasury of the True Dharma Eye: Book XXIX, The Mountains and Rivers Sutra," trans. Carl Bielefeldt, in *The Mountain Spirit*, ed. Michael Tobias (Woodstock, N.Y.: The Overlook Press, 1980), 41–49. Another interesting yet vastly different translation is "Mountains and Waters Sutra," trans. Arnold Kotler and Kazuaki Tanahashi, in *Moon in a Dewdrop: Writings of Zen Master Dōgen*, ed. Kazuaki Tanahashi (San Francisco: North Point Press, 1985), 108–13. Still another version is found in the only complete English edition of the writings of Dōgen: *Dōgen Zenji's Shōbōgenzō*, trans. Kosen Nishiyama and John Stevens, 4 vols. (Sendai, Japan: Daihokkaikaku, 1975–1983).

3. *Cratylus* 412b, in *The Collected Dialogues of Plato*, trans. Benjamin Jowett, ed. Edith Hamilton and Huntington Cairns, Bollingen Series, no. 71 (Princeton: Princeton University Press, 1961), 448.

4. See the section entitled "Anatomy of Non-Duality" in Kazuaki Tanahashi's introduction to *Moon in a Dewdrop* (16–18).

5. René Daumal, *Mount Analogue*, trans. Roger Shattuck (Boston: Shambhala Books, 1986).

6. Maurice Merleau-Ponty, *The Phenomenology of Perception*, trans. Colin Smith (London: Routledge & Kegan Paul, 1962), 16.

7. Merleau-Ponty, *Phenomenology*, 22.

8. Arne Naess, "Modesty and the Conquest of Mountains," in *The Mountain Spirit,* ed. Michael Tobias (Woodstock, N.Y.: The Overlook Press, 1980), 16.

9. See Arne Naess, *Ecology, Community, and Lifestyle: Outline of an Ecosophy,* trans. and ed. David Rothenberg (Cambridge: Cambridge University Press, 1988), chaps. 3 and 7.

3. Dare I Kill the Snake?

1. Padmanabh S. Jain, *The Jaina Path of Purification* (Berkeley: University of California Press, 1979), 167.

2. Ibid., 315.

3. Edward Abbey, *Desert Solitaire* (New York: Ballantine Books, 1971 [1968]), 20.

4. Contact! Contact!

1. Philip Booth, "Distances/Shallows/Deeps," *Ohio Review* (Special Issue on Art and Nature), no. 49, page 18.

2. Henry David Thoreau, *The Maine Woods,* ed. Joseph Moldenhauer with photographs by Herbert Gleason (Princeton: Princeton University Press 1974), 70.

3. Ibid., 70.

4. Ibid., 65.

5. Ibid., 71.

5. Will the Real Chief Seattle Please Speak Up?

1. For further confusion on the circuitous history of the words of Chief Seattle, see William Arrowsmith, "Speech of Chief Seattle, January 9th, 1855," *Arion* 8 (1969), 461–64; Forrest Carter, *The Education of Little Tree* (Albuquerque: University of New Mexico Press, 1990); Eli Gifford, ed., *How Can One Sell the Air? Chief Seattle's Vision* (Summertown, Tenn.: Book Publishing Co., 1992) [contains complete texts of the Smith, Perry,

and Arrowsmith speeches, along with a brief explanation of what happened]; Eli Gifford, *The Many Speeches of Chief Seattle: The Manipulation of Records for Religious, Political, and Environmental Causes,* Occasional Papers of Native American Studies, no. 1 (Rohnert Park, Calif.: Sonoma State University, 1992); Sam Gill, *Mother Earth* (Chicago: University of Chicago Press, 1991); Susan Jeffers, *Brother Eagle, Sister Sky: A Message from Chief Seattle* (New York: Dial Press, 1991); Rudolf Kaiser, "Chief Seattle's Speech(es): American Origins and European Reception," in *Recovering the Word,* ed. Brian Swann and Arnold Krupat (Berkeley: University of California Press, 1987), 497–536; Bruce Kent, "A Fifth Gospel," in *Testimony— Chief Seattle* (London: United Society for the Propagation of the Gospel, 1978), 94–98; Mary Murray, "Little Green Lie," *Reader's Digest,* July 1993, 100–104; Henry Smith, "Scraps from a Diary—Chief Seattle—A Gentleman by Instinct—His Native Eloquence," *Seattle Sunday Star,* 29 Oct. 1887, p. 10; Alexander Wilson, *The Culture of Nature* (Cambridge: Blackwell, 1992); Albert Furtwangler, *Answering Chief Seattle* (Seattle: University of Washington Press, 1997).

6. Melt the Snowflake at Once!

1. Henry Bugbee, *The Inward Morning* (1958; reprint, Athens: University of Georgia Press, 1999), 139.
2. Ibid., 33.
3. Ibid., 121.
4. Philip Kerr, *A Philosophical Investigation* (London: Chatto & Windus, 1992), 170.
5. Bugbee, *Inward Morning,* 121.
6. Ibid., 100.
7. Ibid., 172–73.
8. Ibid., 79.
9. Ibid., 141.
10. Henry Bugbee, "Wilderness in America," unpublished manuscript, 1974.
11. Bugbee, *Inward Morning,* 72–73.
12. Ibid., 140, 155.
13. Chris Marker, "Sunless" [excerpt from script], *Oasis/Semiotexte,* 1983, 39.

7. Who Is the Lone Ranger?

1. Edward Abbey, *Confessions of a Barbarian*, ed. David Peterson (Boston: Little, Brown, 1994), 343.
2. Edward Abbey, *The Fool's Progress* (New York: Avon, 1990), 196.
3. Edward Abbey, *Desert Solitaire* (New York: Ballantine, 1971), x.
4. Edward Abbey, "Manhattan Twilight, Hoboken Night," *The Journey Home* (New York: Dutton, 1977), 95.
5. *Desert Solitaire,* 24.
6. *Confessions of a Barbarian,* 199.
7. *Desert Solitaire,* 205.
8. Edward Abbey, *The Monkey Wrench Gang* (New York: Avon, 1976), 211.
9. *Desert Solitaire,* 286.
10. Ibid., 165.
11. Edward Abbey, *Hayduke Lives!* (Boston: Little, Brown, 1990), 187.
12. See Michael Martin, "Ecosabotage and Civil Disobedience," *Environmental Ethics* 12, no. 4 (1990), 291–310. Also David Rothenberg, "Have a Friend for Lunch: Norwegian Radical Ecology vs. Tradition," *Ecological Resistance Movements* (Albany: SUNY Press, 1995), 201–18.
13. *Desert Solitaire,* 303.
14. Jack Turner, *The Abstract Wild* (Tucson: University of Arizona Press, 1996), 36.
15. See Arne Naess, *Gandhi and Group Conflict* (Oslo: Universitetsforlaget, 1974).
16. See David Rothenberg, *Is It Painful to Think? Conversations with Arne Naess* (Minneapolis: University of Minnesota Press, 1993).
17. On the phone sometime in October 1996.
18. For certainly the most surreal of accounts of this epic swindler, see Michael Binstein and Charles Bowden, *Trust Me: Charles Keating and the Missing Billions* (New York: Random House, 1994).
19. Charles Bowden, "Blood Orchid," *Terra Nova* 1, no. 1 (1996), 110.

8. From the Opaque to the Concrete

1. Michael Zimmerman's *Contesting Earth's Future: Radical Ecology and Postmodernity* (Berkeley: University of California Press, 1994) is the best recent book on this distinction.

2. In a letter to me Naess writes, "The eight points were never meant to describe the core of deep ecology, only some fairly general views which supporters of the deep perspective have in common when we contrast their general views with supporters of environmentalism in general. Unhappily, too much is expected from such points" (Correspondence, Feb. 1996). Thus the overemphasis on the eight points in the critical literature on deep ecology serves to weaken its philosophical core, which is usually ignored in favor of vague political pronouncements. The eight points should be considered a political rallying ground and be judged as such: Do they motivate people? Do they provide a platform upon which members of the movement readily agree?

3. As reported in Arne Naess, "The World of Concrete Contents," *Inquiry* 28 (1986), 418. This brief article is the main source for Naess's views on the subject of concrete contents. Part of this article has been revised by Naess and myself and included in Arne Naess, *Ecology, Community, and Lifestyle* (Cambridge: Cambridge University Press, 1989), 51–57.

4. Arne Naess, "Gestalt-ontology and Gestalt-thinking," unpublished manuscript (Center for Environment and Development, University of Oslo 1989), 4.

5. Italo Calvino, "From the Opaque," in *The Road to San Giovanni*, trans. Tim Parks (New York: Pantheon, 1993), 132.

6. See David Abram, *The Spell of the Sensuous: Perception and Language in a More-than-Human World* (New York: Pantheon, 1996).

7. David Rothenberg, *Is It Painful to Think? Conversations with Arne Naess* (Minneapolis: University of Minnesota Press, 1993), 154.

8. Ibid., 137.

9. Joel Kovel, "The Marriage of Radical Ecologies," in *Environmental Philosophy*, ed. Michael Zimmerman (Englewood Cliffs, N.J.: Prentice-Hall, 1993), 408.

10. Ibid., 145.

11. Tui de Roy, "Where Vulcan Lizards Prosper," *Natural History* 104, no. 1 (1995), 28–38.

12. Ibid., 150.

13. Naess, "Gestalt-ontology and Gestalt-thinking," 3.

14. Ibid., 5.

15. See David Rothenberg, "Ways toward Mountains," *The Trumpeter* 6, no. 3 (1989).

16. Naess, "Gestalt-ontology and Gestalt-thinking," 8.

17. Lawrence Weschler, *Seeing Is Forgetting the Name of the Thing One Sees: The Art of Robert Irwin* (Berkeley: University of California Press, 1982).

18. This exhibit ran at the Mary Boone Gallery in the fall of 1992.

19. Emmanuel Levinas, *Time and the Other,* trans. Richard A. Cohen (Pittsburgh: Duquesne University Press 1987), 63.

20. David Rothenberg, *Is It Painful to Think?,* 164–65.

21. Tomas Tranströmer, "The Gallery," in *Selected Poems, 1954–1986,* ed. Robert Hass, trans. Sam Charters (New York: Ecco Press, 1987), 149.

10. Truth across the Divide

1. Ariel Dorfman and Armand Mattelart, *How to Read Donald Duck: Imperialist Ideology in the Disney Comic* (New York: International General, 1975).

2. Andrew Harvey, *A Journey in Ladakh* (Boston: Houghton Mifflin, 1983).

3. Ibid.

4. Darcy Ribeiro, *Maira,* trans. E. H. Goodland and Thomas Colchie (New York: Vintage, 1984).

5. See "Fred and Barney's Mongolian Adventure," *Harper's,* December 1991, 39.

11. Beyond the Selfish Landscape

1. Alexander Wilson, *The Culture of Nature* (Cambridge: Blackwell, 1992), 91–92.

2. James Howard Kunstler, *Home from Nowhere* (New York: Simon and Schuster, 1996), 185.

3. Betsy Wakefield Teter, "Hub City Writers: Building a Literary Identity for a Southern Town," *Orion Afield* 2, no. 2 (1998).

4. Eben Fodor, *Bigger not Better* (Gabriola Island, B.C.: New Society Publishers, 1999), 135.

5. James Brooke, "Denver Stands Out in Mini-Trend Toward Downtown Living," *New York Times,* Dec. 29, 1998, A10.

12. The Nine Points of Eco-Cultural Restoration

1. Eric Katz, "The Big Lie: Human Restoration of Nature," *Research in Philosophy and Technology* 12 (1992), 231–41.
2. See his contributions to *Beyond Preservation,* ed. Carl Pletsch (Minneapolis: University of Minnesota Press, 1994).
3. Tom Stoppard, *Arcadia* (London: Faber & Faber, 1993), 12.
4. Ibid., 66.
5. Stephanie Mills, *In Service of the Wild* (Boston: Beacon Press, 1995), 35.
6. Ibid., 69.
7. Barry Lopez, foreword to *Helping Nature Heal,* ed. Richard Nilsen (Berkeley: Ten Speed Press, 1991), v.
8. René Daumal, *Mount Analogue,* trans. Roger Shattuck (New York: Penguin, 1974), 116.
9. From Judy Goldhaft, *Water Web,* a performance piece, quoted in *Whole Earth Review* 86 (fall 1995), 108–9.
10. See Raymond O'Brien, *American Sublime: Landscape and Scenery of the Lower Hudson Valley* (New York: Columbia University Press, 1980), 25–31.

14. Why Wild Philosophy?

1. William Cronon, ed., *Uncommon Ground: Toward Reinventing Nature* (New York: Norton, 1995). See also David Rothenberg, "Who's Naive about Nature?", review of *Uncommon Ground,* ed. William Cronon, *Amicus Journal* (spring 1996).
2. J. Baird Callicott and Michael Nelson, eds., *The Great New Wilderness Debate* (Athens: University of Georgia Press, 1998).
3. William Cronon, "The Trouble with Wilderness: A Response," *Environmental History* 1, no. 1 (1996).

15. Knowledge versus Information

1. Tom Stonier, *Information and Meaning: An Evolutionary Perspective* (New York: Springer, 1997), 13.

2. Tor Nørretranders, *The User Illusion: Cutting Consciousness down to Size* (New York: Viking, 1998), 41.

3. Ibid., 42.

4. Ibid., 87.

5. Ibid., 96.

6. Ibid., 98.

7. Ibid., 102.

8. Henry Plotkin, *The Nature of Knowledge: Concerning Adaptations, Instinct, and the Evolution of Intelligence* (London: Penguin, 1994), 117.

9. Ibid., 118.

10. Stonier, op. cit., 128–29.

11. David Rothenberg, "How the Web Destroys the Quality of Student Papers," *The Chronicle of Higher Education,* Aug. 15, 1997; "Use the Web to Connect," *The Chronicle of Higher Education,* July 16, 1999.

16. That's a Damn Talented Elephant!

1. David Gucwa and James Ehmann, *To Whom It May Concern: An Investigation of the Art of Elephants* (New York: W. W. Norton, 1985). This book is much more honest and heartfelt than the more recent, somewhat snide *When Elephants Paint* (New York: Harper Perennial, 2000) by Russian conceptual artist/humorists Komar and Melamid. They describe the opening of an elephant art academy in Thailand, and are as interested in making fun of the art world as they are in supporting elephant conservation. Musician/neuroscientist David Sulzer has also made a recording called *Thai Elephant Orchestra* (Mulatta Records MUL004, 2000; www.mulatta.org for more information), where the Thai elephants are playing marimba-like instruments with mallets in their trunks. So there is no doubt that these elephants are up to something creative. The question is: are we brave enough to try to appreciate it?

19. The Zone

1. In 1996 I was trying to write an introductory textbook in environmental ethics. That project never quite got off the ground, as I found myself caught up in strange convergences that seemed to matter more: the

tenth anniversary of the Chernobyl nuclear accident, the arrest of the Unabomber, the return of the seventeen-year cicadas. Somehow these events all seemed to fit together. Synchronicities led more directly to poetry than to prose. I followed my attention. I was bemused by the fact that the authorities had named the toxic region surrounding the blown-up reactors "The Zone," just like the post-nuclear landscape in a famous Tarkovski film. And then I remember that the visual synthesizer that Chris Marker comes upon in his film *Sans Soleil,* which I keep returning to, was also named "The Zone," specifically an homage to Tarkovski.

We must hold fast to those coincidences that most seem to matter.

ACKNOWLEDGMENTS

Thanks to the editors and referees of all the publications where these essays first appeared in earlier forms, and to all others who have helped to improve them, including Alan Drengson, Simmons Buntin, Satish Kumar, Sabine Hrechdakian, Marta Ulvaeus, Ed Mooney, Wanda Whitten, Joe Grange, Peter Quigley, Alastair Hannay, Andrew Light, Eric Katz, Gayle Young, Huib Ernste, Dieter Steiner, Roger Shattuck, Andrew McLaughlin, Steve Moddemeyer, Adam Clayman, John Davis, Tom Butler, Vance Martin, Finn Alnæs, Howard Mansfield, Jane Brox, Ole Rikard Høisæther, Amy Lee Knisley, Georgia Marsh, Erazim Kohák, and Chris Funkhouser.

Thanks to the New Jersey Institute of Technology for always supporting my unusual trajectories and flights of speculation. Thanks to Andy Singleton for letting me spend time at his cabin on Mt. Desert Island, Maine, where some of these essays were written. Thanks to Barbara Ras and the University of Georgia Press for convincing me that it could all fit together into one book.

Thanks to H. Pittman Floyd for teaching me to sign my correspondence with the salutation "Always the Mountains" at Saltash Mountain Camp in Vermont when I was twelve. I continue the practice unto this day.

"Ways toward Mountains," *The Trumpeter* 6, no. 3 (summer 1989), 71–75.

"The Return of the Sublime" appeared on www.terrain.org (1998) as the first installment of my quarterly online column, *Bull Hill.*

"Dare I Kill the Snake? Regret and Jain Ecology," *Resurgence* no. 172 (fall 1995), 4–5.

"Contact! Contact! Up Katahdin with Thoreau," *The Maine Scholar* 7 (1994), 21–29.

"Will the Real Chief Seattle Please Speak Up?" *Terra Nova* 1, no. 1 (1996), 68–82.

"Melt the Snowflake at Once! A History of Wonder," in *Wilderness and the*

Heart: Henry Bugbee's Philosophy of Place, Presence, and Memory, ed. Edward Mooney (Athens: University of Georgia Press, 1999).

"Who Is the Lone Ranger? Edward Abbey as Philosopher," in *Coyote in the Maze: Tracking Edward Abbey in a World of Words,* ed. Peter Quigley (Salt Lake City: University of Utah Press, 1998). Reprinted courtesy of the University of Utah Press.

"No World But in Things: Naess's Philosophy of Concrete Contents," *Inquiry* 39, no. 2 (1996), 225–72; *Beneath the Surface: Critical Essays in the Philosophy of Deep Ecology,* ed. Eric Katz, Andrew Light, and David Rothenberg (Cambridge, Mass.: MIT Press, 2000).

"Get Out of Whatever Cage: Avant-Garde in Nature," *Musicworks* 58 (spring 1994), 34–40.

"Truth across the Divide: The Fragility of Cultural Identity," in *Pathways to Human Ecology,* ed. Huib Ernste (Bern: Peter Lang, 1994), 189–97.

"The Nine Points of Eco-Cultural Restoration," in *Proceedings, Ecological Restoration Conference 1995* (Seattle: Society for Ecological Restoration, 1996).

"A Plea for Quiet Preservation: Why the Maine Woods Should Not be a National Park," *Wild Earth* (802-434-4077; www.wildlandsproject.org), summer 2000.

"Why Wild Philosophy?" *International Journal of Wilderness* 5, no. 2 (1999), 4–8.

"That's a Damn Talented Elephant!" *Terra Nova* 3, no. 2 (1998).

"The Firefest," *Terra Nova* 3, no. 1 (1998).

"The Zone," *Newark Review* 2, no. 2 (1998), enhanced version online at http:// www-ec.njit.edu/~newrev/v2s2.

Most of the sixteen previously published essays have been revised and transformed for the present volume.

exotic, versus native, 150, 261
experience, 92; delving into it, 66

Faarlund, Nils, 25, 213
fashion, 124–25
FBI, 83
flying, fear of, 218
Fodor, Eben, 138
fragments, 63, 111
Franck, Frederick, 200
friendship, 229–34 passim
Frost, Robert, 154
Fuller, R. Buckminster, 112
future, the, 88, 236

Galapagos, 101
Galileo Galilei, 92
Gandhi, Mohandas, 35–39, 86
Garbo, Greta, 83
gardens, 145, 149
Garrison, New York, 155
Gehry, Frank, 244
gestalt psychology, 220–21
glass bead game, 165
Gleason, Herbert, 43
globalization, 121–30
God, 56–60, 127, 169, 208, 218, 228, 251
Gore, Albert, Jr., 90
Grand Canyon, 18, 20
Grand Central Station, 32
gravity, 231
Great Plains, 13
Griffin, Donald, 198
Gucwa, David, 197–98

Gulf Hagas, 45
Gurdjieff, G. I., 196

Harvey, Andrew, 123
Hasidism, 182
Havel, Václav, 68
health, 149
Heaven's Gate cult, 133
hedonism, 222
Heidegger, Martin, viii, 91, 93, 101, 105, 193, 261
Hesse, Herman, 165
Hiroshima, 235
Hoboken, 78
homelessness, 74
horse, 81–82
Hudson River, 153–55; School of painting, 17, 22, 154, 258
Hudson Valley, 15–34 passim, 153–55, 259–60
humility, 147, 173
Husserl, Edmund, 93

Ignatow, David, 9
iguana, 101
improvisation, 114
indigenous people, 53–61, 125, 171, 195, 198
information, 175–94, 202
inspiration, 190
internet, 183–92; in education, 186–92
introspection, 3–4
intuition, 97
Irwin, Robert, 105

bosoms, 25; hidden, 8; Katahdin, 40–52 passim; Monadnock, 225–34 passim; Rainier, 27; Rushmore, 53; San Gabriel, 70; Sierra Nevada, 19, 85; Slide, 33; Storm King, 15, 154; Suilven, 33; Taurus, 15; unfinished quality of, 11; Ventoux, 2–4; Washington, 21

Moyers, Bill, 48

Muir, John, 18–19, 169; his "mistake," 85

mushrooms, 109, 113, 117–18, 138

music, 109–20

Naess, Arne, 77, 83, 90–108, 213, 220; and deep ecology, 36, 147, 267 (n. 2); in *Hayduke Lives*, 86; on mountains, 14; on the sublime, 226

Nagasaki, 235

Nalungiaq, 195

nature: according to Aristotle, 1; and art, 110; versus humanity, vii; and music, 109–20; contact with, 40–52; love of, 27; turbulent, 41

Nature Conservancy, 158, 163

Nepal, 21, 26, 128

Newark, 78

New Jersey, 136

Niagara Falls, 17, 137

Nietzsche, Friedrich, 46, 217

nonviolence, 84

Nørretranders, Tor, 177

Norway, 25, 125–26, 129, 203–24 passim, 235

nostalgia, 138, 140

nuclear energy, 235–57 passim

Nye, David, 31

Ole Woodsman's Fly Dope, 48

otherness, 130

parks, 151, 156–64

peace, 120

Penobscots, 50

Perls, Frederick, 221

Perry, Ted, 55–58, 60

Petrarch, 1–14 passim, 263 (n. 1)

phenomenology, 13–14, 29, 79, 93–94, 99, 105–6

philosophy: and dialogue, 95; versus literature, 65, 75–89; versus mastery, 69; versus poetry, 97–100, 114, 193–94; wild, 165–74

Pierce, Franklin, 55

pigeons, 119

Pittsford, New York, 135

planning, urban, 131–43

Plato, 7, 80, 96

Plotkin, Henry, 181–82

poetry. *See* philosophy

Prague, 244–48

preservation strategies, 156–64

Protagoras, 92

public transportation, 134

Puget Sound, 55